TRUE CRIME
Diary

G000147444

Also by James Bland

TRUE CRIME DIARY VOLUME 2
CRIME STRANGE BUT TRUE

TRUE CRIME
Diary

180 True Crime Stories

James Bland

WARNER BOOKS

A *Warner* Book

Copyright © James Bland 1986

The right of James Bland to be identified as author of
this work has been asserted by him in accordance with the
Copyright, Designs and Patents Act 1988.

First published in Great Britain in 1987
by Futura Publications
Reprinted 1987 (twice), 1988, 1989, 1990 (twice), 1992
This edition published by Warner Books in 1992
Reprinted 1992, 1993

ISBN 0 7515 0338 X

Printed in England by Clays Ltd, St Ives plc

Acknowledgements
Almost all the stories in this book were
originally published in the magazines *True Crime Monthly*,
True Detective and *Master Detective*

Warner Books
A Division of
Little, Brown and Company (UK) Limited
165 Great Dover Street
London SE1 4YA

CONTENTS

PREFACE

True Crime Diary recounts a large number of modern murder stories, many of them already famous. The subjects have been chosen according to my own preferences, with due regard for variety, oddities of character and quirks of fate. It is, as far as I know, the first time that such a collection has been arranged as a book of anniversaries, though about a third of the contents were originally published as a series with the same title in *True Crime Monthly*.

I have no doubt that some readers will notice discrepancies between my own accounts of certain cases and those currently available by other authors. This is always irritating to anyone with a keen interest in the subject, and it must be admitted that some authors in this field are not above presenting fiction as fact. As I do not wish to be regarded as one of them, I feel obliged to say that I have confined myself to using information which I believe to be accurate and that if I have erred at all, I have done so in good faith.

I make no apology for the fact that some of the stories are shocking, for nobody acquainted with the subject would expect otherwise. It is not only the cases of mass murder to which I am referring; many others, such as those of the Papin Sisters or Dr Geza de Kaplany, were so horrifying as to be incomprehensible to any normal person. I have no fresh insights or theories to offer in respect of such crimes; as with all the other cases, I have been content to describe them in a concise and, I hope, interesting manner. If the reader finds them absorbing, then the book is as I intended it to be.

Inquest on Margaret Lofty, 1915

On 1 January 1915, a man calling himself John Lloyd and claiming to be an estate agent told a London coroner's court of the tragic death of his wife, Margaret Elizabeth Lloyd, formerly Lofty, in a house in Highgate fourteen days earlier.

Weeping copiously, he said that on the day before her death he and his wife had moved into rooms at 14, Bismarck Road after travelling from Bath, where they had just been married. He had found her lying dead in the bathroom when he returned to the house after going out to buy some tomatoes.

A local doctor, who had been called to the house, told the court that Mrs Lloyd's death had been caused by drowning, and suggested that she had fainted as a result of getting into a hot bath while she was suffering from influenza.

The coroner's jury, having no reason to suspect foul play, accepted this explanation and brought in a verdict of death by misadventure. But that was not the end of the matter.

A report of the inquest, published in the *News of the World*, was read by a Buckinghamshire fruit-grower, Charles Burnham, whose daughter Alice had died in similar circumstances in Blackpool a year earlier, after marrying a man named George Smith. This George Smith, who claimed to be a bachelor of independent means, had insured Alice Burnham's life for £500 on the day before the marriage. Burnham informed the police that he suspected that George Smith and John Lloyd were the same person. As a result, an extensive investigation was started, and Charles Burnham's suspicions soon proved to be justified.

Moreover, a third case came to light — that of Beatrice

Williams, formerly Mundy, who had died in almost identical circumstances in Herne Bay in July 1912. Her husband, who called himself Henry Williams and claimed to be a picture-restorer, had gained £2500 by her death. Henry Williams was now also found to have been George Smith.

Margaret Lloyd's life had been insured for £700, and she had made a will in her husband's favour just a few hours before her death

On 23 March 1915, following police inquiries in many towns, George Joseph Smith, aged forty-three, was charged with three murders. At his trial on one of those charges, which began at the Old Bailey on 22 June, 112 witnesses and 264 exhibits were produced. Smith was shown to be a callous, predatory individual, who had committed bigamy several times in order to deprive lonely or unhappy women of their savings, and no one was left in any doubt that he was also a murderer.

In a demonstration of how he could have drowned his victims without leaving any signs of a struggle, a nurse was placed in a bath and pulled under the water by her feet. The rushing of water into her nasal passages produced immediate unconsciousness, and she had to be revived by artificial respiration.

Despite frequent outbursts, Smith was convicted and sentenced to death. He was hanged at Maidstone Prison on 13 August 1915.

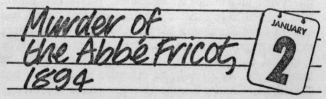

Murder of the Abbé Fricot, 1894

JANUARY 2

On the evening of 2 January 1894, the Abbé Fricot, rector of the parish of Entrammes, near Laval, sat down to make up his accounts in the company of his curate, the Abbé Albert Bruneau. What passed between the two priests is not known for certain, but it was clearly of some importance. At half past six a choir practice was cancelled without notice, the choir having already turned up at the rectory. Half an hour later, on being told that supper was ready, Bruneau said that Fricot had gone out. He then began playing the organ before going to have supper on his own. Though he appeared shaken at this point, it was also noticed that he had a good appetite. Later, when Fricot had still not appeared, a search of the premises was started, with neighbours being called in to help.

The search went on all night to no avail. In the morning Bruneau suggested that Fricot might have committed suicide and led his neighbour, a man named Chelle, to a well in the garden. There, under thirty feet of water, and concealed by logs, lay the body of the missing rector; his head had been battered with a heavy instrument. There were bloodstains on the edge of the well.

Bruneau was immediately suspected of the murder. His hand had been cut, but he claimed this had happened as he looked into the well at three o'clock in the morning, before leading Chelle to it. But there were also bloodstains on the keys of the organ, which Bruneau had played the previous evening. In his desk were found 1300 francs, which he appeared to have stolen from the rector's strong-box. A nun who visited the rectory had been told by Bruneau that Fricot had committed suicide — a mortal sin — and that his death had been made to look like murder in order to avoid a scandal.

Bruneau's character could hardly have helped to allay suspicion. A man of peasant origin, he was found to be a liar, a thief and a frequenter of brothels — at one of which he had contracted gonorrhoea. He had been a curate in Astillé, in the same province, for some years and during that time had used a bequest of 16,000 francs, intended for charity, for his own purposes. It was also while he was there that the rectory was burgled four times. He had taken up his post in Entrammes at the age of thirty-one in November 1892, his arrival being quickly followed by the theft of 500 francs from a strong-box. It is likely that Fricot knew Bruneau to be the thief.

Neighbours claimed that on the night of the rector's death they heard groans coming from the rectory garden. It was supposed that Fricot, in making up his accounts, had decided that something had to be done about his curate's criminal activities, and that Bruneau had killed him after hearing what Fricot had to say on the matter.

Bruneau was brought to trial on 9 July. His sordid past was exposed, with prostitutes telling the court that he was a regular customer, and a brothel-keeper stating that he was not the only priest to turn up at her premises wearing his cassock. He was found guilty and sentenced to death, his execution on 29 August 1894, being attended by 16000 people. He died with dignity, declaring his innocence to the last.

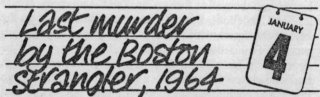

Last murder by the Boston Strangler, 1964

On 4 January 1964, the man known as the Boston Strangler committed his last murder. The body of the victim, Mary Sullivan, aged nineteen, was found in a Boston apartment. She had been stripped naked, tied up, raped and strangled; finally, a broom handle had been thrust into her body and, as a cruel act of mockery, a New Year greetings card placed against her right foot. Albert DeSalvo, a non-drinking, non-smoking schizophrenic with uncontrollable sexual urges, later confessed to being the Strangler. He was to remember that as Mary Sullivan lay dead 'she

12

was looking like she was surprised and even disappointed with the way I had treated her'.

It was his thirteenth murder in just over eighteen months, though at the time it was believed to be only his eleventh, the other two not having been attributed to him. His victims had all been women and, though several were either elderly or middle-aged, all had been raped or sexually abused. He gained admission to their homes by posing as a workman, and invariably managed to avoid leaving fingerprints. Generally, the weapon he used was a ligature made from stockings, its ends being left in a bow under the victim's chin. Some of the victims were also found to have been beaten over the head, stabbed or bitten.

As the pattern became familiar, public tension mounted. The police searched their records for known sexual deviants and questioned many suspects, but they received only false confessions. One woman, in February 1963, had successfully fought off the Strangler, but was suffering from a partial loss of memory as a result of her ordeal. After the death of Mary Sullivan, when the murders suddenly stopped, it was feared that the culprit would never be caught.

Then, on 27 October the same year, a young married woman in Cambridge, Massachusetts, was tied up and sexually assaulted by an intruder. The description she gave of him led police to DeSalvo, who had a record for breaking and entering. This, in turn, led to his photograph being circulated to neighbouring states, with the result that scores of women, all victims of sex attacks, identified him as their assailant. But DeSalvo, even then, was not suspected of being the Strangler. Held on rape charges, he was sent to the Boston State Hospital at Bridgewater for observation. On 4 February 1965, after confessing to a great many crimes, he was judged to be not competent to stand trial and committed to the hospital by court order. It was only then that he confessed to being the Strangler.

He gave details of the murders, in some cases making a sketch of the victim's home. He demonstrated the knot he had used when strangling his victims. But the police, while convinced that he was telling them the truth, could not find any evidence to support his confessions. The state therefore reached an agreement with DeSalvo's attorney that no charges would be brought in connection with the murders, but that DeSalvo would be brought to trial for some of his other crimes instead.

The hearing began on 30 June 1966, with reporters and other observers from all over the world present. At the end of it DeSalvo, pleading for medical treatment, was sent to prison for life. In 1973, at the age of forty-two, he was stabbed to death by a fellow prisoner in Walpole State Prison.

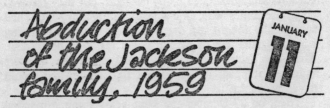

Abduction of the Jackson family, 1959

On 11 January 1959, Carrol Jackson, driving along a road near Apple Grove, Eastern Virginia, with his wife and two little daughters — one aged five, the other eighteen months — was forced to a halt by the driver of an old blue Chevrolet who had pulled over in front of them and stopped suddenly. Before Jackson could reverse and drive away, the other driver jumped out into the road and, threatening them with a gun, made the whole family get into the trunk of his own car. Later, when Jackson's car was found abandoned, a police search started, but no member of the missing family was to be seen alive again.

The bodies of Jackson and the younger girl were found in a ditch near Fredericksburg seven weeks later; Jackson had been shot in the head, the child had died of suffocation lying underneath him. Seventeen days after that the other two members of the family were found in a shallow grave near Annapolis, Maryland; the mother had been raped and murdered, the child beaten to death with a blunt instrument. The grave was not far from the place where another woman had been shot dead and then sexually assaulted in June 1957, and police were quick to suspect that the same person was responsible for both crimes.

During the investigation that followed, an anonymous letter was received from Norfolk, Virginia, accusing Melvin Rees, a jazz musician, of the crimes, but police searched for Rees without success. The following January the letter-writer contacted them again, this time giving his name as Glenn L. Moser and informing them that Rees was working as a salesman in a music shop in West Memphis, Arkansas. Rees was immediately arrested and identified by a witness to the 1957 murder; a search of his parents' home in Hyattsville resulted in the discovery of the gun used to kill Jackson, together with detailed notes about this and other crimes.

Melvin Rees, a former university student, was known to his friends to be a mild-mannered, intelligent man. He played the piano, the guitar, the saxophone and the clarinet, taking work wherever he could find it. But he had an unusual 'philosophy' of murder: 'You can't say it's wrong to kill,' he had once remarked. 'Only individual standards make it right or wrong.'

Glenn Moser, who knew Rees well, had had cause to ask him outright if he had murdered the Jacksons, and had received an evasive answer. It now became clear that he was a sadist, responsible not only for these and the Annapolis murder, but also for the sex-murders of two teenage girls abducted near the University of Maryland, and two others whose bodies had been recovered from Maryland rivers.

The 'Sex Beast', as he was to be called, was tried for murder, firstly in Maryland, where he was given a life sentence, then in Virginia, where he was sentenced to death. He was executed in 1961, at the age of twenty-eight.

Trial of Clifford Olson concluded, 1982

In the Supreme Court of Vancouver, British Columbia, on 12 January 1982, the trial of Clifford Olson, an ex-convict accused of the murder of eleven young people, was brought to a swift conclusion when the defence counsel informed the court that his client, who had earlier denied the offences, wished to change all of his pleas to guilty. When the judge asked the reason for this, he explained that the accused wanted to spare the families of his victims the ordeal of listening to details of the crimes. The pleas were formally registered and a sentence of life imprisonment passed on each charge. The judge recommended that Olson should never be released on parole.

Olson, who was forty-two years old, already had a long record of violent crimes and had, in fact, spent almost all his adult life in jail. Since his release two years earlier, there had been many reports of the disappearance of children and young people in the Vancouver area, and the discovery of three bodies — two boys and a girl — at Weaver Lake, fifty miles east of the city, led to intensive police action.

Olson, living on the outskirts of Vancouver with his wife and baby son, was kept under surveillance. He was arrested in August 1981, after being identified by an eighteen-year-old girl who had been raped while she was out hitch-hiking two months previously. Searching his apartment, police discovered a number of articles belonging to one of the Weaver Lake victims.

Confronted with this evidence, Olson confessed that he was guilty of all three of the murders, and many others, too. He offered to show police where another eight victims had been buried, but only if he was paid $10,000 for each corpse, together with an extra $30,000 for the three which had already been found.

The police refused the offer outright, pointing out that they already had enough evidence to convict him of murder. But, to their astonishment, the Attorney-General, Alan Williams, accepted it, insisting only that $90,000 of the proceeds should be placed in trust for Olson's son. When the money had been paid, and his lawyer was satisfied that it could not be recovered, Olson led police to the sites of eight different graves.

Olson's crimes caused widespread revulsion. His victims, aged between nine and eighteen, had been picked up at random and beaten, stabbed, strangled or mutilated. The revelation, at the end of his trial, that he had been paid $100,000 out of public funds, despite protests from the police, caused much anger. The unprecedented offer was, however, defended by the Solicitor-General, Robert Kaplan, on the grounds that the parents of the victims were entitled to give their children Christian burials.

Two weeks after the payment had been made known to the public, Olson offered the police a 'bargain deal': in return for a further $100,000, he would take them to the graves of twenty other victims. But this time, though he was suspected of many other murders, the offer was not taken up.

A year later, in January 1983, the man who, according to his counsel, had wanted to spare the feelings of his victims' parents, caused further anger by announcing that, in collaboration with a freelance writer, he intended to write a book about his crimes for publication. This led to demands for the law to be changed in order to prevent anyone making a profit out of crime.

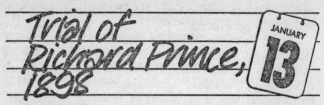

At the Old Bailey on 13 January 1898, Richard Prince, an out-of-work actor, was brought to trial for the murder of William Terriss, an immensely popular member of the same profession, at a rear entrance of the Adelphi Theatre, London, on 16 December previously.

Prince, aged thirty-nine, had been born on a farm near Dundee, where his father was a ploughman; his real name was Richard Millar Archer. He was neither a good actor nor a lucky one, and had never been anywhere near the heights to which he aspired; he had made, at best, a meagre living out of occasional small parts.

Of late he had been maintained by payments from the Actors' Benevolent Fund, pawning all but one set of his clothes and existing on meals of bread and milk; his landlady, out of sympathy, had reduced his rent from 4s (20p) to 3s (15p) a week. When his grant was suddenly terminated he became desperate.

He saw Terriss, who had once had him thrown out of a play for making an offensive remark, as the cause of his misfortune. 'He had kept me out of employment for ten years, and I had either to die in the street or kill him,' he was afterwards to declare.

On the evening of his death Terriss, aged fifty, arrived at the theatre where he was appearing in a play called *Secret Service*, in the company of a friend. He intended to enter by a pass-door in Maiden Lane, in order to avoid his fans. But as he inserted his key in the lock, Prince, who had been watching for him, rushed across the street and thrust a kitchen knife into his back with great force.

Terriss turned and fell, a second blow slashing his side and a third inflicting a wound in his chest. He died inside the theatre a little while afterwards. The evening's performance had to be cancelled.

Prince, who had offered no resistance, was handed over to a policeman and taken to Bow Street Police Station. There, having admitted responsibility for the crime, he asked for something to eat. At the committal proceedings the following morning he was subjected to shouts and jeers from the crowds that filled the court.

At his trial Prince wore an Inverness cape. He made a plea of 'guilty with provocation' at first, but changed this on the advice of his counsel to one of not guilty by reason of insanity. Members of his own family and others told the court that his behaviour was unusual, his mother stating that he was 'soft in the head', and medical evidence was given of his 'insane delusions'.

The accused conducted himself throughout in a theatrical manner, as if pleased at having suddenly obtained in real life the leading part which had for so long escaped him on the stage.

The trial lasted one day, the jury deliberating for half an hour before informing the court that they found the accused guilty of the crime but not responsible for his actions. He was committed to the criminal lunatic asylum at Broadmoor and hastily removed from the courtroom after attempting to make a speech of thanks.

He was happier in the asylum than he had been outside and took a keen interest in the entertainments put on by the inmates.

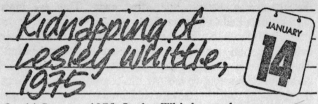

Kidnapping of Lesley Whittle, 1975

On 14 January 1975, Lesley Whittle, aged seventeen, was found to be missing from her home in the village of Highley, in Shropshire. She had not appeared for breakfast that morning and was not in her bedroom. A ransom note, demanding £50,000 for her return, was found on a piece of tape with embossed lettering; it ordered the family not to contact the police and said that a telephone call would be made to a shopping centre in Kidderminster that evening.

Ronald Whittle, the victim's brother, informed the police and later went to the shopping centre to take the call. In the meantime, however, the kidnapping had been reported on television and, as a result, the call was not made.

Two days later, at 11.45 p.m., Ronald Whittle received a telephone call at home, telling him to take the ransom money to a telephone kiosk in Kidsgrove, near Stoke-on-Trent, where he would find another message. He arrived there early in the morning and found the message on a piece of Dynotape, telling him to drive to the nearby Bathpool Park and make contact with the kidnapper by flashing the lights of his car. He followed the instruction, but the kidnapper did not appear.

A further telephone call gave Ronald an opportunity to ask the kidnapper for proof that Lesley was with him. The man agreed to get him the proof — the answer to a certain question — and call back, but he never did so.

By this time the kidnapper was known to have committed other serious crimes. On the night of 15 January a security guard at a transport depot in Dudley, Worcestershire, had seen a shabby little man hanging around the premises and asked him what he wanted. Receiving an unsatisfactory answer, he turned away from the man, intending to call the police, but was shot six times in the back. A stolen car which had been parked nearby was found to contain Lesley's slippers, more messages from the kidnapper, and a tape-recording made by Lesley asking her family to co-operate with him.

Moreover, an examination of the cartridge cases found at the depot showed that the same gun had been used by a notorious criminal called the 'Black Panther', who specialized in sub-post office burglaries and was known to have committed three murders.

An intensive police search led to the discovery, on 7 March 1975, of Lesley Whittle's body in the network of sewage tunnels underneath Bathpool Park; it was hanging, naked, by a wire rope below a narrow ledge. The sewage system had been the kidnapper's hide-out and his victim's place of captivity.

On 11 December the same year two policemen driving through Mansfield Woodhouse, Nottinghamshire, late at night noticed a suspicious-looking man loitering near the post office and stopped to speak to him. The man produced a sawn-off shotgun and ordered them to drive him to Blidworth, six miles away. But they managed, with the help of two members of the public, to overpower him, and found in his possession two hoods of the sort known to have been used by the Black Panther.

The man turned out to be Donald Neilson, aged thirty-nine, of Grangefield Avenue, Thornaby, Bradford, a married man with a teenage daughter. Neilson, who had changed his name from Nappey, was a joiner and occasional taxi-driver. But in his attic police found more guns and hoods, together with burglary equipment.

Neilson was tried in Oxford in June 1976 for the kidnapping and murder of Lesley Whittle, for which he was sentenced to twenty-one years' imprisonment. He was then tried for the murders of three sub-postmasters and sentenced to life imprisonment for each offence. No charge was brought against him in connection with the shooting of

21

the security guard in Dudley, as the victim in this case had lived for fourteen months after the offence had been committed.

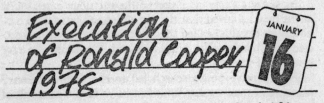

Execution of Ronald Cooper, 1978

Ronald Frank Cooper, who was hanged in South Africa on 16 January 1978, was a fantasist who wanted to become a mass murderer. Fortunately for the rest of society, he was assailed by doubt and misfortune in his attempts to put his ideas into practice.

Cooper had a troubled childhood: he is known to have hated his father and to have tried, at the age of eleven, to strangle a girl. Early in 1976 he was an unemployed labourer living in a hotel in Berea, Johannesburg. It was then that he committed his first-known crime as an adult.

Following a ten-year-old boy into an apartment block in a different district of Johannesburg, he pulled out a gun and forced the child to accompany him to a nearby park. There, however, he suddenly gave up whatever he had in mind and allowed his victim to go home. The boy, Tresslin Pohl, was later taken out in a police car to look for him, but without success.

A month later, on 17 March 1976, Ronald Cooper made a long entry in his diary, no doubt to convince himself that he was now more resolute than he had been before. He began, falteringly enough: 'I have decided that I think I should become a homosexual murderer ...' Then, taking the bull by the horns, he continued: '... and shall get hold of young boys and bring them here where I am staying and I shall rape them and then kill them.'

22

Soon his imagination was running wild: 'I shall not kill all the boys in the same way. Some I shall strangle with my hands. Other boys I shall strangle with a piece of cord or rope. Others again I shall stab to death, and others I shall cut their throats. I can also suffocate or smother other boys ...'

He went on and on, listing different ways in which he would dispose of his victims, finally stating that after killing thirty boys, he would turn his attention to the opposite sex and kill at least six girls or women. Yet, in spite of this, he remained as half-hearted as ever in practice.

Four days after making this entry Cooper followed another ten-year-old boy into a block of flats. Pushing him against a wall, he pressed a knife against his chest, inflicting two minor wounds, but ran off when the boy screamed. At his next attempt, in a block in his own district, he pulled a boy out of the lift and tried to strangle him, but once again took to his heels when the victim screamed.

On 16 May, in yet another apartment block, he grasped Mark Garnet, aged twelve, by the throat. When the boy lost consciousness Cooper tied a rope round his neck and made an unsuccessful attempt at sodomy. Afterwards he loosened the rope, hoping that the boy was still alive. But this time the attack had been fatal.

Overcome with remorse, Cooper described the murder in three different diaries — a clear sign of mental conflict. 'I only wish I can undo what I did,' he wrote in one of them. 'It's a really dreadful thing that I did. I never want to do such a thing again.'

He was not to have any more opportunities, for Tresslin Pohl, a schoolfriend of Mark Garnet's, had discovered where Cooper was living: he had followed him home after seeing him in a cinema and, surprisingly, kept this information to himself. But now, hearing of Mark's death, he decided to go to the police.

Police officers went immediately to the hotel and waited in a car near the entrance. When Cooper emerged he took fright at the sight of them, and after a brief chase, was taken into custody. The diaries found in his room left no doubt about his guilt.

Cooper was twenty-six years old at the time of his execution.

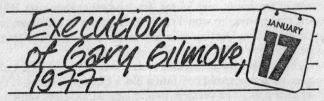

On 17 January 1977, Gary Gilmore, a double murderer, was executed by firing squad in the State of Utah, at his own insistence. It was the outcome of a successful legal battle over what he called 'the right to die' and brought an end to a ten-year moratorium on the death penalty in the United States. The case was, of course, highly publicized and provided Norman Mailer with a subject for a very successful book, *The Executioner's Song*.

Nine months earlier Gilmore, aged thirty-five, had been released on parole from the federal penitentiary in Marion, Illinois, after serving over eleven years. A violent and dangerous man, he had, in fact, spent more than half of his life in detention, and during his last term, he and a friend had beaten and knifed a fellow-convict so badly that he had almost died.

He had, it seems, no intention of making good. He drank heavily and began stealing from stores, the thefts being the result of habit rather than need. The two murders were committed in July 1976, robbery being the motive in each case.

The first murder was that of Max Jensen, a law student working at a service station in Orem, Utah; Gilmore held him up, forced him into the men's room, and shot him in the back of the head while he lay on the floor. The second

24

which took place the following evening, was that of Ben Bushnell, the manager of the City Centre Motel in Provo, a few miles away; the victim was shot dead in the same way. In each case Gilmore stole about $125 in cash.

On the latter occasion he was seen by the victim's wife and a guest at the motel. Afterwards, in disposing of the gun, he accidentally shot himself in the hand. The wound was noticed at a nearby garage when he went to collect his truck, which had been left for servicing, and was later reported to the police. Gilmore was arrested without difficulty while trying to leave the state by road.

His determination to avoid a commutation of sentence was due not to remorse, but to a fear of further long-term imprisonment. He told his brother, who intended to apply for a stay of execution on his behalf: 'I've spent too much time in jail. I don't have anything left in me.'

At one point he persuaded a girl with whom he was in love to smuggle drugs in to him, so that they could both commit suicide at a pre-arranged time. But the attempt failed and the girl was removed to a mental hospital for treatment.

As a result of his demand to be executed, Gilmore became a celebrity, selling the rights to his life story for about $50,000. On the night before his death he gave a farewell party inside the prison for his relatives and friends. Early the following morning he instructed his lawyers to appeal against a last-minute stay of execution; they did so, and the order was set aside.

The execution was carried out in a local cannery to which Gilmore had been taken by van. He was strapped down in an old office chair, with a dirty mattress behind the backboard to prevent ricochets. A light was shone on to him, while everyone else was in semi-darkness. When a hood had been pulled over his face, the members of the firing squad took aim from behind a screen, training their guns on a white ring pinned above his heart.

Murder of Julia Wallace, 1931

On the evening of 20 January 1931, Julia Wallace, the fifty-year-old wife of an insurance agent, was found battered to death in the sitting-room of her home in Wolverton Street, Liverpool. She had been struck over the head eleven times — many of the blows being dealt when she was already dead — and the walls, furniture and carpet of the room were drenched with blood. An iron bar which the couple had kept for cleaning the fireplace was missing from the house, and it appeared that about £4 in cash had also been taken. The iron bar, which was never found, was almost certainly the murder weapon.

Her husband, William Herbert Wallace, aged fifty-two, informed the police that a telephone message had been left for him at his chess club the previous evening by an unknown man calling himself Qualtrough. The message was that Qualtrough wanted to speak to him on a matter of business and that the insurance agent should call at his home in Menlove Gardens East, Mossley Hill, at 7.30 p.m. the following day. Wallace had accordingly left his own home about 6.50 p.m. and travelled by tramcar to the Menlove Gardens area of Liverpool, only to discover that Menlove Gardens East did not exist.

Arriving back at his own home about 8.45 p.m., Wallace had called for assistance from his neighbours, Mr and Mrs Johnston, saying that he was unable to get into his house because the doors wouldn't open. But when they went to help him they found that his back door, at least, opened without difficulty. The body was discovered a moment later, Wallace being strangely calm at the sight of it.

The police were suspicious of Wallace's account of his movements, especially as they could find no sign of a forced entry. It also seemed, from the pathologist's report, that Mrs Wallace had been killed before her husband left the house that evening. As for the telephone call to his chess club, that was found to have been made from a telephone box less than a quarter of a mile from Wolverton Street. So Wallace could easily have made it himself.

After continuing their investigation for two weeks, the police arrested Wallace and charged him with the crime. He was brought to trial at St George's Hall, Liverpool, on 22 April. But the case proved not to be very strong, and the judge, in his summing-up, suggested to the jury that it was insufficient to justify a conviction.

Wallace had had no motive for killing his wife. They had been a devoted couple, leading conventional lives, and he had stood to gain nothing from her death. Mrs Wallace, according to the evidence of a milk delivery boy, had still been alive at 6.30 that evening; her husband had boarded a tramcar at Smithdown Junction, a ten-minute walk from the house, at 7.10. Later, when the murder was reported, no bloodstains had been found on any of his clothes, except a macintosh on which his dead wife's body had actually been lying.

Yet, incredibly, the jury disregarded the judge's advice and returned a verdict of guilty. Wallace, under sentence of death, appealed against the conviction, and won his case before the Court of Criminal Appeal. He died two years later, claiming to the end that he knew the real identity of his wife's murderer.

The case is still the subject of much speculation.

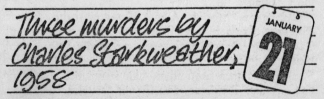

Three murders by Charles Starkweather, 1958

JANUARY
21

On 21 January 1958, Charles Starkweather, a nineteen-year-old garbage collector of Lincoln, Nebraska, called at the home of his girlfriend, Caril Ann Fugate, aged fourteen. She was not there at the time, so her mother and stepfather, Velda and Marion Bartlett, allowed him into the house to await her return. He was carrying a hunting rifle, and began to play with it while he was waiting.

Being only 5 feet 2 inches tall, and having red hair, Starkweather was known as 'Little Red'. He drove a hot-rod and read comics; the film star James Dean was his personal hero. But his girlfriend's mother was evidently uneasy in his presence, for she shouted at him, telling him to stop fiddling with his gun. At this, Starkweather shot both Mrs Bartlett and her husband dead. He then went on waiting until Caril returned.

Caril Fugate knew what Starkweather was like, for a few weeks earlier she had joined him in carrying out a robbery at a gas station, during the course of which the attendant had been murdered. She was not distressed when she arrived home and found that he had killed her mother and stepfather, and apparently raised no objection when he went into one of the bedrooms and choked her two-year-old stepsister to death. The couple calmly put a notice on the front door, stating: 'Every Body is Sick with the Flu'. They then made some sandwiches and sat down to watch television, as if oblivious of the corpses lying around.

A few days later the two teenagers drove off in Stark-weather's hot-rod, making their way across America. The police broke into the house in Lincoln and raised an alert, but it was several days before the couple were arrested and during that time the former garbage collector killed seven more people.

The first of these was August Meyer, a wealthy farmer. The next two were a teenage couple, Robert Jensen and Carol King; the girl was raped repeatedly before being beaten to death. Then C. Lauer Ward, head of the Capital Steel Works, his wife and their maid were killed after being tied up and mutilated. Finally, in Douglas, Wyoming, Merle Collison, a shoe salesman, was shot dead.

Attempting to get away from the scene of this last

crime, Starkweather found that his car would not start, and tried to force a passer-by to help him. The passer-by, an oil agent named Joseph Sprinkle, grabbed his rifle and held on to it until the police arrived. There were, by this time, 1200 police and members of the National Guard in pursuit of the couple, and they were quickly arrested, Starkweather surrendering after being grazed by a bullet.

Starkweather at first tried to protect the girl by telling the police that he had taken her hostage, but he stopped doing so when she called him a killer. He made a confession, declaring his hatred of the society he knew, which seemed to him to be made up entirely of 'Goddam sons of bitches looking for somebody to make fun of'. He was executed in the electric chair at the Nebraska State Penitentiary on 25 June 1959.

Caril Fugate, who claimed to be innocent of the crimes to which Starkweather had confessed, was sentenced to life imprisonment. She was released on parole in 1977.

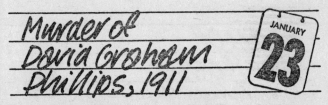

Murder of David Graham Phillips, 1911

JANUARY 23

The murder of David Graham Phillips, on 23 January 1911, was a ludicrous crime, committed as a result of a false assumption on the part of his killer, Fitzhugh Coyle Goldsborough, who killed himself immediately afterwards.

Phillips, aged forty-three, was a popular author whose novel, *The Fashionable Adventures of Joshua Craig*, was among the best-sellers of the time. He had an apartment in Gramercy Park, Manhattan.

Goldsborough, aged thirty, was a member of a rich Philadelphia family. He had no occupation and no apparent aim; much of his time was spent lying in bed, either reading love stories or turning neurotic ideas over in his mind. He did not know Phillips personally.

Somehow, Goldsborough had conceived the notion that his unmarried sister, whom he adored, had been used as a real-life model for a flippant society girl in Phillips' novel, and this he regarded as a slight which had to be avenged.

The murder took place just after Phillips left his apartment on the day in question. Goldsborough, according to witnesses, confronted him with a pistol, shouting, 'Here you go!' He then shot Phillips five times before turning the gun on himself. As he fired his last shot he screamed, 'Here I go!'

Phillips was taken to hospital, where he lived for some hours. As he died he remarked, 'I can fight one bullet, but not five.'

When Goldsborough's parents were told what had happened they revealed the reason for his astonishing conduct.

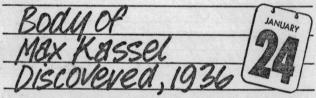

Body of Max Kassel Discovered, 1936

JANUARY 24

About ten o'clock on the morning of 24 January 1936, a man's body was discovered in a country lane near St Albans, Hertfordshire. He had died from gunshot wounds a few hours earlier, having been beaten up beforehand. There was nothing in his pockets to reveal his identity, and all marks had been removed from his clothes. It was speculated in the press that he had been the victim of a gang killing.

Three days later he was identified as Émile Allard, a

dealer in cheap jewellery. Émile Allard, however, turned out to be one of many aliases of an international crook named Max Kassel, generally known as 'Red Max'.

Kassel was a Latvian, born in 1879. He had a criminal record in France, where he had been imprisoned in 1922 for drug-trafficking, and was also known to have been involved in a vice racket in South America. More recently he had lived in Soho, arranging marriages — or, at least, marriage ceremonies — for Frenchwomen who wanted to obtain British nationality. He had been seen in Soho about 7.30 p.m. on 23 January.

During the course of their inquiries police officers learnt that Kassel had been accustomed to using the car-hire services of a Frenchman named Alexandre, who, on being interviewed, gave the impression of knowing more about the affair than he was willing to divulge.

Investigating his background, they found that he held the lease of a two-floor flat in Little Newport Street, occupied by Suzanne Naylor, a Frenchwoman married to an Englishman. Mrs Naylor was known to have a lover named Georges Lacroix, who normally lived with her at the Little Newport Street address. But neither of them were to be found there when the police went to see them.

Suspicious, the police broke in and searched the place, finding some broken window-panes and specks of blood in the bathroom. But there were no fingerprints anywhere and no clothes in the cupboards. The couple had cleaned the flat as thoroughly as possible and fled.

From a Ministry of Health insurance card, found behind a chest of drawers, the police traced a second French-woman, Marcelle Aubin, who had been employed as Suzanne Naylor's maid. Marcelle Aubin informed them that her employer had left for France on 25 January.

Alexandre was questioned further and obliged to surrender his American car for examination. When blood-stains were found in it he decided to tell the police what had happened.

He said that Lacroix had telephoned him late at night

on 23 January and told him to go to the flat in Little Newport Street. When he arrived there he was shown Kassel's body and told to return at 4 a.m. to help dispose of it, Lacroix threatening him with a gun. At 4 a.m. he and Lacroix had taken the body, wrapped in a blanket, out to his car. They had then driven to St Albans together.

Kassel, he explained, had owed Suzanne Naylor £25. Lacroix had started to beat him up because he had failed to pay it back, and had shot him when Kassel resisted. The victim had broken the window in an attempt to call for help.

This account was confirmed by Marcelle Aubin, who now admitted that she had been present and that she had heard the fighting, the shots and a constant groaning from another room. She had stayed in the flat all night, helping Suzanne to remove traces of the crime, she said.

Suzanne Naylor was located in France, where she was known to the police as Paulette Bernard. She had been legally married in France before coming to England, and so was still a French citizen. Georges Lacroix proved to be an alias of Robert Vernon, a Frenchman with a record of larceny with violence, who had escaped from Devil's Island in 1927.

As extradition was impossible, it was arranged that they would both be tried in Paris, Vernon for murder and his mistress for being an accessory after the fact. Chief Inspector F.D. Sharpe of the Flying Squad had therefore to give evidence against them before a French court.

In April 1937 Robert Vernon was convicted of the murder and sentenced to ten years' hard labour and twenty years' banishment to French Guiana. Paulette Bernard, who claimed to have been an unwilling participant, was acquitted.

Mass Poisoning in Tokyo, 1948

Just before closing time on 26 January 1948, a man entered a branch of the Imperial Bank in north Tokyo, claiming to be one of the city's public health officials. Announcing that there had been an outbreak of dysentery in the area, he induced all sixteen of the bank's employees to drink a solution of potassium cyanide. He then proceeded to rob the tills as his victims collapsed around him, and made off with a large amount of money in cash and cheques. Only four members of the staff survived.

Seven months later Sadamichi Hirasawa, a fifty-six-year-old artist of Otaru, Hokkaido, was arrested in connection with the murders. Normally a poor man, Hirasawa was unable to explain a comparatively large sum of money found in his possession, and eventually confessed to the crime. He afterwards retracted the confession, saying that it had been obtained after thirty-seven days of intensive questioning, but he was convicted and sentenced to death.

The sentence was confirmed in 1955 but never carried out, as successive Justice Ministers, for some undisclosed reason, refused to give their approval to the execution order. Sadamichi Hirasawa has remained in prison ever since and his sentence has never been commuted. He is said to have been on Death Row longer than anyone else in the world.

But many doubts have been expressed about his guilt, and there have been many demands for a retrial. Of the four surviving members of the bank staff, three said only that he bore a resemblance to the person responsible for the crime, while the fourth could see no resemblance at all. Moreover, it is now known that the Japanese police did not believe him to be guilty, either.

33

Following his retirement in 1963, Hideo Noruchi, the police officer in charge of the investigation, revealed that his team of detectives had believed the culprit to be experienced in the use of poisons, and had suspected a member of the 731st Regiment of the Imperial Japanese Army. This regiment had been involved in chemical warfare research during the Second World War, using Chinese prisoners in its experiments. But its war record had been ignored by General MacArthur's Occupation Force in return for the information which had been gained.

It appears from contemporary documents which have recently been discovered in the United States that MacArthur's General Headquarters also believed the poisoner to have been a member of the 731st Regiment, but forced the Japanese police to frame an innocent man rather than allow the connection to be exposed. Japanese newspapers which tried to investigate the case at the time were censored — also on orders from MacArthur's GHQ. And an American soldier with whom Hirasawa claimed to have been playing cards on the afternoon in question was recalled from Japan before the trial started in 1949.

In February 1984 Hirasawa, then aged ninety-two, was reported to be confined to bed and going blind in Sendai Jail. A plea for clemency was made on his behalf by a group of supporters called the Save Hirasawa Committee, whose members include Takeshiko Hirasawa, the artist's adopted son. The plea was unsuccessful.

In May 1985 an attempt was made to get him released under Japan's Statute of Limitations, as thirty years had elapsed since his death sentence had been confirmed. But this also failed because the thirty-year rule was interpreted as applying only to accused persons who had not been captured or who had escaped from custody.

It seems likely that the fight to clear Hirasawa's name will continue long after his death.

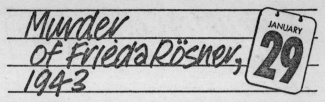

Murder of Frieda Rösner, 1943

On 29 January 1943, a woman's body was found in a wood near the village of Köpenick, near Berlin. Frieda Rösner, aged fifty-one, had been out collecting firewood; her death was caused by strangulation. There were no obvious suspects, so the police officer in charge of the case began questioning known criminals from the village. One of these was Bruno Lüdke, a laundry roundsman who had earlier been sterilized after being arrested for sexual assault.

Lüdke, who was mentally defective, admitted that he had known the victim and that he had seen her in the woods. On being asked if he had killed her, he became violent and had to be restrained. He then admitted the crime and went on to confess that he was guilty of eighty-four other murders in different parts of Germany. Some of these murders were found to be on record as unsolved crimes; others were found to be offences for which innocent men had been arrested. At any rate, after an investigation lasting a year, it was concluded that Lüdke's confession was true.

Born in 1909, Lüdke had committed his first murder in 1928. His victims had all been women, rape being his usual motive, although he also robbed them; their deaths were normally caused either by strangulation or by stabbing. On another occasion he had derived pleasure from running a woman down with his horse-drawn delivery van. In addition to all this, he had been in the habit of torturing animals.

Instead of being brought to trial, Lüdke was removed to a hospital in Vienna, where he was used for experiments. He was finally put to death by means of an injection on 8 April 1944.

The Nazis treated the case as a state secret.

Kenneth Neu, who was hanged in New Orleans on 1 February 1935, was an aspiring night-club singer with a record of mental illness. On 2 September 1933, while he was out of work in New York, he met Lawrence Shead, a homosexual theatre-owner. Shead took him for a drink, offered him a job, and invited him back to his apartment. There, however, it became clear that his real interest in him was a sexual one. Neu smashed in Shead's skull with an electric iron, put on one of his suits, and made off with his watch and wallet.

Two weeks later, in New Orleans, he met Eunice Hotter, a young waitress with whom he spent the next three nights. Eunice wanted to go to New York and Neu promised to take her there, but by now he was out of money again and decided to try blackmail.

In the lobby of the Jung Hotel, he became acquainted with Sheffield Clark, a Nashville store-owner aged sixty-three. Calling on Clark later in his room, he demanded money from him, threatening to accuse him of making homosexual advances. When Clark reached for the telephone to call the police, Neu hit him with a blackjack and strangled him. He took $300 and Clark's car keys and went to the car park to get his car, telling the attendant that he was the owner's son. He then set out for New York with Eunice Hotter, having first replaced the number plate of the stolen car with a notice chalked on a piece of cardboard: 'New Car in Transit'.

Driving through New Jersey, he was stopped by the police, who asked what the notice meant. Unable to give a satisfactory explanation, he spent the night in jail — as did Eunice Hotter and a hitch-hiker who had been in the car with them. It was then noticed that he fitted the description of a man wanted in connection with Shead's murder.

Asked if he knew Shead, Neu replied, 'Sure ... I killed him. This is his suit I'm wearing now.' He went on to confess that he had also killed Sheffield Clark. 'He seemed like a nice old man,' he said. 'But I was desperate for money.' In view of Shead's homosexuality, it was decided that Neu should be sent back to New Orleans to be tried for Clark's murder.

Neu, aged twenty-five, was a handsome man with an engaging manner. It was partly because of this that his trial, which opened on 12 December 1933, attracted a lot of attention. He appeared in court wearing Shead's suit and pleaded insanity, evidence being given that he had suffered mental deterioration as a result of syphilis. As if to emphasize the point, Neu sang on his way to and from the courtroom. He was, however, convicted, and an appeal was turned down.

On Death Row he remained cheerful, singing and tap-dancing in his cell, and receiving visits from a young woman who had apparently fallen in love with him. At the gallows he sang a verse which he had composed himself, beginning, 'I'm fit as a fiddle and ready to hang'.

While under sentence of death he had also become a Roman Catholic.

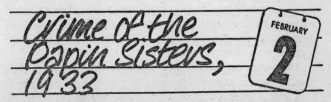

Crime of the Papin Sisters, 1933

FEBRUARY 2

On the evening of 2 February 1933, René Lancelin, a French attorney living in Le Mans, arrived for dinner at the home of a friend. He had been away all day on business and expected that his wife and twenty-seven-year-old daughter Geneviève, who had also been invited, would meet him there. But they had not turned up and his friend had had no word from them.

M. Lancelin waited for a little while, then tried to telephone his home. He received no reply. Becoming worried, he excused himself and went to find out what had happened. He found his own house in darkness, except for a faint glow from an upstairs room occupied by their maids, the sisters Christine and Lea Papin. Moreover, he was unable to get into the house as the front door had been locked from the inside. He therefore called the police.

An inspector came to his assistance, forcing his way into the house. He found the ground floor to be deserted. But on the first floor landing lay the bodies of the attorney's wife and daughter, revoltingly mutilated: the walls and doors had been splashed with blood to a height of over seven feet. The police officer immediately went in search of the maids and, finding their room locked, broke down the door. Inside, the two women lay huddled together, naked, in a bed.

They both confessed to the crime, which appeared to have been committed because Madame Lancelin had rebuked them over a blown fuse. 'When I saw that Madame Lancelin was going to jump on me I leapt at her face and scratched out her eyes with my fingers,' said Christine Papin. She then realized that she had made a mistake and quickly corrected herself: 'No ... it was on Mademoiselle Lancelin that I leapt, and it was her eyes that I scratched out. Meanwhile, my sister Lea had jumped on Madame Lancelin and scratched her eyes out in the same way.'

After this, she continued, she had brought up a knife and a hammer from the kitchen, and with these two instruments she and her sister attacked their victims afresh. 'We struck at the head with the knife, hacked at the bodies and legs, and also struck with a pewter pot, which was standing on a little table on the landing. We exchanged one instru-

38

ment for another several times. By that I mean that I would pass the hammer over to my sister so that she could hit with it, while she handed me the knife — and we did the same with the pewter pot.'

She said that she had locked the attorney out because she wanted the police to be the first to arrive on the scene, and that they had taken their clothes off because they were stained with blood. 'I have no regrets — or, rather, I can't tell you whether I have any or not ... I did not plan my crime and I didn't feel any hatred towards them (the victims), but I don't put up with the sort of gesture that Madame Lancelin was making at me that evening.'

Lea corroborated Christine's account. 'Like my sister, I affirm that we had not planned to kill our mistresses,' she said. 'The idea came suddenly, when we heard Madame Lancelin scolding us.'

Christine Papin, aged twenty-eight, and her sister Lea, twenty-one, were brought to trial in Le Mans in September 1933. They were already regarded as notorious criminals by this time, and the newspapers referred to them as 'the diabolical sisters', and 'the lambs who had become wolves'. As the details of their crime were given in the courtroom, there were murmurs of horror and demands for their execution from the spectators. The prisoners listened impassively.

The judge questioned them about their motive, finding it impossible to believe that they could have made such ferocious attacks on their victims just because they were being scolded over a blown fuse. They had, after all, both agreed that they had been well paid and well treated by the family, and bore no resentment as a result of being their servants.

Observing that the prisoners had led unusually isolated lives for young people, with no social activities and no contact with members of the opposite sex, the judge asked whether they had had a sexual relationship with each other. But Christine replied, with a shrug, that they were just sisters; there was nothing else between them.

As no satisfactory explanation of the crime emerged, the defence naturally pleaded that the prisoners were not of sound mind. The jury, however, returned verdicts of guilty against both of them, though with extenuating circumstances in Lea's case, as she had been dominated by Christine. The judge then sentenced Christine to death and Lea to ten years' hard labour.

Christine's sentence was afterwards commuted to hard labour for life, but she began to show signs of insanity not long afterwards and died in a psychiatric hospital in 1937. Lea was released after serving her term.

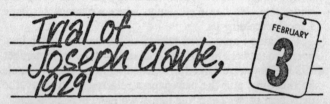

Trial of Joseph Clark, 1929

On 3 February 1929, Joseph Clark, aged twenty-one, was brought to trial at the Liverpool Assize Court, charged with the murder of Alice Fontaine, his former landlady. He pleaded guilty, against the advice of his counsel, and was sentenced to death. It was one of the shortest murder trials on record, lasting just four and a half minutes. He was afterwards hanged.

Clark was an amateur hypnotist who lived off his many girlfriends. He had been brought up by relatives in the United States, but worked his passage back to England in 1927. He seems to have had little difficulty inducing girls to part with their money; one of them said later, 'I could not resist him, and would do anything he suggested ... I gave him money whenever he wanted it ...'

In Birkenhead he tried to marry a girl who was under twenty-one by presenting her older sister's birth certificate at the registrar's office. When the attempt was discovered he became enraged and tried to strangle the girl with a pyjama cord, shouting, 'If I can't have you nobody else shall!' No charge was brought against him over this, as the girl was afraid of the publicity which would result from it.

Clark became a lodger at Mrs Fontaine's house in Northbrook Street, Liverpool, after meeting her daughter whose name was also Alice; he was now calling himself Kennedy. He failed to pay for his keep and constantly borrowed money. When he was finally turned out — after the discovery of a letter from one of his other victims — he sent obscene letters to both mother and daughter.

Shortly afterwards, in October 1928, Clark suddenly appeared in the daughter's bedroom as she was getting ready to go to church. He tried to strangle her, again using a pyjama cord, and after a struggle she lost consciousness. She recovered a little later and found that he had also attempted to cut her throat. Her mother's body was found downstairs, Clark's attempt to strangle Mrs Fontaine having been more successful.

After being arrested Clark made a confession. He claimed that in her last moments, after he had relaxed his grip on her throat, Mrs Fontaine had smiled at him and asked him to take care of her daughter.

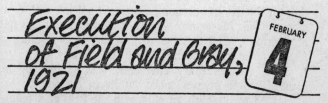

Execution of Field and Gray, 1921

FEBRUARY 4

On 4 February 1921, Jack Alfred Field, aged nineteen, and William Thomas Gray, twenty-nine, were hanged at Wandsworth Prison for a brutal murder committed on a stretch of shingle near Eastbourne on 19 August the previous year.

41

Their victim, Irene Munro, a Scottish-born typist from London, was seventeen years old. She had been spending a week's holiday at an Eastbourne boarding-house, and on the afternoon of the day in question was known to have been carrying her holiday money in her handbag.

A number of people noticed her in the company of two men, one of whom wore a herring-bone suit. Her body was afterwards found in a shallow grave; she had been battered to death with a stone, and her money had been stolen. It was the landlady of the boarding-house who identified the body.

Field and Gray were local residents, both out of work. They were initially questioned by police as a result of Gray's herring-bone suit, but were not regarded as suspects at this stage. Later, however, it was learnt from a barmaid at the Albemarle Hotel that they had been out of money on the morning of 19 August, but apparently affluent a few hours afterwards.

Then, during a house-to-house inquiry, a labourer stated that he had seen Gray, whom he knew personally, walking towards the shingle that afternoon with another man and a girl. The two culprits were arrested and charged with the crime.

They appeared for trial at the Lewes Assizes on 13 December 1920, denying the offence. Though witnesses had seen them in the girl's company, Field told the court that on the day in question he had had a drink with Gray after drawing his unemployment benefit, and that they had afterwards walked together to Pevensey — a distance of about four miles — meeting nobody on the way.

Gray, an unsavoury character, was advised by his counsel not to give evidence. While in custody he had attempted to establish an alibi with the help of a fellow-prisoner; during the course of the trial he fell asleep and was rebuked by the judge. His counsel suggested to the jury that an educated and refined girl like Irene Munro was unlikely to have associated with down-and-out men like the prisoners.

While under sentence of death the two ruffians both accused each other of the girl's murder. We do not know which of them was telling the truth.

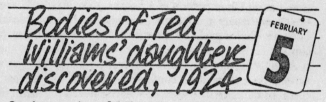

Bodies of Ted Williams' daughters discovered, 1924

FEBRUARY 5

On the morning of 5 February 1924, Edward Williams, a poor music teacher living in a suburb of Sydney, was returning from Mass when he stopped to speak to a crossing-sweeper named Tonkin, and offered to buy him a drink. Tonkin was surprised, for Williams did not normally drink and was known to be having a very hard time. However, he went with him to a working-men's bar where the music teacher ordered two glasses of stout.

During the course of their conversation Williams said that he was taking his three daughters to Brisbane, where he had been offered a position as choirmaster. Tonkin, he said, could have his furniture in settlement of a debt; he could go and collect it from his lodgings. The crossing-sweeper was impressed and gave Williams enough money to get the four of them to Brisbane. Later, after parting company with him, he took a handcart to the music teacher's lodgings to move the furniture.

His arrival threw Williams' landlady, Florence Mahon, into a state of confusion. She rushed upstairs to Williams' room, to see what he had to say about it. But Williams wasn't there. Instead, she found his three little girls lying together in bed, all with their throats cut. Their blood had soaked through the mattress on to some newspaper which had been spread underneath it.

The police started a search for Williams, but he was

nowhere to be found. He was still at large when the bodies of the children were buried.

Among those who knew him, the crime caused dismay as well as horror, for Ted Williams had loved his children: they had been a source of great pleasure to him, in spite of his otherwise troubled existence. A neighbour who had seen him on the afternoon of 4 February was to recall: 'He looked extremely tired until he smiled at his daughters. Then his whole face lit up and the tiredness seemed to leave him.'

After being on the run for several days Williams gave himself up and made a confession. He said that he had killed his daughters because he was frightened for them. 'I knew what I was doing,' he said. 'I was doing it for the best, because I loved them.' He was charged with murder.

Ted Williams, aged fifty-two, was a man prone to misfortune. His income had never been high and he had always found it difficult to make ends meet. For the last two years his wife, Florence Mahon's sister-in-law, had been confined in an asylum, and he and his three daughters, the eldest of whom was five and a half, had lived and slept in one room. While he went hungry to ensure that they had an adequate amount of food, he was treated with contempt by his brother-in-law who regarded him as 'a bum'. By 4 February he was close to the end of his tether.

On that day, Florence Mahon, who looked after the children for him while he went out to give lessons, said that she would do it no more: he would have to find somebody else. Later the same day her husband suggested that he should send them to an institution because they were now too old to sleep in the same room as him.

To Ted Williams, Mahon's remark was a shattering blow. When he came up for trial at the Central Court in Sydney, he told the jury: 'I saw if my girls went to an institution they would be separated. They would not be able to sit at the same table together, and when they came out they would be tools for the first smooth-tongued person who came along. I know — and you know, gentlemen — that

44

the majority of prostitutes are the women who were raised in public institutions such as my girls would have been sent to had I been agreeable. I saw it all, and saw beyond it.' Rather than allow that to happen, he had murdered them in their sleep.

He denied that he was insane; he denied that he had tried to escape justice. 'I intended to give myself up, but decided not to do so until the Monday, in order that I might learn that my children were properly buried,' he explained.

Ted Williams was convicted and sentenced to death. Many thousands of letters were sent to the Minister of Justice, Thomas Ley, asking for the sentence to be commuted. But they were brushed aside, the execution being carried out at Long Bay Jail.

Thomas Ley was later convicted of murder himself and died in Broadmoor. An account of his crime also appears in this book (see 30 November).

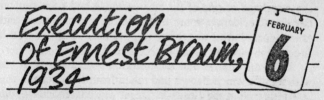

Execution of Ernest Brown, 1934

FEBRUARY 6

Ernest Brown, who was hanged on 6 February 1934, at the age of thirty-five, had been employed as a groom by Frederick Morton, a wealthy cattle-dealer of Saxton Grange, an isolated farmhouse near the village of Towton, in Yorkshire. While working in that capacity he had been having an affair with Dorothy Morton, the cattle-dealer's wife. But he proved to be a possessive man with a violent temper, and Mrs Morton found this irksome.

In June 1933 he became indignant at being asked to mow the lawn, which he did not consider to be one of his duties; he promptly left Morton's employment. A little while afterwards he sought, with Mrs Morton's help, to get the job back, but found that his former employer would now only accept him as an odd-job man. Brown therefore returned to Saxton Grange seething with resentment and promising himself revenge.

On the evening of 5 September, while his employer was away, he started an argument with Dorothy Morton because she had been out swimming with another man; he struck her and she fell to the ground. The same evening the telephone was found to be out of order and Brown began firing a shotgun outside the house, saying that he was shooting at rats. Dorothy Morton became frightened, having only her baby and her young help, Ann Houseman, for company, and soon the two women took the child and locked themselves in upstairs rooms.

At 3.30 a.m. there was an explosion outside and they saw that the garage was on fire. They left the house in terror, running into the nearby fields. In the morning the ruins of the garage, which had been completely destroyed, were examined, and the cattle-dealer's body was found in the wreckage of one of his two cars. He had been shot in the chest, evidently some hours before the explosion had taken place. Petrol was found to have been used to fuel the fire, and it was this which had caused the explosion.

It was also found that the telephone wires had been cut with a knife which Brown had taken from the kitchen.

At his trial at the Leeds Assizes it was contended that he had cut the wires after killing Frederick Morton about 9.30 p.m., and then frightened the women to prevent them leaving the house. His own claim, that Morton had caused the fire himself as a result of being drunk, was not taken seriously.

Ernest Brown's execution took place at Armley Prison in Leeds. While on the scaffold he was asked by the chaplain if he wanted to confess any other crimes before being hanged. His reply, 'Ought to burn!' or 'Otterburn!' has given rise to the idea that he may have been the murderer of Evelyn Foster. Unfortunately, the trap opened before he could make himself clear on this point.

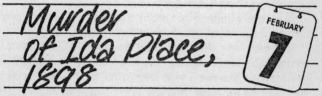

Murder of Ida Place, 1898

Just after 6.30 p.m. on 7 February 1898, a New York City policeman arrived at the Brooklyn home of William Place, a prosperous forty-seven-year-old insurance adjuster, accompanied by a neighbour who had reported hearing screams and cries for help from inside. He rang the bell and waited for a moment, then, hearing a moan himself, got the neighbour to help him force an entry.

Inside the house, a few feet from the front door, the two men found Place lying unconscious on the floor. He had serious head injuries and his face was smeared with blood. There was a smell of gas about the place.

Sending the neighbour to summon an ambulance, the patrolman tended the injured man. The precinct commander and two detectives arrived soon afterwards and began to search the premises, leaving Place in the hands of the ambulance crew. There appeared at first to be nobody else in the house, but tracing the smell of gas to one of the front bedrooms, the police officers found Place's wife Martha, also unconscious, wrapped in a quilt on the floor. She too, was taken to hospital, to be treated for gas poisoning.

But with the windows open and the gas cleared, another smell — that of carbolic acid — caused the police to force open the locked door of one of the other bedrooms. There, under the mattress of a disordered bed, they found the body of Place's daughter Ida, aged seventeen.

Ida Place had been dead for several hours. Her face had

been disfigured with acid burns while she was still alive; she had also received a heavy blow on the left temple. But her death had been caused by strangulation.

The police found no sign of a forced entry, and were unable to find the acid container. The following morning, however, a bloodstained axe was discovered in the side yard of the adjoining property; it appeared to have been thrown from one of Place's windows.

Inquiries revealed that Martha was William Place's second wife; his first had died when Ida was eleven, and he had married Martha a year later, after employing her as a housekeeper for some months. There had been many bitter quarrels between them, Martha behaving so aggressively that her husband, a year earlier, had brought charges against her, though without success.

The police also learnt from Hilda Jans, who had been a servant in the house, that she had been dismissed from her position on the day of the murder, being given a month's wages in lieu of notice, together with a bonus of $5 for having packed in readiness to leave by 5 p.m.

Asked about the smell of carbolic acid, Hilda said that she had been out in the back yard after breakfast and had first noticed it when she returned to the house around 9.15 a.m. She had not seen Ida Place afterwards, and had later found her bedroom door locked.

As soon as he regained consciousness William Place, not realizing that Ida was dead or that his wife was a patient in the same hospital, told police that Martha had tried to kill him and begged them to protect his daughter.

When he was well enough to speak to them at greater length he said that Martha had complained of Ida showing her neither affection nor respect, and resented the way in which he indulged her; that was one of their differences. Another was Martha's practice of hoarding money in her own bank account and, at the same time, running up excessive bills for him to pay.

On the day that she attacked him, he said, he had arrived home from his office to find the house in darkness.

He let himself in, calling out to his wife, his daughter and the servant — for he did not know that Hilda had been dismissed, and then, hearing nothing, went to look in the kitchen. He was going back towards the front door when he heard somebody creeping down the stairs, and, turning round, saw that it was Martha. He spoke to her, unaware that she had an axe in her hand, but she suddenly rushed forward and began to strike him with it.

The police, after listening to his account, had the unpleasant duty of informing him that his daughter had been murdered.

They were now satisfied that Martha had planned to kill both her husband and her stepdaughter, and that she had tried to kill herself when she realized that William's cries for help had been loud enough to be heard by the neighbours. She was therefore charged and taken into custody.

On 5 July she was brought to trial, dressed entirely in black. She admitted the attacks, pleading intense provocation in each case, but refused to say where she had obtained the acid or how long it had been in her possession. She was found guilty, with no recommendation of mercy, and on 20 March 1899, she was executed in Sing Sing Prison.

She was the first woman ever to die in the electric chair.

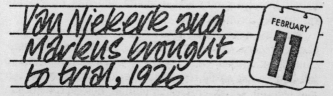

Van Niekerk and Markus brought to trial, 1926

FEBRUARY
11

On 11 February 1926, two ex-convicts, Andries Van Niekerk and Edward Markus, were brought to trial in Pretoria, accused of murdering the two occupants of a Transvaal farmhouse on the night of 2 December previously. The crime had been a callous one, and the farmhouse had been set on fire afterwards. The trial, which lasted eight days, was therefore followed with much interest.

Waterval Farm, in the Transvaal's Potgietersrust district, had been managed by sixty-year-old Bill Nelson for its absent owner; Nelson's companion, Tom Denton, a fifty-five-year-old former soldier, had run a small general store on the property, selling goods to its native workers. Both were evidently kind and friendly men, for when the two ex-convicts appeared at the farm in search of work they were treated with sympathy and generosity.

Nelson hired them to decorate the outside walls of the farm and gave them food and beds. He did not expect them to start work on the day of their arrival, and the next day he and Denton took them on a shooting trip, providing them with guns. On the evening of the second day they all dined together and retired early. Then, just after midnight, the sound of shots was heard, but nobody went to the scene until it was realized that the buildings were on fire. Two men were then seen running away from the premises.

Van Niekerk, aged thirty-four, was a habitual criminal with a long history of housebreaking, theft and violence: he had spent nearly half his life in prison and had been whipped on a number of occasions. A man of low mentality, he had delusions of persecution and superiority, and was given to outbursts of fury. It was contended on his behalf that his sanity was in doubt and that he was not responsible for his actions.

Markus, aged twenty-four, was a weaker man with a shorter record. On being arrested, he had made a confession, claiming that Van Niekerk — who had threatened to kill him — was solely responsible for the deaths of Nelson and Denton. Under cross-examination, however, he began to contradict himself, and it soon appeared that a confession which Van Niekerk had made in revenge — 'both Markus and I committed the crime' — was more credible.

Towards the close the question of whether Van Niekerk

was in such a condition that he would not know the nature and quality of his actions was put to a medical expert. The witness replied, 'I have seen an imbecile of the mental age of three or four years commit an act and know it was wrong. Therefore a person of higher age must know it.'

After an absence of just over two hours the jury found both defendants guilty and they were sentenced to death. Van Niekerk, pleased that Markus was to suffer the same fate as him, then waved his handkerchief towards relatives in the courtroom. The prisoners were both hanged on 14 April 1926.

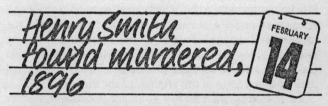

Henry Smith found murdered, 1896

On the morning of 14 February 1896, Henry Smith, a seventy-nine-year-old widower, was found dead in the kitchen of his neglected mansion in Muswell Hill, north London. He had been struck on the head twelve times during the course of a struggle and had afterwards been bound and gagged, his attackers evidently not realizing that they had killed him. His bedroom had been ransacked and money had been taken from his safe.

The culprits had entered the house through a kitchen window after trying unsuccessfully to open two other windows with a jemmy, and Mr Smith, awakened by the noise, had come downstairs in his nightshirt to investigate. Two penknives, which had been used to cut strips from a tablecloth, were found beside the body; the intruders had also left behind a toy lantern. Mr Smith's body had been found by his gardener.

Police investigating the crime soon learnt that two

strange men had been seen in the neighbourhood during the previous two days, and these were seen as the most likely suspects. Further inquiries revealed that they were Henry Fowler, aged thirty-one, and Albert Milsom, thirty-three, two known criminals from Kentish Town who were both missing from their homes. The toy lantern found at the scene of the crime was identified by Milsom's fifteen-year-old brother-in-law as his own. A warrant was then obtained for the arrest of both men, and they were apprehended in Bath on 12 April.

Fowler, an ex-convict who had been released on licence on 16 January previously, was a tough individual; he resisted arrest and was not overpowered until he had been struck several times over the head with a police revolver. But his companion, a shifty little man, gave no trouble and afterwards made a statement in which he admitted the robbery and accused Fowler of the murder. Fowler, he said, had killed the old man while he (Milsom) was outside the house. He also revealed that he and Fowler had buried their burglary tools in the grounds of the mansion.

Infuriated by what he saw as an act of betrayal, Fowler claimed that the murder had been committed by Milsom; the 'dirty dog' had put his foot on the old man's neck and made sure that he was dead, he declared. Besides the evidence of the toy lantern and their own statements, they were both identified as the men who had been seen in the neighbourhood two days before the discovery of the crime, and a £10 note found in Fowler's possession was known to have been stolen from the victim's home.

Their trial began at the Old Bailey on 19 May and lasted three days, the judge remarking in his summing up that the evidence of the two penknives indicated that two people had been engaged in tying up Mr Smith. When the jury retired to consider their verdict, Fowler fell upon Milsom and tried to strangle him. He had to be forcibly restrained by warders and policemen, the struggle continuing for twelve minutes. The jury returned a verdict of guilty against each of them and they were sentenced to death.

Henry Fowler and Albert Milsom were hanged at Newgate Prison on 9 June 1896, together with another murderer named Seaman, who was placed between them on the scaffold. An accident occurred at the execution, the hangman's assistant falling through the trap with the condemned. But he escaped unhurt, having instinctively grapped the legs of the prisoner in front of him.

It was the last triple execution to be carried out at Newgate.

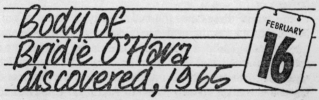

Body of Bridie O'Hara discovered, 1965

FEBRUARY 16

On 16 February 1965, the body of a naked woman was found in a patch of bracken on the Heron Trading Estate in Acton, west London. Bridie O'Hara, a twenty-seven-year-old prostitute of Agate Road, Hammersmith, had died of suffocation after an unsuccessful attempt at strangling; some of her teeth were missing and sperm was found in her throat. It appeared that she had died in a kneeling position, and also that her body had been kept somewhere cool before being taken to the place where it was found. Bridie O'Hara, a native of Dublin, had last been seen alive five weeks earlier.

At the time of this discovery police were investigating the cases of seven other prostitutes who had died mysteriously in the London area during the previous six years. The first of these, Elizabeth Figg, aged twenty-one, had been found strangled beside the Thames between Barnes and Chiswick on 17 June 1959; the skeleton of the second, Gwynneth Rees, aged twenty-two, during the clearing of a rubbish dump at Mortlake, also beside the Thames, on 8

November 1963. In the case of Gwynneth Rees the cause of death had not been established with certainty, but the fact that she too, had been a prostitute caused police to wonder whether the two cases were connected.

The other five bodies had all be found in 1964: Hannah Tailford, thirty, in the Thames at Hammersmith on 2 February; Irene Lockwood, twenty-six, also in the Thames (about 300 yards from the same place) on 9 April; Helene Barthelemy, twenty-two, near a sports ground in Brentford on 24 April; Mary Fleming, thirty, outside a garage near Chiswick High Road on 14 July, and Margaret McGowan, twenty-one, behind a car park in Kensington on 25 November.

In each of these cases the body had been found naked. There was no specific evidence of murder in two of them, for Hannah Tailford may have committed suicide, and Irene Lockwood had died from drowning. But the police regarded them as probable murder cases just the same, and when a caretaker named Kenneth Archibald confessed to having killed Irene Lockwood, he was arrested and brought to trial. He was found not guilty, having retracted his confession in the meantime.

In the case of Mary Fleming the body had been found in a sitting position in a cul-de-sac, close to a site where painters had been working the previous night. The painters had seen a man standing near a van, and when he became aware of their presence he had driven away hurriedly, almost colliding with a car. Though the driver of the car had reported the matter to the police, he had failed to make a note of the van's registration number, so the suspect could not be traced.

The deaths of Helene Barthelemy, Mary Fleming, and Margaret McGowan were all similar to that of Bridie O'Hara: teeth were missing from the bodies — false teeth in the case of Mary Fleming — and sperm was found in each of their throats. Traces of paint of a type used for spraying cars were found on the body in each case, leading police to speculate that they had been left in a garage or factory at some stage.

It seemed that the killer was a pervert who enjoyed strangling or choking his victims during oral sex, then repeating the sexual act later after forcing out some of their teeth. The fact that he removed all articles of clothing from the dead bodies led to him being called 'Jack the Stripper'.

The police were already engaged in a large-scale operation aimed at catching him, but it was not until the death of Bridie O'Hara that they located the place where the bodies had been kept — a transformer building near a paint-spray shop on the estate where Bridie O'Hara had been discovered.

The police then concentrated their efforts on the estate itself, taking note of all the vans seen in the area and paying particular attention to any which appeared there more than once. It was hinted on television that they were very near to bringing the culprit to justice. But, in fact, they never did so.

It was later claimed that one of the three main suspects, a forty-five-year-old security guard whose rounds included the paint-spray shop, had committed suicide while inquiries at the Heron Trading Estate were in progress. The man, who was unmarried, was not named, and his identity has not been made known to the public since. It is known, however, that he left a note saying he was 'unable to stand the strain any longer'.

With his death this shocking series of murders came to an end.

On 18 February 1949, John George Haigh, aged thirty-nine, a resident at the Onslow Court Hotel in South Kensington, London, committed the crime for which he was to be hanged. It was by no means his first offence, for Haigh was a professional criminal who lived by fraud and theft and had resorted to murder several times before. To the other residents at the hotel, however, he was a man of charm and good manners who appeared to have made a success of running his own engineering business. They had no reason to suspect him of any wrong-doing.

His victim, Mrs Olive Durand-Deacon, was a rich widow of sixty-nine. She and Haigh were on friendly terms as a result of having adjacent tables in the dining-room, and when she told him of a scheme to manufacture artificial finger-nails of her own design he suggested that she visit his factory in Crawley, Sussex, where she could chose the necessary materials. This idea appealed to Mrs Durand-Deacon, and she agreed to go with him.

On the day in question they left London about 2.30 p.m., travelling in Haigh's Alvis car. About 4.15 p.m. they were seen together at the George Hotel in Crawley. But that was the last time that Mrs Durand-Deacon was seen by anyone except Haigh.

Haigh's 'factory', in Leopold Road, was actually a building which he did not own, but was occasionally allowed to use as a storeroom in connection with his 'experimental engineering' work. It contained various articles, including three carboys of sulphuric acid, a forty-five gallon drum which had been specially lined to hold corrosive chemicals, a stirrup pump, a pair of gloves and a rubber apron. If Mrs Durand-Deacon found any of these things suspicious, it did not prevent her turning her back on him, for Haigh, taking a revolver from his pocket, was able to kill her with a single shot in the back of the neck. He then removed all her valuables — a Persian lamb coat, rings, a necklace, earrings and a cruciform — before putting the body into the drum. The sulphuric acid was put in afterwards with the use of the stirrup pump.

Haigh immediately set about disposing of the valuables and paying off debts, returning to Crawley several times in the next few days in order to make sure that the body was dissolving in the acid. In the meantime he was obliged to go to the police, in the company of another resident, to report his victim's disappearance.

The police were suspicious of Haigh from the start, and were not surprised to learn that he had served three terms of imprisonment. Searching the 'factory' in Crawley, they found his revolver, some ammunition and a receipt for a Persian lamb coat which had been left at a cleaners' in Reigate. They also traced the victim's jewellery, which had been sold to a jeweller in Horsham, a few miles away.

On being taken to Chelsea police station for questioning, Haigh told the police how he had dissolved Mrs Durand-Deacon's body, evidently in the mistaken belief that if the body could not be found a murder charge could not be brought against him. An examination of the sludge outside the storeroom then led to the discovery of a human gallstone and some fragments of bone, showing that the disintegration had not been complete. These remains were later identified as those of Mrs Durand-Deacon.

Charged with the murder, Haigh confessed that he had also killed a Mr William Donald McSwann in London in 1944, Mr McSwann's parents, also in London, in 1945, and a Dr Archibald Henderson and his wife in Crawley in 1948. He claimed that he had committed these murders, like that of Mrs Durand-Deacon, because he wanted to drink the blood of the victims, but it was found that his real motive in each case had been financial gain.

He later claimed to have killed three other people, all of

whom were strangers to him, but the existence of these people was never proved.

At his trial in Lewes, in July 1949, for the murder of Mrs Durand-Deacon, Haigh pleaded that he was insane. The jury, however, took only fifteen minutes to reject this defence and returned a verdict of guilty. Haigh's execution took place at Wandsworth Prison on 6 August.

Execution of Jean Lee and her accomplices, 1951

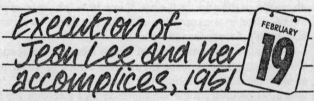

On 19 February 1951, Jean Lee, a thirty-three-year-old Australian murderess, and her two accomplices, Robert David Clayton and Norman Andrews, were hanged for the murder of William Kent, a bookmaker aged seventy-three, in his hotel room in Carlton, New South Wales, in November 1949.

Jean Lee, an attractive woman, had taken to prostitution during the Second World War after the failure of her marriage; Clayton, her lover, was a petty criminal who lived off her earnings from the servicemen of various nations who were stationed in Australia at the time.

After the war they turned to blackmail, Jean Lee enticing men into compromising situations, and Clayton, pretending to be her irate husband, bursting in on them to demand compensation. Andrews, a thug, did not join them in their criminal activities until 1949.

The murder of William Kent took place on the night of 7 November. Jean Lee and her companions met him in the bar of his hotel and later she retired to his room with him and got him drunk so that she could pick his pockets. However, the old man kept a tight grip on his money and she was unable to get it away from him until she hit him on the head with a bottle. She then tied him up and let Clayton and Andrews into the room.

The two ruffians tied the old man's thumbs together with a bootlace, kicked him repeatedly and slashed him several times with a broken bottle before he finally died. The room was ransacked.

After the discovery of the body, members of the hotel staff gave descriptions of the three culprits to the police and they were soon identified and arrested in Sydney. They all made confessions and were brought to trial in March 1950, a retrial being granted as a result of the manner in which two of the confessions had been obtained. The second trial had the same result as the first, and the High Court confirmed the death sentences passed on each of them.

Their executions took place at Pentridge Jail.

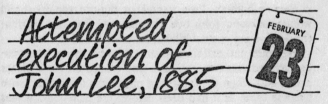

Attempted execution of John Lee, 1885

FEBRUARY
23

On 23 February 1885, John Lee, a prisoner in Exeter Jail, was due to be hanged for the murder of Emma Keyse, an elderly spinster of Babbacombe, near Torquay, by whom he had been employed as a footman. The body of his victim had been discovered during the course of a fire at her home in the early hours of 15 November previously. Her throat had been cut so deeply that the vertebrae of her neck were notched; she had also been beaten over the head with a hatchet. Lee, a young man with a prison record for theft, had killed her because she had found fault with his conduct and reduced his wages from 2s 6d (12½p) to 2s (10p) a week. He had afterwards set fire to the house, probably in the hope of concealing the crime.

As the time appointed for his execution approached, Lee showed no sign of fear; the strain which the imminence of such an event always produced among the prison staff did not affect him at all. Just before 8 a.m. he was taken from his cell and the solemn procession to the scaffold began, the chief warder leading the way. Lee, accompanied by two other warders, walked behind the prison chaplain, the Reverend John Pitkin. Various officials, including the hangman, the prison governor and the under-sheriff, together with several more warders followed.

At the place of execution Lee's legs were strapped together and the white cap pulled over his face. James Berry, the hangman, then adjusted the rope round his neck and asked if he had anything to say. Lee replied that he had not. As the chaplain concluded his service the hangman pulled the lever which operated the two trap-doors. To everyone's amazement, they failed to open. The prisoner remained motionless.

Berry moved the lever to and fro, but the trap-doors still would not open. John Lee was removed from the scaffold to an adjoining room while an examination of the drop was carried out, and certain adjustments were made. Then the condemned was brought back and placed on the scaffold again. But when the hangman pulled the lever, the result was the same as it had been before: the trap-doors would not budge.

Once again the culprit was taken from the scaffold, this time to the prison basement. Further adjustments were made. After a few more minutes the prisoner was brought back for a third attempt, the drop having been tested and found to be in working order. The chaplain started the service for the third time. James Berry pulled the lever. But the trap-doors still remained closed. The third attempt had failed, too.

Everyone concerned, except the condemned, was now in a state of consternation. They had no idea what to do for the best. Finally, the chaplain told the under-sheriff that he would have nothing more to do with the execution. It had therefore to be postponed, as it could not be carried out without the chaplain being present. Mr Pitkin accompanied the prisoner as he was taken back to his cell.

Outside the prison, there was much surprise when the black flag did not appear, and this was followed by great excitement when it was heard that there had been three unsuccessful attempts to hang the prisoner. Newspaper offices were afterwards besieged by people wanting to know the latest news of the affair, and it was said that there was a general feeling that the prisoner's life should be spared after the ordeal which he had suffered. It was announced later the same day that John Lee had been reprieved and that his sentence would be commuted to life imprisonment.

The failure of the scaffold has never been satisfactorily explained. Some said it was caused by damp, others that it was due to faulty construction.

John Lee remained in prison for the next twenty-two years, and was released on 18 December 1907. The following year he published a book about his life, making himself out to be innocent of the murder of which he had been convicted. It sold well, but was not taken seriously by people acquainted with the case. His guilt had been too firmly established by the evidence.

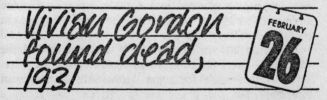

Vivian Gordon found dead, 1931

On the morning of 26 February 1931, Vivian Gordon, an attractive divorcée with expensive tastes, was found dead in a ravine in New York City's Van Cortlandt Park, having been strangled with a piece of clothes-line some hours earlier. Her mink coat, diamond ring and $665 wrist-watch were all missing, giving the impression that robbery had been the motive for the murder. However, the discovery of a five-volume diary in her Manhattan apartment, together with other pieces of evidence obtained elsewhere, caused police to suspect that this was not the case at all.

Vivian Gordon, who had once been convicted on a vice charge and sent to a reformatory, was found to have been both a blackmailer and a money-lender. It was also found that a few days before her murder she had given inform-ation to a committee investigating police corruption in New York City, claiming that her conviction eight years earlier had been the result of fabricated evidence. It there-fore appeared that any one of a good many people could have had cause to want her out of the way.

The crime proved to be New York's most sensational murder for five years, with several well-known figures being regarded as suspects and many lurid details of the victim's life published. At one point the lawyer Bernard Gervase and a thief known as 'Knucklehead' Kaufman were arrested on suspicion, only to be released later. All this became too much for Vivian's sixteen-year-old daugh-ter in New Jersey, and drove her to suicide.

Eventually it was discovered that in July 1929 Vivian Gordon had made a loan of $1500 to an ex-convict named Howie Schramm — known to her as Charles Reuben — and that this had never been repaid. Schramm, aged thirty-two, had a long criminal record, his crimes including the attempted strangling of a Bronx housewife during the course of a robbery in 1921.

Schramm and an associate — a thief named Dutchie Ginsman — were placed under surveillance, but no further headway was made for some weeks until an unknown informant put the police on to Herman Schwartz, a garment jobber, who said that Schramm had tried to sell him a mink coat, and had also had a diamond ring and an expensive wrist-watch for sale, on the morning of 26 February. Turning down the offer because the pelts were marked on the inside, Schwartz had taken Schramm to meet a diamond dealer and a Broadway dressmaker. The police officers investigating the crime had no doubt that the valuables in question had been those stolen from Vivian Gordon.

Another associate of Schramm's was found to be Harvey Sawyer, a young man with no criminal record. It was learnt that he had hired a Cadillac on the night of 25 February and returned it the following morning, and also that Schramm had been giving him occasional sums of money. When Schramm and Ginsman were finally interrogated in connection with the murder, they denied all knowledge of it. But Sawyer made a confession.

He revealed that the murder of Vivian Gordon had been planned beforehand, and that Schramm had taken her to Van Cortlandt Park — where Ginsman and Sawyer were waiting in the hired car — believing that she was to meet a potential victim of her own. Having introduced her to Ginsman, Schramm had got into the back of the car with her and strangled her there as they drove towards the ravine where her body was found.

Sawyer, whose own part in the affair had been confined to hiring and driving the car, believed that the murder had been carried out on behalf of 'Knucklehead' Kaufman. He also revealed that Schramm had been unable to sell the mink coat and had therefore burnt it.

Schramm and Ginsman were charged with murder and brought to trial in June 1931. Sawyer, Schwartz, the diamond dealer and the dressmaker all gave evidence, and it appeared that the prosecution's case was overwhelming. But then Howie Schramm's twenty-two-year-old sister appeared for the defence, stating that her brother had taken her out on the night of the murder and had remained in her company until daylight the following morning.

Ginsman's sister then gave *him* an alibi, testifying that he had spent the night at her home in the East Bronx. In this, she was supported by her sixteen-year-old son and a neighbouring shopkeeper.

To the amazement and disgust of the district attorney and the police officers concerned, the jury found both defendants not guilty. The case therefore remains officially unsolved.

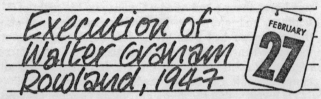

Execution of Walter Graham Rowland, 1947

FEBRUARY 27

On 27 February 1947, Walter Graham Rowland, a thirty-nine-year-old labourer, was hanged at Strangeways Prison for the murder of Olive Balchin, a prostitute aged about forty, whose body had been found on a bomb-site in Cumberland Street, near Deansgate, Manchester, on 20 October previously. The crime had been committed with a cobbler's hammer, which the culprit had left a few feet from the body, and had evidently taken place because Rowland was suffering from venereal disease and believed he had contracted it from the victim.

Rowland had been in trouble before and had, in fact, occupied the condemned cell at Strangeways on an earlier occasion. At the age of nineteen he had been sent to Borstal for three years for attempting to strangle sixteen-year-old Annie Schofield whom he married after being released; then, in 1934, he had strangled their daughter Mavis, aged two, with a stocking, and been sentenced to death. This latter sentence had been commuted to life imprisonment, and Rowland remained in jail until 1940, when he was freed after volunteering to serve in the army.

Demobilized from the Royal Artillery in June 1946, Rowland went to stay at the Services Transit Dormitory in

Manchester, and it was there that police went to find him after learning that he had been behaving suspiciously. 'You don't want me for murdering that woman, do you?' he asked, on being woken up. He admitted knowing Olive Balchin and said he suspected that she had given him venereal disease, but denied having killed her.

However, he was identified by a dealer in second-hand goods from whom he had bought the hammer, and also by two people who had seen him in the company of Olive Balchin on the night of 19 October. Two hairs found on Rowland's jacket matched the victim's own hair; a blood-stain on one of his shoes proved to be of the same group as Olive Balchin's blood. Moreover, samples of brick-dust, cement, charcoal and clinker from the turn-ups of his trousers matched other samples taken from the site where the body had been found.

While Rowland was awaiting trial on this occasion his wife divorced him on the grounds of cruelty. The divorce court had to sit *in camera* so that the jury at the forth-coming murder trial would not be prejudiced by disclosure of the prisoner's criminal record.

Rowland appeared for trial at the Manchester Assizes in December 1946, the case lasting five days. When the jury returned a verdict of guilty, he made a speech from the dock, claiming that he was innocent. 'The killing of this woman was a terrible crime, but there is a worse crime being committed now because someone with the knowledge of this murder is seeing me sentenced today for a crime which I did not commit,' he declared.

The case was made all the more extraordinary on 22 January 1947, when somebody else confessed to the murder of Olive Balchin. David John Ware, a thirty-nine-year-old man with a history of mental illness, was serving a sentence for theft at the time of Rowland's trial and sent his confession to the prison governor. He later retracted it, admitting that he had lied for the sake of publicity. In the meantime an inquiry had been held to discover whether there were grounds for thinking that Rowland's conviction had been a miscarriage of justice. It concluded that there were no such grounds. Rowland nonetheless persisted in denying his guilt to the end.

Four years later David John Ware was tried for the attempted murder of another woman and found guilty but insane. He was sent to Broadmoor, where he committed suicide in April 1954.

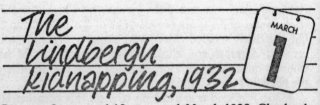

The Lindbergh kidnapping, 1932

Between 8 p.m. and 10 p.m. on 1 March 1932, Charles A. Lindbergh Jr, twenty-month-old son of the famous aviator, was abducted from his nursery at the Lindbergh Estate in the Sourland Mountains of Hunterdon County, New Jersey. The nursery was on the second floor of the house, and the child's disappearance was discovered by his Scots nurse, Betty Gow; a ransom note, demanding $50,000, was found on the window-sill.

The kidnapper had used a crudely-made ladder to gain access to the nursery, and had left no fingerprints. The ransom note — which was followed by another on 6 March increasing the demand to $70,000 — contained spelling mistakes, and was believed to have been written by a German of little education.

Colonel Lindbergh appealed to the kidnapper to start negotiations, and appointed Dr John F. Condon of the Bronx, New York, to act as an intermediary. The kidnapper sent Condon a note saying that he was agreeable to this, and later, at a meeting, gave his name as John. He sent Condon the missing child's night clothes as proof that he was the person concerned.

At a second meeting, in a cemetery in the Bronx in April, Condon offered 'John' $50,000 for the child's return. The offer was accepted and the money handed over, 'John' giving Condon a note informing him that the child was to be found on a boat called *Nellie* anchored off Martha's Vineyard, Massachusetts. He then hurried away in the darkness.

Colonel Lindbergh set off immediately, and the following day a search was carried out in the area indicated. But there was no sign of either the child or the boat. On 12 May the child's body was found in a shallow grave about five miles from the Lindbergh Estate. He had been killed by a blow on the head about two months earlier.

On 18 September 1934, a cashier at a petrol station in the Bronx received a note from a customer which he recognized as part of the ransom money. He informed the police, and the following day Bruno Richard Hauptmann, a former machine-gunner in the German army who had entered the United States illegally in 1923, was arrested. More of the ransom money was found in his possession, and his handwriting was found to be the same as that on the ransom notes. It was also discovered that he had a criminal record in Germany, his known offences including robbery and burglary.

Hauptmann was brought to trial for murder and kidnapping in January 1935. The proceedings lasted six weeks, and on 13 February he was found guilty on both charges. He was executed in the electric chair at Trenton State Prison, New Jersey, at the age of thirty-six, on 3 April 1936.

In January 1983 it was reported that his widow, Anna Hauptmann, aged eighty-four, was seeking damages for his death, and had accused the State of New Jersey and several former state and federal officials of conspiring to wrongfully convict an innocent man.

Klaus Grabowski brought to trial, 1981

On 3 March 1981, Klaus Grabowski, a thirty-five-year-old butcher with a history of child-molesting, was brought to trial in Lübeck, West Germany, charged with the murder of seven-year-old Anna Bachmeier. The child had failed to return home after going out to play in the morning of 5 May the previous year, and Grabowski, who lived only a block away, was later held for questioning in connection with her disappearance. He eventually confessed to having killed Anna, and led police to a piece of waste ground where her body was found. She had been strangled with her own tights.

Grabowski denied that the crime had been a sex murder and his counsel demanded that the charge be reduced to one of manslaughter. It was stated in court that following an earlier offence — his second — he had agreed to be castrated, but later had his sex drive restored by means of hormone injections. Omitting to explain why he had taken off Anna's tights, he claimed that he had had no sexual feelings towards her. He had invited her to his apartment because he loved children, and had killed her in a panic because she tried to blackmail him, he said.

All this was too much for Marianne Bachmeier, the child's mother. After listening to the case for three days in an apparently calm collected manner, she suddenly crossed the courtroom on 6 March, pulled out a Beretta pistol and fired seven bullets into the prisoner, killing him instantly. Frau Bachmeier, a former barmaid, then lowered the gun and waited passively to be arrested. The scene was witnessed by schoolgirls on an educational visit to the court, who began to cry hysterically. Later the same day the public prosecutor announced that Marianne Bachmeier was to be charged with murder.

Frau Bachmeier's life had not been a happy one even before Anna's death. The daughter of a former SS officer, she had been sexually assaulted at the age of nine and thrown out of home when she became pregnant at sixteen. Two years later she was raped while pregnant for the second time, the father in this case being a different man. Of the two children, one had been adopted, the other placed in an orphanage.

When these facts were reported, public sympathy, which was already strongly in her favour, became overwhelming, and large sums of money were donated to the defence fund started on her behalf. However, this sympathy began to wane when it was learnt that her fellow prisoners found her arrogant and suspected that she did not really care about Anna at all. Even so, when her trial began in November 1982, it was followed with intense interest.

Marianne Bachmeier — 'the Avenging Mother', as the press called her — was convicted of manslaughter on 2 March 1983, and sentenced to six years' imprisonment. The trial judge, in an hour-long account of his findings, said that she had not planned to kill Grabowski but decided to do so when she saw him sitting in the dock. The defence had earlier claimed that she had bought the pistol with the intention of committing suicide.

She was released on parole in June 1985.

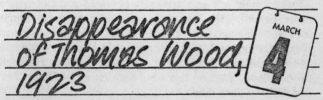

Disappearance of Thomas Wood, 1923

MARCH 4

On 4 March 1923, Thomas Wood, aged three, was reported missing from his home in Glossop, a coal-mining town in Derbyshire. The report led to a search of the town and surrounding countryside, but no trace of the missing child was found. The circulation of his description to other districts, in the hope that he might be found wandering further afield, brought no results; likewise, the dragging of the River Goyt, which runs through Glossop, revealed nothing. After the search had been going on for nine days, a local man went to the police and told them that he knew something about the boy's disappearance.

Albert Edward Burrows, a farm labourer, said that on the day in question, a Sunday, he had taken Thomas Wood for a walk to Simmondley, a village about a mile from Glossop. He had left him on his own for a few minutes near a disused mineshaft on Symmondley Moor and then been unable to find him, he continued. He gave no satisfactory reason for having failed to report this earlier.

Burrows was already known to the police in connection with other offences. Four years earlier he had been sent to prison for bigamy after going through a ceremony of marriage with a woman from Nantwich, Cheshire, by whom he had had an illegitimate child. After returning to his lawful wife on release, he had been sent to prison again, this time for failing to pay maintenance to the child's mother.

The woman, Hannah Calladine, had another child, besides the one which Burrows had fathered. In December 1919, fourteen months after her second confinement, she suddenly turned up in Glossop with both children and all her belongings, and moved into Burrows' home. At this, Burrows' wife left and promptly obtained a maintenance order herself. Her husband, being a poor man, found himself at the age of fifty-seven in danger of being sent to prison yet again. But after three weeks Hannah Calladine and her children disappeared, and Mrs Burrows returned to the house. Nothing had been seen either of Hannah or her children since then.

With great difficulty, the police searched the mineshaft which Burrows had indicated, and eventually they recovered the body of Thomas Wood. He had been sexually assaulted and then murdered, probably by strangulation, before being thrown into the shaft.

The police, going to interview Burrows again, found him about to leave the house, perhaps for good. He stuck to the story he had told them before, but could not convince them he was telling the truth. On 28 March he was charged with murder.

While he was awaiting trial the police began to investigate the disappearance of Hannah Calladine and her children. It was learnt that on 11 January 1920, Burrows had taken Hannah and the younger child for a walk, and that this was the last time anyone else had seen them. Early the following morning he had taken the older child, a girl of four, for a walk — and that had been the last time anyone had seen her.

Six weeks after Burrows had been arrested the police began searching the mineshaft on Symmondley Moor again, and a fortnight later the remains of Hannah and her children were discovered there. They, too, had been murdered, probably by strangulation, though this could not be established with certainty. Burrows, who for three years had kept up a pretence that they were all still alive, was then charged with their murders.

He was brought to trial for the murder of Hannah and the younger child at the Derby Assizes in July 1923. The case against him included the evidence of another prisoner, whom Burrows had tried to persuade to forge a letter from Hannah, saying that she was still alive. The defence called no witnesses, but contended that Hannah had committed suicide. But Burrows was convicted and sentenced to death.

He was hanged in Nottingham, at the age of sixty-two, on 8 August 1923.

Murder of Gertrude Yates, 1922

On the morning of 6 March 1922, Gertrude Yates, a prostitute aged twenty-five, was found dead in the bathroom of her basement flat in Fulham, London. She had died of asphyxia, a towel having been rammed down her throat and a dressing-gown cord tied around her neck; she had also been beaten over the head with a blunt instrument. The body was naked.

In her bedroom, there was blood everywhere; a rolling-pin, with which the blows to her head had been inflicted, lay under the eiderdown. The dressing-table had been ransacked and some jewellery stolen. The body had been discovered by the victim's daily help, Miss Emily Steel, who knew Mrs Yates as Olive Young.

Miss Steel had arrived at the flat about 9.15 a.m., letting herself in with her own key. She had gone to the kitchen and started to cook sausages for her own breakfast, tidying the sitting-room as she did so. While she was thus occupied a man known to her as Major True entered the room and told her that Miss Young was still asleep and should not be disturbed, as they had had a late night together; he would send round his car for her at midday. He then put on his coat, with Miss Steel's help, and gave her half-a-crown (12½p) before leaving to get a taxi. Miss Steel found the body shortly afterwards and ran out to get help.

The man Miss Steel had seen in the flat was, in fact, Ronald True, a mentally-ill man of thirty who was not a major at all. He was already known to the police, his wife — who was alarmed at his deteriorating state of mind — having reported him missing only three days earlier. He was arrested at the Palace of Varieties in Hammersmith within twelve hours of the body being discovered; the police found a loaded revolver in his hip pocket.

True, a former pupil at Bedford Grammar School, was a compulsive liar and a morphia addict. His stepfather, a wealthy man, had several times sent him abroad to learn work of some sort, but he was incapable of holding any job for long. In 1915 he joined the Royal Flying Corps, but on his solo flight he crashed the plane, suffering severe concussion. A month later he was involved in another crash. After his second spell in hospital he had a nervous breakdown, and was discharged from the service. He then worked briefly at one thing after another, in various countries, but finally his stepfather reconciled himself to giving him a regular allowance for doing nothing.

He was always popular with young women, and invariably managed to impress them with lies about himself. One such woman was an actress named Frances Roberts, whom he married soon after leaving the Royal Flying Corps. She, however, could not have been taken in for very long, for he was becoming increasingly abnormal and was regularly seeking treatment for his drug-addiction — treatment which never worked. In September 1921, he was fined in Portsmouth for using forged prescriptions to obtain morphia.

He began to talk about another Ronald True, an imaginary figure whom he believed to be his enemy. This 'other' Ronald True, he said, had been impersonating him and forging his signature on cheques which bounced. At the same time he was becoming violent towards his wife and hostile towards their two-year-old son. Suddenly, early in 1922, he decided to leave home.

For the next few weeks he stayed in hotels in London, frequenting clubs and bars in the West End and committing a variety of thefts. Though apparently having a good time, he was increasingly preoccupied with the 'other' Ronald True, and bought the gun that was later found in his possession in order to protect himself against this imaginary figure.

On the night of 5 March, just before midnight, he arrived at Gertrude Yates' flat in a chauffeur-driven car which he had been using for four days. He sent the driver away and stayed the night with Mrs Yates, from whom he had earlier stolen £5. In the morning he made tea for them both, then took Mrs Yates' cup into the bedroom; it was as she sat up to drink it that he attacked her with the rolling-pin. He afterwards drank his own cup of tea and ate some biscuits.

True was brought to trial at the Old Bailey in May 1922. He pleaded insanity, producing two psychiatrists to give evidence that he was suffering from a congenital mental disorder, aggravated by his addiction to morphia. But he was found guilty and sentenced to death.

Though his appeal was dismissed by the Lord Chief Justice, he was examined by three specialists on the orders of the Home Secretary and found to be insane. He was therefore reprieved and sent to Broadmoor.

He remained there for the rest of his life, a cheerful man who took part in the social activities and was popular with the other inmates. He died, at the age of sixty, in 1951.

Bodies of Dr. Petiot's victims found, 1944

MARCH 11

On 11 March 1944, a resident of the Rue Lesueur in Paris complained to the police about greasy black smoke coming from the chimney of a neighbouring house owned by Dr Marcel Petiot. The police arrived at the house to investigate and found a card pinned to the door, directing callers to an address in the Rue Caumartin where Dr Petiot lived and also had a consulting room. They contacted him by telephone.

Dr Petiot said that he would come to the Rue Lesueur immediately, but before he appeared the chimney caught fire and the fire brigade was called to the scene. Breaking into the house, the firemen entered the cellar, where a fire had been left to burn in a stove. There they found a large number of corpses, most of which had been dismembered.

When Petiot finally turned up he was told that he would be taken into custody. Unperturbed, he said that the bodies were those of pro-Nazis and collaborators killed by the French Resistance. The police were taken in by this, and made the mistake of letting Petiot go free. Petiot, his wife and their seventeen-year-old son promptly left their home in the Rue Caumartin and went into hiding. His wife was later found in Auxerre but Petiot managed to avoid being arrested for several months.

After the fall of Paris the newspapers gave a lot of publicity to the case, and Petiot wrote to one of them, stating that he was an officer of the Resistance and that the corpses found in his cellar had been placed there by the Gestapo. The handwriting of the letter was found to correspond with that of a Captain Henri Valéry, who had joined the Free French Forces just six weeks earlier and was serving in Reuilly. Petiot was thus discovered and arrested on 2 November.

On being taken to the Quai des Orfèvres for questioning, he said that as a member of the Resistance he had killed sixty-three people, and that the twenty-seven bodies in his cellar had been mostly those of German soldiers. He also said that he had helped many Frenchmen to escape from France. This time, however, nobody was taken in.

Marcel Petiot, a qualified doctor and former Mayor of Villeneuve, was a man with marked criminal tendencies. As a schoolboy he had stolen from his classmates; as an army conscript during the First World War he had stolen drugs from a casualty clearing station, and as Mayor of Villeneuve he had robbed his electric light meter and stolen from a municipal store. Later, in Paris, he was convicted of drug-trafficking and also of stealing a book.

The bodies discovered in his cellar were found to be the remains of people who had gone to his house with all their money and valuables, thinking that he would help them to escape from the Germans. They had each been given a lethal injection, then left in a sound-proofed room built specially for the purpose. Petiot had made himself a fortune out of all these murders; in all likelihood, he had also derived enjoyment from watching through a spyhole as his victims died in agony.

After seventeen months in custody, Petiot was brought to trial at the Seine Assize Court on twenty-seven charges of murder. The trial lasted three weeks and, on 4 April 1946, the jury returned verdicts of guilty on twenty-four of those charges. Petiot, aged forty-nine, was executed by guillotine on the morning of 26 May.

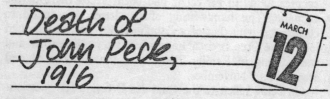

Death of John Peck, 1916

MARCH 12

On 12 March 1916, John Peck, a seventy-two-year-old timber millionaire of Grand Rapids, Michigan, died at the home of his son-in-law, Dr Arthur Warren Waite, a New York dentist. The cause of his death was diagnosed as a kidney disease and arrangements were made for the body to be cremated. But Peck's son Percy, whose mother had also died in Waite's home only a few weeks earlier, demanded its return to Michigan for burial, and afterwards requested an autopsy. When this was carried out, the body was found to contain arsenic.

Waite, aged twenty-seven, had studied at Glasgow University and worked in South Africa for some years before his marriage to Clara Peck in September 1915. In addition to having a dental practice in New York's fashionable Riverside Drive, he worked on germ-culture research at Cornell University. However, he lived extravagantly, having affairs with other women, and as his wife now inherited half of her father's fortune, he was suspected of having murdered both of her parents.

On 23 March the fashionable dentist was found suffering from an overdose of drugs, having apparently tried to take his own life. When he recovered he was charged with the murders of John and Hannah Peck and later brought to trial. Having pleaded not guilty, he then made an extraordinary confession, stating not only that he had murdered both of his wife's parents, but also that he had intended to murder his wife as well.

He had murdered his mother-in-law by putting diphtheria, tuberculosis and influenza germs in her food, he explained. He had then used the same methods in an attempt to kill his father-in-law, even using a nasal spray containing tuberculosis bacteria in his case. When these and other attempts proved unsuccessful, he had finally disposed of John Peck with the use of arsenic.

Waite revealed that it was for the sake of their money that he had murdered Clara's parents, and said that he would have murdered Clara next because he intended to have a more beautiful wife. Asked if he was crazy, he replied, 'I think not — unless it is crazy to want money'.

It was nonetheless on grounds of insanity that appeals were made on his behalf when he was convicted and sentenced to death. But these were unsuccessful and his execution in the electric chair was carried out at Sing Sing Prison on the night of 24 May 1917.

Four poisoned in Lund, 1949

MARCH
13

On 13 March 1949, two medical students and two children in Lund, Sweden, were taken ill as a result of eating chocolate which had been poisoned with arsenic. The two students, Odvar Eiken and Anders Muren, and one of the children recovered after receiving hospital treatment, but the other child died. The investigation which followed involved the police of Norway and Denmark, as well as Sweden.

Eiken and Muren, both Norwegians in their late twenties, were room-mates lodging with a family named Svendson, and Eiken was engaged to Muren's sister Randi — a student at a teachers' training college in Kristiansand, Norway — though their engagement had not yet been formally announced. The chocolate, which had been sent to Eiken through the post, appeared to have been a gift from Randi.

Odvar Eiken had given a little of the chocolate to Muren and eaten some of it himself; the rest had been given to his landlady's eight-year-old daughter Marianne who, in turn, had given some to her friend Barbro Jakobson. It was Marianne Svendson who failed to recover from its effects.

Randi Muren denied sending the chocolate to Eiken, but agreed that handwriting on the gift card which had accompanied it was similar to her own. She revealed that since making her engagement known to friends she had received a number of anonymous letters suggesting that her fiancé was having affairs with girls in Sweden, and a further letter from a woman named Signe Lundgren claiming that she was expecting Eiken's child. At the same time Eiken, who said that he did not know anybody named Signe Lundgren, had been receiving anonymous letters of the same type about her.

The investigating officers, both Swedish and Norwegian became convinced that these letters and the poisoned chocolate were connected, and — observing that Randi Muren was an extremely attractive girl — suggested that they might have been the work of a jealous rival. Further questions elicited the information that a young Dane named Flemming Rosbörg, who had worked in Norway for a year, had recently threatened to commit suicide after failing to persuade her to marry him. As his present whereabouts were unknown, the Copenhagen police were asked to make inquiries about him.

He was soon arrested and handed over to the Swedish police for questioning, but then released after giving a satisfactory account of his movements. In the meantime, it had been learnt that shortly before the arrival of the poisoned chocolate, Odvar Eiken had received (also through the post) a small bottle of whisky inside a cigar-box. He had been ill after drinking some of it, but had not realized that the illness was connected with the whisky. When the rest of the whisky was handed to the police, together with the cigar-box, it was found to contain arsenic.

Several women named. Signe Lundgren had been traced, but none of them knew Odvar Eiken or Randi Muren. Nor could any other woman be found in Sweden to substantiate the accusations which had been made against Eiken. But then another case of arsenic poisoning was reported, this time in Kristiansand.

Carstein Brekke, a friend of Randi Muren and her fiancé who was also a student at the teachers' training college, claimed that he, too, had received chocolate through the post and been ill after eating some of it. He produced a box containing several pieces which were found to have been poisoned, though with smaller amounts of arsenic than the chocolate sent to Eiken. Brekke could think of no reason why anyone should want to poison him, other than the fact that he was a friend of the other victims, he said.

The matter was further complicated by the discovery of a paid advertisement which had appeared in a Stavanger newspaper, announcing that Carstein Brekke and Randi Muren had become engaged — which both parties said they were unable to explain. However, when a police officer showed Randi the cigar-box in which the poisoned whisky had been sent to Eiken, she said that it was Brekke who owned it.

Brekke, though a close friend of Randi's, also turned out to be another of her rejected suitors. A letter which he had sent to his mother on 13 March contained information about Eiken's poisoned chocolate, though this was not known by Randi until the following day. Moreover, a note-book which he had discarded was found to have been used for imitations of Randi's handwriting. After being questioned intensively for some hours, he admitted having sent Eiken the poisoned chocolate. However, he refused to allow a police officer to take down his confession, saying that he wanted to write it himself in a more intellectual manner.

The written statement which he then made gave details of an unsuccessful attempt to get Randi Muren — the only woman in his life, he claimed — to break off her engagement, followed by an equally unsuccessful attempt to poison his rival.

Charged on a number of counts, Carstein Brekke was brought to trial in Kristiansand in October 1949, and convicted of manslaughter and attempted murder. He was then sentenced to twelve years' imprisonment and ten years' loss of rights as a citizen. The sentence of imprisonment was later increased to fifteen years when the case was taken to the Norwegian Supreme Court.

Shooting of Gaston Calmette, 1914

On the afternoon of 16 March 1914, Henriette Caillaux, the wife of the French Finance Minister, entered the offices of the daily newspaper *Le Figaro* and asked to see Gaston Calmette, the editor-in-chief. That very morning *Le Figaro* had published a facsimile of an indiscreet love letter which Madame Caillaux had received from her husband before their marriage, and Calmette assumed that she would try to come to an arrangement with him to prevent the publication of other such letters which she knew to be in his possession. He therefore agreed to see her.

A moment later the sound of shots was heard, and other members of staff rushed into Calmette's office to see what had happened. They found him lying on the floor, covered with blood. Madame Caillaux made no attempt to escape. 'I shot Calmette deliberately because he wanted to destroy my husband and me,' she confessed to the police. The following day Calmette died of his wounds. Henriette Caillaux, one of the best-known women in Paris, was charged with his murder; she was brought to trial four months later.

Joseph Caillaux, a former Prime Minister, was a very unpopular man. The rich had hated him for years because, during an earlier period as Finance Minister, he had introduced an income tax. More recently he had become widely despised as a result of his opposition to the impending war with Germany.

Gaston Calmette had been the most implacable of his opponents. He had repeatedly accused Caillaux of betraying his country and, on acquiring some of the Finance Minister's private letters written during the course of his previous marriage, had been determined to use them to bring about his downfall.

At her trial Henriette Caillaux said that the attacks on her husband had caused both of them much unhappiness. Joseph Caillaux, on learning that the letters were in Calmette's hands, had bought a pistol, saying that he would kill Calmette if they were published. She had been unable to get him to part with it.

On the day of the shooting, she claimed, she had found the newspaper on the breakfast table, her husband having left without waking her. She went to his desk, where she knew that the pistol was normally kept in a locked drawer, but found the drawer open and the gun missing. After two unsuccessful attempts to see him at his ministry she decided to confront Calmette, and bought a gun herself for the purpose of threatening him. She claimed — in spite of her original confession — that she had not intended to kill him.

The trial took place during the week preceding the declaration of war between Austria–Hungary and Serbia, and its outcome depended less on the events of 16 March than on the motives of Joseph Caillaux and Gaston Calmette. There were some sensational developments in this respect, and soon the case became — for a few days, at least — the main preoccupation of the whole country.

One of Calmette's editors told the court that documents proving that Caillaux had betrayed France had been placed in the hands of the President of the Republic. This was to be refuted the following day by a statement, authorized by the Government, that the President had received no such papers. In the meantime, Caillaux was called as a witness and caused much indignation.

'Calmette has accused me of betraying my country to the Germans,' he said. 'Therefore, I am forced to tell the truth. I state here and now that *Le Figaro* has accepted German money!'

The publisher of the newspaper, called to deny the allegation, was forced to concede that *Le Figaro* had German shareholders. The admission was made with the utmost reluctance.

Later, just before the closing speeches, Caillaux re-appeared with a copy of Calmette's will, revealing that the victim of the shooting had avoided paying taxes on a very large inheritance. He also produced a contract which had been drawn up between Calmette and the Government of Austria–Hungary, by which Calmette pledged himself to write articles serving the interests of that government in return for money. The presiding judge read the contract aloud, remarking that there could be no doubt about its authenticity.

These revelations caused an uproar in the court, with spectators leaping to their feet, crying out that Calmette had been a traitor and that shooting had been too good for him. The jury considered the case for only a quarter of an hour before returning a unanimous verdict of not guilty. Caillaux and his wife did not leave the court in triumph, however, for the verdict was immediately overshadowed by the news that Austria–Hungary and Serbia were at war.

Caillaux returned to his political life after an enforced withdrawal. He was later to be imprisoned by Clemenceau for corresponding with the enemy.

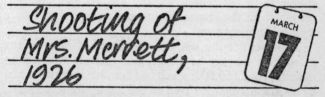

Shooting of Mrs. Merrett, 1926

MARCH 17

On the morning of 17 March 1926, Mrs Bertha Merrett, a woman of private means, was rushed to hospital from her furnished rooms in Buckingham Terrace, Edinburgh, with a bullet wound in her right ear; she was alive but unconscious. The wound appeared to have been self-inflicted, and when her son, John Donald Merrett, aged seventeen, informed the police that she had tried to kill herself because she was in financial difficulties, they saw no cause to disbelieve him.

Mrs Merrett was kept in isolation at the Royal Infirmary. When she recovered consciousness she was asked no questions about the bullet wound, but made a statement of her own accord to one of the doctors. 'I was sitting down, writing letters, and my son Donald was standing beside me,' she said. 'I said, "Go away, Donald, and don't annoy me." And the next thing I heard was a kind of explosion, and I don't remember anything more.' She died on 1 April.

Despite her statement, her death was regarded as suicide, until the discovery of one of her cheque-books in Donald Merrett's bedroom caused police officers to suspect otherwise. During the investigation which followed it was found that the signatures on many of Mrs Merrett's cheques had been forged. At the same time tests were carried out on the pistol that killed her.

Eventually, on 1 February 1927, Donald Merrett, now aged eighteen, was brought to trial in Edinburgh. He was charged with his mother's murder, and also with forging twenty-nine cheques on her account. The prosecution claimed that the absence of powder-blackening round the bullet wound proved that the gun had not been fired closely enough to be consistent with suicide, but the jury found the charge to be not proven. Donald Merrett was, however, convicted on the second charge and sentenced to twelve months' imprisonment.

This was not the last that was heard of him, by any means. At the age of twenty-one Merrett received an inheritance of £50,000, which had been left in trust for him by his grandfather. He lived on this money for some years, then, having spent most of it, returned to a life of crime. Now known as Ronald John Chesney, he committed a variety of offences — blackmail, fraud, theft and smuggling — before going into the Royal Naval Volunteer Reserve during the Second World War. After the war he lived in Germany, and was mainly engaged in black-market activities. Then, in 1954, he decided to murder his wife.

Merrett had married Vera Bonnar, the daughter of one of his mother's friends, in 1928. At the time of his inheritance he had made a settlement of £8400 on her, the money to revert to him in the event of her death. They had long since separated, and Vera Merrett, known as Vera Chesney, ran an old people's home in Ealing with her mother, who called herself Lady Menzies.

Merrett came to England in disguise, using a false passport. He visited his wife, got her hopelessly drunk, and drowned her in a few inches of water in her own bath, intending to make her death appear to have been the result of an accident. But as he was leaving the house he was seen by his mother-in-law, and realized that he would have to kill her too. After a desperate struggle he managed to overpower and strangle her. He then escaped from the house and flew back to Germany.

But he had been seen in the neighbourhood, and it was not long before the police were after him. On 16 February 1954, less than a week after the double murder, he was found dead in a wood near Cologne; he had shot himself. His arms were scratched and bruised from the struggle with his mother-in-law, and pink fibres from her scarf were found on his clothing. His German mistress, Gerda Schaller, said that Merrett had confided to her that he was guilty of the murder of his mother twenty-eight years earlier.

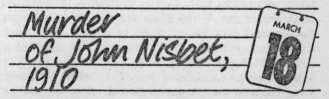

Murder of John Nisbet, 1910

On the morning of 18 March 1910, John Nisbet, a forty-four-year-old cashier working for the Stobswood Colliery

Company, left his employers' Newcastle office to deliver £370 in wages to a colliery at Widdrington, thirty-five miles away. It was a journey he made every Friday, leaving Newcastle by train at 10.27 a.m. and carrying the money in a black leather bag. On this occasion, however, he did not alight at Widdrington because he was dead by the time the train arrived there. His body was discovered by a porter when the train reached Alnmouth.

Nisbet had been shot five times, his body hidden under a seat and the bag of money stolen. It was established that John Alexander Dickman, a former secretary of a colliery syndicate, had travelled in the same compartment, leaving the train at Morpeth. The post-mortem examination revealed that the bullets found in Nisbet's body had been fired from two different guns.

Dickman, a married man with two children, lived in Jesmond. He made his living out of betting on horses and was often in financial difficulties. It was also found that he had recently owned a revolver. He was therefore an obvious suspect.

On the day of the murder Dickman had had to pay excess fare at Morpeth, as he had only bought a ticket to Stannington, the previous stop. Asked to explain this, he told police that he had intended getting out at Stannington, in order to attend an interview for a job with the overseer at the Dovecot Moor colliery, but had gone on to Morpeth by mistake. This proved to be a lie, the overseer at Dovecot telling police that no such interview had been arranged.

Dickman was arrested and charged with murder. A search of his home failed to produce either of the guns, the black bag or any of the stolen money. But it was soon discovered that he had managed to pay off one or two debts to money-lenders almost immediately after the murder.

Brought to trial at the Newcastle Summer Assizes on 4 July, Dickman denied the offence. The case for the prosecution depended upon circumstantial evidence, but was strong enough to convince the jury of his guilt. He was sentenced to death.

On 9 July the black leather bag which had contained the stolen money was found in a disused mine-shaft between Morpeth and Stannington; it had been cut open — the key having been left in the victim's pocket — and all the money removed. Its discovery convinced the police that they had made no mistake in arresting Dickman. But the guns which had been used were never found.

There were many other people who felt that the evidence against Dickman was insufficient to warrant a conviction, and attempts were made to get him reprieved. But these were unsuccessful, and he was hanged at Newcastle Prison on 10 August 1910.

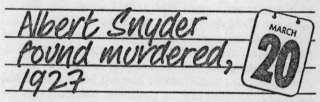

Albert Snyder found murdered, 1927

Getting up on the morning of 20 March 1927, Lorraine Snyder, aged ten, of Queen's Village, Long Island, came out of her bedroom and found her mother lying bound and gagged at the top of the stairs. She let out a scream, then telephoned some neighbours, who immediately came to her assistance. On being untied, Ruth Snyder, aged thirty-two, said that she had been attacked and knocked unconscious by an intruder — a big man with a moustache, looking 'like an Italian' — who had entered her bedroom while she was asleep. She supposed that she must have been dragged out of the bedroom while she was still unconscious.

Entering the bedroom themselves, the neighbours found that Mrs Snyder's husband had been murdered. Albert Snyder, forty-four-year-old art editor of *Motor Boating* magazine, lay on the bed, his head having been so savagely battered that he was almost unrecognizable. When the police were called to the scene, it was also discovered that a piece of picture wire had been tied tightly round his neck and pieces of cotton wool, soaked in chloroform, stuffed into his mouth and nostrils. Clearly, it was a case of premeditated murder, and it was not long before the police began to have doubts about Ruth Snyder's story.

Searching the house for clues, they found pots and pans scattered about the kitchen and the contents of a bureau strewn about the living-room floor. But there was no sign of a forced entry. Jewels which Mrs Snyder claimed had been stolen were found hidden under her mattress, and some scraps of paper, pieced together, turned out to be a love letter which she had received from somebody signing himself 'Judd'. Ruth Snyder, on being questioned at length, then confessed that she had been having an affair with a salesman named Henry Judd Gray, who was an employee of the Bien Jolie Corset Company.

Gray, a timid man of thirty-five, was questioned about the murder, but denied having had anything to do with it. However, the police told Ruth Snyder that he had broken down and made a confession, blaming her for what had happened. She then made a statement, admitting that she had conspired with Gray to kill her husband but claiming that she had taken no part in the crime itself.

On being confronted with this, Gray made a statement, saying that they had committed the murder together, but that he had been under her influence at the time. 'She had this power over me,' he said. 'She told me what to do and I just did it.' Thus, the truth about what had happened gradually emerged.

Ruth Snyder and Judd Gray, both unhappily married, had begun to have an affair in 1925. Mrs Snyder disliked her husband, who often compared her unfavourably with a former fiancée, and had made a number of unsuccessful attempts to kill him on her own before finally getting Gray to help her. She had also taken out life insurance policies by which she stood to gain $96,000 after the murder had been carried out.

On the night of 19 March Gray entered the house while his mistress and her husband were out at a party. When they returned he kept himself concealed until after they had gone to bed. He then entered the bedroom and, taking Snyder by surprise, struck him over the head with a sash weight. After the murder Ruth Snyder helped to disarrange the room and allowed herself to be tied up and gagged before Gray left the house.

On 25 April the two prisoners were brought to trial for murder, the case being given a tremendous amount of publicity. As the sordid details were made known, Ruth Snyder was seen to be a callous schemer who had turned a weak man into a murderer by means of 'drink, veiled threats and intensive love'. As such, she became an object of fascination among ordinary people, and received 164 proposals of marriage.

The trial ended on 9 May with both defendants being found guilty; they were sentenced to death. Both were executed in the electric chair at Sing Sing Prison in January 1928.

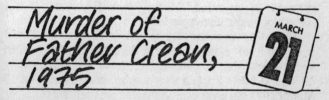

Murder of Father Crean, 1975

MARCH 21

On 21 March 1975, Father Anthony Crean, a Catholic priest, was brutally murdered at his home in Gravesend, Kent, his assailant striking him over the head with an axe and also stabbing him several times with a knife. The police suspected a twenty-two-year-old psychopath named Patrick Mackay, whose mother lived locally, and arrested him two days later. Mackay soon confessed, not only to that crime, but to two other murders as well, and was brought to trial for all three in November the same year. He was sentenced to life imprisonment.

Mackay, the son of a drunken clerk, had a long record of theft and violence. As a schoolboy, besides being a bully, a liar and a thief, he had taken to torturing animals and on one occasion had been put on probation for setting fire to a church. At thirteen he was admitted to a mental hospital after attacking his mother and sisters, and at fifteen — by which time he had committed a number of other violent crimes — he was described by a Home Office psychiatrist as 'a cold psychopathic killer'. Thereafter he became an admirer of the Nazis, drank heavily, took drugs and committed a great many burglaries and muggings.

In 1973 Father Crean, then aged sixty-three, befriended him, but not long afterwards Mackay broke into his house and stole a cheque. When he was arrested for this the priest tried to prevent him being prosecuted, and Mackay was merely fined £20 and set free.

On the day of the murder Mackay entered the house, which had been left open in Father Crean's absence. The victim, on returning, became nervous and tried to leave again, but Mackay attacked him and chased him into the bathroom, where further blows were struck. 'I must have gone out of my mind,' Mackay said afterwards. 'It was something in me that exploded.'

The other two murders to which Mackay confessed were both of elderly women: Isabella Griffiths, aged eighty-four, who was stabbed to death on 14 February 1974, and Adele Price, a widow, who was strangled on 10 March 1975. In each case the victim was murdered in her own home for no particular reason. 'I felt hellish and very peculiar inside,' said Mackay, referring to the murder of Adele Price.

Besides the three murders for which he was sent to prison, Mackay was believed to have committed eight others, but no charges were brought against him in connection with any of them.

Double murder in West Shelby, 1915

On the morning of 22 March 1915, Margaret Wolcott, a housekeeper, was found dead on her employer's farm at West Shelby, in Orleans County, New York; she had been shot with a revolver and was lying in her nightgown outside the door of a cottage occupied by Charles E. Stielow, a hired man. The farm-owner, Charles B. Phelps, aged seventy, lay in his nightshirt in the farmhouse kitchen, fatally injured, also by shooting; he died in hospital later, having been unable to speak from the time of his discovery. His desk had been broken open and all his money stolen.

Stielow, a thirty-seven-year-old German immigrant, lived with his wife, child, mother-in-law and brother-in-law; he was a strong but simple-minded man. Discovering what had happened, he had sent his brother-in-law, Nelson Green — who was equally simple minded — to inform the Orleans County Sheriff, Chester D. Bartlett. But he also got Green to hide his revolver, rifle and shotgun, as he was afraid that he might otherwise be accused of the murders himself.

The county had had no other serious crime within living memory, and the sheriff, having no idea how to conduct a murder investigation, hired an unscrupulous private detective named Newton, from Buffalo, to do it for him. Newton promptly had Green arrested, terrified him into revealing the whereabouts of his brother-in-law's guns, then forced him to make a confession that he and Stielow had killed Phelps and his housekeeper. Newton and Bartlett then arrested Stielow and had him interrogated for two days without food or sleep until he, too, confessed to the murders.

On 12 July Stielow was brought to trial. The stolen

money had not been recovered and the prisoner's confession, which he retracted, was regarded with suspicion by the judge. However, the prosecution introduced the evidence of a charlatan named Albert Hamilton, who purported to be a ballistics expert, as well as an expert in nearly every other branch of forensic science. He told the court that the bullets removed from Phelps' body had been fired from Stielow's revolver; they could not have been fired from any other weapon, he declared. Stielow was convicted and sentenced to death.

His case was taken up by members of a penal reform society and several reprieves followed, one of them arriving after he had been strapped in the electric chair at Sing Sing Prison. A tramp named King confessed that he and his companion, both of whom were now serving prison sentences for other crimes, were guilty of the West Shelby murders — but retracted the confession after being taken away for questioning by Newton and Bartlett. By this time, however, the case was causing much disquiet, and Governor Whitman of New York appointed an independent commission to look into it.

During the course of their inquiry Stielow's revolver was examined by a New York City detective, Captain Jones, who said that it had not been fired for three or four years. When test shots were fired the bullets — unlike those from Phelps' body — were found to be covered with dirt from the barrel, and when the two sets of bullets were compared it was found that their markings were entirely different. It was then clear that Stielow was innocent, and eventually, after three years in jail, he was pardoned and set free.

Though King once more confessed to the murder of Phelps and his housekeeper — and there was evidence to show that he and his friend had known about the crime before it became general knowledge — a grand jury refused to indict him. The county's one serious crime in a whole generation was thus left officially unsolved, saving the cost of a fresh trial.

Murder of William Munday, 1905

On 23 March 1905, William Munday, an elderly gentleman, was held up by a tramp with a gun between Tooringa and Toowong, in Queensland. He resisted and was shot in the stomach, but managed to give a description of his attacker before dying in hospital the same evening. Later that night the tramp was arrested after trying unsuccessfully to draw a gun on the police officer concerned. The tramp was Robert Butler, a man with a long criminal record, who had spent most of his life in jail. He was charged with murder.

Butler, a native of Kilkenny, in Ireland, was an intelligent and literate man, but bitter and destructive. Arriving in Australia at the age of fourteen, he had spent thirteen of the next sixteen years in jail for crimes which included highway robbery and burglary. He then went to New Zealand, where he was given four years' hard labour for burglary, and later eighteen years' imprisonment, of which he served sixteen, for burning down the home of a solicitor. He was also tried for the murder of a young couple and their baby, but in this case he was acquitted; he had conducted his own defence.

Returning to Australia in 1896, he was given fifteen years, later reduced to ten, for burglary. At the same time he was acquitted on a charge of highway robbery, again after defending himself. He was released in 1904.

Brought to trial for the murder of Mr Munday, he was convicted and sentenced to death. While awaiting execution, he declared that he could not have the consolation of religion at his death, as there was 'an impassable bar' between himself and any religious organization. This incorrigible criminal was about sixty years old when the sentence was carried out.

About 7.30 a.m. on 27 March 1905, Thomas Farrow, an elderly tradesman, was found dead in the back parlour of his chandler's store in Deptford, south-east London; he had been battered over the head, and his body was covered with blood. His wife, Ann, was found unconscious in her bed upstairs, having been similarly attacked; she died in hospital three days later. The crime was discovered when a boy employed as an assistant in the store turned up for work.

It had taken place only half an hour earlier, the culprits knocking on the door of the shop and forcing their way in when Mr Farrow opened it. An empty cash-box, which had been broken open, showed that robbery had been the motive: it had earlier contained a few pounds. The main clues to the identities of those responsible were two black masks, made from silk stockings, and a thumbprint, in blood, on the cash-box tray. The masks suggested to the police that the crime had been committed by local men, afraid of being recognized.

The police questioned known criminals in the Deptford area and checked their alibis, and before long suspicion fell on Alfred Stratton, aged twenty-two, and his brother Albert, aged twenty, both of whom had convictions for house-breaking and burglary. Though both had disappeared, the police were able to speak to Alfred's girlfriend who had a black eye and was frightened. She informed them that the two brothers had both been out all night prior to the murder and that Alfred had afterwards destroyed his coat and dyed his brown shoes black.

On the Sunday following the murder a police officer found Alfred Stratton in a public house full of seamen, criminals and prostitutes; asking him to step outside, he promptly arrested him. Albert was found in a lodging-house in Stepney, and he, too, was arrested. Both were questioned and fingerprinted at Tower Bridge police station, and it was found that Alfred Stratton's right thumbprint matched the one found at the scene of the crime. They were charged with murder.

At their trial at the Old Bailey in May 1905, the thumb-print was an important part of the evidence, but its value was disputed by the defence. The jury, however, were impressed by a demonstration given by Inspector Collins of the newly-formed Finger-Print Branch at Scotland Yard and found both of the defendants guilty. Both blamed the other for the murders, and both were hanged. It was the first time that a conviction for murder had been obtained by fingerprint evidence in a British court.

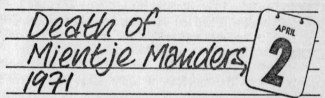

Death of Mientje Manders, 1971
APRIL 2

On 2 April 1971, a girl named Mientje Manders died in Utrecht, Holland, after suffering from stomach pains for some days. It appeared that food poisoning was the cause of her death, but three months earlier another girl, Willy Maas, had also died in Utrecht after suffering from the same symptoms. Both girls had been engaged to a young man named Sjef Rijke, who was apparently grief-stricken on each occasion, but nonetheless married a third girl, eighteen-year-old Maria Haas, three weeks after the death of the second. Six weeks after that Rijke's wife left him and began divorce proceedings, having found him to be abnormally jealous.

Since the death of Mientje Manders the Utrecht police had been taking an interest in Rijke, and his wife was now interviewed. On being asked whether she had experienced any stomach pains, she revealed that she *had* had such pains from the time of her marriage but that they had stopped when she left her husband. Not long afterwards it was learnt that another girl, who had moved into Rijke's home in his wife's place, and begun to suffer similarly, had had a jar of peanut butter analysed at the local health department's laboratory where it was found to contain rat poison.

Even so, the police were not certain that Rijke was responsible, for he seemed to have no motive for poisoning any of these girls: they therefore arrested his middle-aged cleaning woman as well as him, releasing the cleaner only when a local store-owner informed them that Rijke had bought rat poison from him on a number of occasions.

Rijke then admitted that he had been responsible for the deaths of Willy Maas and Mientje Manders, and also that he had poisoned his wife and the girl who had lived with him after his wife had left. He denied that he had intended to murder anyone, saying that the poisonings had only taken place because he enjoyed watching women suffer.

Brought to trial in January 1972, Sjef Rijke was convicted of the murders of Willy Maas and Mientje Manders and sentenced to life imprisonment for each crime.

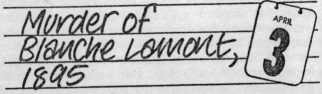

Murder of Blanche Lamont, 1895

APRIL 3

On 3 April 1895, Blanche Lamont, a twenty-one-year-old student teacher and regular church-goer, was murdered in

San Francisco's Bartlett Street Emmanuel Baptist Church, where her body lay in the belfry for the next eleven days. Before its discovery Miss Lamont's friend Marion Williams, known as 'Minnie', was also killed in the same building. It was the body of Miss Williams, whose murder had taken place on 12 April, which was found first.

Blanche Lamont, who lived with her uncle and aunt, Mr and Mrs Noble, had been seen entering the church in the company of William Durrant, a twenty-four-year-old medical student and church official, on the afternoon of her death. Durrant afterwards offered to help Mrs Noble to find her, but cautioned her against telling others about the girl's disappearance. Three rings belonging to Miss Lamont were received by her aunt on the morning of 13 April, having been sent through the post anonymously.

Minnie Williams left a friend's house to go to church about eight o'clock on the evening of 12 April. The following morning the new pastor, J. George Gibson, reported finding that a door of the church had been forced, and later a female volunteer worker found Miss Williams' body in the library; she had been strangled, then mutilated with a table-knife. It was afterwards alleged that the police were not informed of this discovery until after Gibson had made an unsuccessful attempt to get the body removed secretly by a local undertaker.

On 14 April a patrolman on duty at the church climbed to the belfry and found the naked body of Blanche Lamont, who lay with her hands crossed on her breasts. She, too, had been strangled, but not mutilated, and nobody doubted that the two murders had been committed by the same person.

Durrant was arrested and brought to trial on 22 July. The case lasted until 1 November, but the jury took only twenty minutes to find him guilty of first-degree murder; he was sentenced to death. The trial received much publicity, the 'Demon in the Belfry' making news in Europe as well as the United States. After four stays of execution, he was hanged at San Quentin Prison on 7

January, 1898, protesting his innocence to the end.

The execution was followed by a number of false confessions, and the idea that Gibson rather than Durrant had murdered the two girls gained a certain amount of support.

Horrifying murder in Barking, 1968

APRIL 4

On the morning of 4 April, 1968, Suchnam Singh Sandhu, a thirty-nine-year-old Punjab Sikh living in Barking, Essex, murdered his teenage daughter Sarabjit in a horrifying manner. Sarabjit, who lived away from home, had been staying with her family for a few days and had been left in her father's company while her mother was out and her two younger sisters were at school. Following a bitter argument — over a married man living in India — Sarabjit told her father that she had taken poison and written a letter blaming him for her impending death. Suchnam Singh, who was still in his pyjamas, then lost his temper and struck her twice with a hammer.

Having done so, he dressed quickly and went out, returning to the house half an hour later with a high-tensile hacksaw which he had just bought for the purpose of dismembering his daughter's body. Sarabjit, at this stage, was not dead and when he started to cut her neck she tried to grasp the saw, cutting her thumb in the attempt. But Suchnam Singh, now wearing his pyjamas again, went on sawing until he had cut off her head, then cut through her body at the waist and severed her legs at the knees. The dismemberment was carried out with the body in a large plastic bag, so that Sarabjit's blood could afterwards be poured into the bath.

With this frightful task accomplished, Suchnam Singh put the upper part of his daughter's body into one suitcase, the lower part, together with the severed legs, into another, and her head into a duffel bag, ready for disposal. The blood-stained pyjamas and the hacksaw were put into his dustbin.

That night the first suitcase was taken by public transport to Euston Station, London, where it was placed on the 10.40 p.m. train to Wolverhampton; the other was thrown into the River Roding from a bridge at Ilford. The following morning — by which time the first suitcase had been opened at Wolverhampton — the duffel bag was left near a roadside on Wanstead Flats, in Essex.

After the discovery of part of Sarabjit's remains, the police made a public appeal for information about a young Asian woman who might recently have left home or disappeared from a boarding-house. They later issued a photofit picture of a coloured man whom a ticket-collector at Euston remembered seeing with a suitcase before the departure of the Wolverhampton train.

When the second suitcase was found, also on 5 April, it was quickly established that the contents of both were parts of the same body. From an examination of the stomach contents it was learnt that the young woman had taken a fatal dose of phenobarbitone but that she had died before this had been absorbed into her system. It also appeared, from a scar on the inside of one of her legs and the fact that her pubic hair had been shaved off three or four months earlier, that she had received gynaecological treatment.

Detectives then began checking on Indian and Pakistani women who had received such treatment, and eventually the corpse — the head of which was discovered by a cyclist on 8 May — was identified by a doctor whom Sarabjit had been to see in Ilford in November 1967. Sarabjit, who had been pregnant at the time, had been sent to a consultant gynaecologist at Barking Hospital, where she had afterwards failed to keep an appointment for ante-natal treatment. It appeared that she had had an abortion during the next few weeks, though the police never discovered who had performed it.

On 11 May Suchnam Singh, a machine-minder, was questioned by police about his missing daughter. He said that Sarabjit had left home in February 1968, and that he did not know her whereabouts. He also denied knowing that she had been pregnant and refused to identify the suit-cases or items of clothing found with her remains. Two days later, however, he made a full confession. He was then charged with murder.

Sarabjit, it was learnt, had been Suchnam Singh's favourite child, and he — an educated man who had formerly been a schoolmaster — had wanted her to become a doctor. But then she had become pregnant, thus bringing the family into disgrace, and had further angered her father by saying that she was in love with a man who was already married, and wanted him to divorce or kill his wife so that he could marry her.

At the time of the murder Suchnam Singh, having struck his daughter with the hammer, had done his best to follow an old Sikh custom — that of dismembering one who had disgraced the family and sending parts of the body on trains going in different directions.

He was later brought to trial at the Old Bailey, where the evidence against him was shown to be overwhelming, and after retiring for ninety minutes the jury found him guilty of murder. He was sent to prison for life.

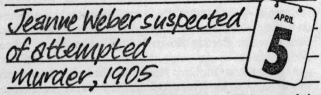

Jeanne Weber suspected of attempted murder, 1905

On the afternoon of 5 April 1905, Maurice Weber, aged six months, was taken to the Bretonneau Hospital in Paris suffering from acute asphyxia. He had been left in the care of an aunt, Jeanne Weber, who lived in a slum in the Passage Goutte d'Or, and shortly afterwards had been found blue in the face and choking. Jeanne Weber, aged thirty, had been sitting beside him with her hands under his vest.

The resident physician examined the child and found a reddish mark on his neck which made the doctor suspect that an attempt had been made to choke him. Later, when the child had recovered, the doctor questioned the mother at length and learnt of the deaths of four other children, all related, in the previous few weeks. All had died mysteriously after being left in Jeanne Weber's charge.

The first had been Georgette Weber, a niece aged eighteen months, who had died on 2 March while her mother was working in the public laundry; the cause had been diagnosed as 'convulsions'. Georgette's sister Suzanne, a year older, had died in similar circumstances on 11 March; her death had also been put down to 'convulsions'. On 26 March a third niece, Germaine Weber, seven-month-old daughter of another brother-in-law, had died while her mother was out shopping, and this, too, had been put down to the same cause. Finally, on 27 March, the day on which Germaine was buried, Jeanne Weber's own seven-year-old son, Marcel, had fallen ill and died, the diagnosis in this case being diphtheria.

The doctor found all this information disturbing. The following morning, after examining the child again, he consulted the doctor in charge of the children's ward, who made his own examination and came to the same conclusion. As a result, the police were informed and Jeanne Weber taken into custody. It was then discovered that she had had two other children besides Marcel, both of whom had died, and that two others had died while in her care in 1902.

The interviewing of witnesses produced other startling pieces of information. On the day that Georgette died the child's mother had been called away from the laundry by a neighbour, who had entered the apartment after hearing screams; she had arrived home to find Georgette's tongue hanging out and foam on her lips, but had then gone back to the laundry after holding her in front of an open window for a while. A similar thing had happened *twice* on consecutive days before Germaine's death, except that in this case a doctor had been called each time.

Though Dr Léon Thoinot, the pathologist appointed to examine the exhumed bodies of the four children, found no signs of strangulation or choking, the examining magistrate was convinced of Jeanne Weber's guilt and determined to have her brought to trial. But when the trial took place, in January 1906, Thoinot's evidence proved to be devastating and the accused was acquitted. Soon afterwards she disappeared.

The following year, using a different name, she appeared in the village of Chambon, near Villedieu, where she became the housekeeper and mistress of a peasant named Bavouzet, who had three children. A few weeks later one of the children, a boy of nine, died suddenly, his death being put down to 'convulsions resulting from an irritation of the meninges'. The case was investigated when Jeanne Weber's identity was discovered; the child was then found to have died of strangulation. Jeanne Weber was arrested and brought to trial again, but with the same result as before.

The year after that she arrived in Commercy with a lime-burner named Émile Bouchery, who introduced her as his wife. The couple rented a room at an inn, but Bouchery had to go out that evening and said he would return late at night; the innkeeper and his wife therefore allowed their seven-year-old son to sleep in the room, to keep Jeanne company. They were later summoned by another lodger who had heard the child screaming.

Breaking into the room, the innkeeper and his wife found their son lying on the bed with his face discoloured and blood streaming from his mouth. Jeanne Weber lay beside him, her hands and her petticoat bloodstained. The boy died soon afterwards, his death having been caused by strangulation. The bleeding had been caused by his biting his tongue.

When the case was reported in the newspapers there was a storm of indignation. Jeanne Weber, however, was not brought to trial this time; instead, she was declared insane and committed to a mental hospital. She remained there until she committed suicide two years later.

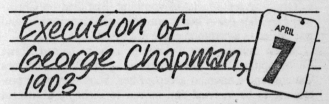

Execution of George Chapman, 1903

APRIL 7

George Chapman, who was hanged on 7 April 1903, was a philanderer and bigamist who poisoned three women with antimony, probably because he had grown tired of them. It has been suggested that he was also responsible for the 'Jack the Ripper' murders.

Chapman was a native of Poland, his real name being Severin Antoniovitch Klosovski. The son of a carpenter, he had been apprenticed to a surgeon at the age of fifteen, but failed to get a degree. After his arrival in London in 1888 he worked as a barber's assistant in the East End.

He was already married by this time, but had left his wife in Poland. Later, when she joined him in England, she found him living with another Polish woman, Lucy Baderski, whom he had also married. The two women lived in the same house with him for a short while, until the legal wife left.

Klosovski and Lucy Baderski went to America together in 1890, but parted company the following year, Klosovski coming back to England in 1892. He changed his name to George Chapman after living for a year with a girl named Annie Chapman.

In 1895 he took up with a married woman, Mary Spink, who had been deserted by her husband. They lived together, claiming to be married, and Mrs Spink — who had private means — allowed him to use some of her money to open a hairdressing shop in Hastings in 1897.

Though this proved popular, with Mrs Spink playing the piano for the benefit of customers, they gave it up six months later and moved back to London, taking the lease of the Prince of Wales Tavern, off City Road.

Towards the end of the year Mrs Spink became ill, suffering severe attacks of vomiting. She died on Christmas Day, her death being put down to consumption, and was buried in a common grave at Leyton.

A few months later a domestic servant named Bessie Taylor applied for a job as barmaid at the Prince of Wales Tavern, and Chapman accepted her. Soon they were pretending to be married and moved to Bishop's Stortford, but then returned to London, where Chapman set himself up in the Monument Tavern, in Borough.

Bessie's health was deteriorating by this time and Chapman treated her violently. When she died, in February 1901, 'exhaustion from vomiting and diarrhoea' was stated to be the cause.

After another few months Chapman met Maud Marsh, whom he also employed as a barmaid. The daughter of a labourer in Croydon, she soon became his mistress, though only after he had threatened to dismiss her. They began to live as man and wife not long afterwards.

The following year, 1902, they moved to a new pub, the Crown, which was in the same road as the Monument Tavern. Maud had also begun to suffer from vomiting and diarrhoea and, although she recovered in hospital, she became ill again after being discharged.

Her mother, who was nursing her, became ill herself after drinking a glass of brandy and soda which Chapman had prepared for Maud. This made her suspicious enough to ask her own doctor to examine Maud, and he, having done so, warned Chapman's doctor that she was being poisoned. When Maud died, on 22 October 1902, Chapman's doctor refused to issue a death certificate.

Chapman was arrested three days later and charged with her murder; he was later charged with the murders of Mary Spink and Bessie Taylor, too. His trial began at the Old Bailey on 16 March 1903, and lasted four days. He was hanged at Wandsworth Prison, at the age of thirty-seven.

Superintendent of Milford Sanatorium poisoned, 1949

During the late afternoon of 9 April 1949, the superintendent of the Milford Sanatorium at Godalming, in Surrey, found a brown-paper parcel containing part of a fruit pie in his office. His secretary was not there, as it was Saturday, and there was no message to tell him who had sent it. He therefore assumed that it was from one of his friends and, taking it home with him, started to eat it. Before long he was seized with pain and began to be violently sick.

He spent the rest of the weekend in bed, feeling very ill and unable to eat anything else, and on Monday, when he returned to work, he was still weak and suffering from a stomach ache. He was then given a letter which had been left in his secretary's in-tray two days earlier. It was from a Mrs Formby, and explained the arrival of the fruit pie, which the superintendent already suspected to have been the cause of his illness.

Mrs Formby was a friend of Mrs Margery Radford, an inmate of the sanatorium, who had received the pie from her husband and been ill herself after eating some of it. Fearing it to be poisoned, she had asked Mrs Formby to have its contents analysed, informing her that she had been ill on several other occasions after receiving food or drink sent by her husband. But Mrs Formby, after consulting her own husband, had decided not to send it to Scotland Yard, as her friend had requested, but to the superintendent instead.

Having read the letter and spoken to Margery Radford, who was now close to death, the superintendent called the Surrey police. The following day the remains of the fruit pie were sent to the laboratories at Scotland Yard, where they were found to contain arsenic. Margery Radford, having suffered from tuberculosis for seven years, died on the very day that this discovery was made. It was then found that she had been systematically poisoned over a period of three months.

Her husband, Frederick Gordon Radford, was a laboratory technician at a hospital about a mile from the sanatorium. He had not been attentive to his ailing wife and was believed to have a mistress; the pies and mineral drinks which Mrs Radford had received, though bought by her husband, were delivered by her father, a Mr Kite. On being told that arsenic had been found in one of the pies and also in his wife's body, Radford held his face in his hands, denying all knowledge of the matter.

'Why should I want to kill my wife?' he asked. 'I knew she was going to die anyway. I would not be such a fool as to use arsenic with my experience, as I know the police could find it easily enough.' He then challenged Detective Superintendent Roberts, head of the Surrey CID, to charge him 'and let a judge and jury decide'.

Superintendent Roberts was not yet ready to make an arrest, as it was just possible that the suspect was telling the truth. Frederick Radford was therefore driven home by police officers after agreeing to attend the inquest the following day. In the morning, however, he was found dead, his body already cold. He had poisoned himself with cyanide.

Murder of David Blakely, 1955

On the night of 10 April 1955, Ruth Ellis, a twenty-eight-year-old divorcée and night-club hostess, peered through a window of a public house in Hampstead, London, and saw her former lover inside. She waited outside for him, and when he emerged she produced a gun and fired at him six times in quick succession. David Blakely, a twenty-five-year-old racing driver, was killed instantly, and a passer-by was wounded in the hand.

Ruth Ellis was immediately apprehended and taken to Hampstead police station, where she admitted the shooting. 'I am guilty,' she said, adding: 'I am rather confused.' At her trial at the Old Bailey in June she was asked what her intention had been when she fired the shots. 'I intended to kill him,' she replied.

Blakely and Ruth Ellis had been lovers for the previous two years, and a few weeks earlier had set up home together in Egerton Gardens, Kensington. However, neither of them had been faithful to the other and both had resented the other's affairs. After many bitter quarrels, Blakely left without telling her where he was going. At the beginning of April she had a miscarriage.

On Good Friday — 8 April — she tried to see him at a house in Tanza Road, Hampstead, where she knew that he was spending Easter in the company of friends. But he refused to see her, and when she became noisy the police were called. It was from the same house that Blakely went out to the pub on the evening of 10 April.

Ruth Ellis was convicted and sentenced to death. Despite many petitions for a commutation, she was hanged at Holloway Prison on 13 July 1955, the execution causing much astonishment and disgust. It was the last time that a

107

woman was hanged in Britain.

In July 1983, Ruth's daughter, then aged thirty-one, gave a newspaper interview to the *Sunday Mirror*, in which she spoke of the anguish which she had suffered as a result of knowing that her mother had been hanged.

'For most of my life I have tried to face up to the image of the hangman peering through the peephole into her cell, trying to work out how much rope he should use to make sure that frail little neck was broken,' she said. 'As for the scene on the gallows, I just blank it out.'

Her half-brother, born in 1944, had had similar problems, though he had been brought up separately. He took his own life in 1982, after years of depression.

Beginning of Adelaide Bartlett's trial, 1886

APRIL
12

On 12 April 1886, the trial of Adelaide Bartlett, aged thirty, for the murder of her husband, began at the Old Bailey. Edwin Bartlett, a forty-year-old grocer, had been found dead at the couple's lodgings in the Pimlico district of London on 1 January the same year. He had died as a result of taking a large dose of liquid chloroform.

The accused was the illegitimate daughter of a well-born Frenchwoman; she had been brought up in France and had come to England to complete her education. Her marriage had taken place in 1875.

Edwin Bartlett was an ambitious businessman and a staunch Wesleyan. Though good-humoured, he gave his wife less attention than she would have liked, with the result that she was often bored. For a period of five years her father-in-law lived with them, her husband having invited him to do so without consulting her. However, they gave the impression of being a contented couple.

In 1885 they became acquainted with a young Wesleyan minister, the Reverend George Dyson, who visited them frequently. Dyson and Adelaide were attracted to each other and began to have an affair — with Bartlett's knowledge and approval. Bartlett made a will, leaving everything to his wife and naming her lover as the executor. He also made it clear that he wanted Dyson to have Adelaide in the event of his own death.

In December Bartlett was seriously ill, but recovered well enough to celebrate Christmas. On the day before his death he visited his dentist and appeared to be in good health. It was afterwards revealed that on 29 December Dyson had given Adelaide a large amount of chloroform which he had bought in small amounts from three different chemists.

Though Dyson had also been charged with the murder, no evidence was offered against him when the case came to court. Adelaide claimed that she used chloroform in order to resist her husband's sexual demands — by getting him to inhale it. As no traces of it were found in the dead man's mouth or windpipe, the jury, at the end of the six-day trial, concluded that while grave suspicion attached to the defendant, there was insufficient evidence to show how or by whom the chloroform had been administered. She was therefore acquitted.

A study of the case by Yseult Bridges, entitled *Poison and Adelaide Bartlett,* puts forward the theory that Edwin Bartlett was induced to drink the chloroform while under the influence of hypnotic suggestion.

Death of Sarah Ricketts, 1953

On 14 April 1953, Sarah Ricketts, a seventy-nine-year-old widow of Devonshire Road, Blackpool, died of phosphorus poisoning, her death occurring at 3.15 a.m. in the presence of Louisa Merrifield, her housekeeper. Mrs Merrifield, aged forty-six, did not call in a doctor until nearly eleven hours later, but tried unsuccessfully to get an undertaker to cremate the body 'at once'. Later, when the bungalow and garden were being searched by police, she made arrangements for members of the Salvation Army to play *Abide With Me* outside.

Louisa Merrifield and her third husband Alfred, aged seventy-one, had moved into Mrs Ricketts' home only a few weeks earlier, Mrs Merrifield having obtained the job after seeing it advertised in a newspaper. Mrs Merrifield had had twenty similar jobs in the previous three years; she also had a criminal record, having served a prison sentence for ration-book frauds. Mrs Ricketts, despite feeling that she was not being properly looked after — she complained that she was not given enough food — had since changed her will in the couple's favour.

'We are landed', Mrs Merrifield told an acquaintance a few days before Mrs Ricketts' death. 'We went living with an old lady and she died and left me a bungalow worth £4000.' When asked which old lady she was talking about, she replied, 'She's not dead yet, but she soon will be'.

During a medical examination on the day before her death Mrs Ricketts was found to be in reasonably good health.

The search of the bungalow failed to reveal any trace of the poison, but a substance attached to a teaspoon in Mrs Merrifield's handbag was found to be the residue which resulted from phosphorus being mixed with rum. Alfred Merrifield was identified by a Blackpool chemist's assistant from whom he had purchased a tin of rat poison which contained phosphorus.

Louisa and Alfred Merrifield were brought to trial in Manchester in July, both pleading not guilty to the murder; the case lasted eleven days. Louisa stated that she had found Mrs Ricketts on the floor of her bedroom at 3.15 a.m. on the day of her death, and went on to tell the court: 'I picked her up and put her into bed. She said she was thankful to me. Those were the last words she spoke.' On being asked why she had not immediately gone for help, she replied, 'Well, it was not such a nice time in the morning to go out on the streets and call a doctor.'

Though the defence contended that Mrs Ricketts had died from cirrhosis of the liver, the jury found Louisa Merrifield guilty of murder and she was sentenced to death. In the case of her husband they were unable to reach agreement; the judge therefore ordered that he should be retried at the following assizes, but the case against him was finally dropped. Louisa Merrifield was hanged at Manchester's Strangeways Prison on 18 September 1953.

Alfred Merrifield, on being released, received his half-share of Mrs Ricketts' bungalow, and later appeared in sideshows in Blackpool. He died, aged eighty, in 1962.

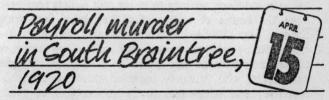

Payroll murder
in South Braintree,
1920

APRIL
15

On the afternoon of 15 April 1920, two employees of the Slater and Morrill Shoe Company were shot and fatally wounded by two other men while delivering the $16,000 weekly payroll to the company's factory in South Braintree, Massachusetts. The two killers, having grabbed the money, escaped in a car with a third gunman who had taken no active part in the crime; another two men were also seen in the car with them. The two victims were Frederick A. Parmenter, the paymaster, and Alexander Berardelli, an armed guard.

The two men who had fired the shots were both described as 'foreign-looking', one of them being clean-shaven and the other having a moustache. It was as a result of these descriptions that a police officer boarded a streetcar in the same district on 5 May and arrested two Italian immigrants, Nicola Sacco, a shoemaker aged twenty-nine, and Bartolomeo Vanzetti, a fish-pedlar aged thirty-two. Both were found to be armed with guns, Sacco having a .32 Colt automatic and Venzetti a .38 revolver; both were also found to be anarchists.

Though each was initially charged with possessing a firearm without a permit, Sacco was later brought to trial for taking part in an attempted payroll robbery in Bridgewater, near Boston, the previous Christmas. On being convicted of this offence, he was sentenced to ten to fifteen years' imprisonment. By this time he and Vanzetti had been charged with the South Braintree murders.

Their trial, which began in Dedham, Massachusetts, on 31 May 1921, made headline news in many countries. Some sixty witnesses appeared for the prosecution, and nearly 100 for the defence. The prosecution produced ballistics evidence, seeking to prove that bullets recovered from the bodies of both victims had been fired from Sacco's gun. While the value of this evidence was challenged by defence witnesses, the political sympathies of the defendants made bias inevitable. The conduct of the trial judge, who privately regarded them as 'anarchist bastards', was afterwards to be the subject of much criticism. Sacco and Vanzetti were both found guilty of first-degree murder and sentenced to death.

There were immediate demands for another trial. Organizations were set up to raise funds for their defence and a campaign of agitation began. During the next six years many petitions for clemency were presented and many protests staged. In legal circles disquiet was expressed at the verdict and the means by which it had been reached. But, on 9 April 1927, after no fewer than seven motions for a new trial had been heard and dismissed, the death sentences were confirmed. Sacco and Vanzetti were executed in the electric chair on 23 August 1927.

The controversy to which the case had given rise continued long after their deaths, and has never been forgotten. In 1977 their names were cleared in a special proclamation issued by the Governor of Massachusetts.

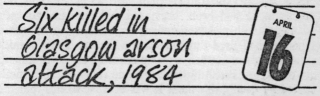

Six killed in Glasgow arson attack, 1984

During the early hours of 16 April 1984, an arson attack was made on a Glasgow council flat, resulting in the deaths of six people. The flat, which was the home of a family named Doyle, was on the top floor of a block in Backend Street, Ruchazie. As the front door was its only exit, and petrol had been poured through the letter-box and ignited, the people inside were trapped. One of the survivors, twenty-one-year-old Stephen Doyle, only managed to escape the blaze by jumping fifty feet to the concrete below, injuring his back and legs in the process.

Stephen's brother Anthony, aged fourteen, and his twenty-five-year-old sister, Mrs Christine Halleron, both died in the flames; his father, James Doyle, aged fifty-three, his brothers James and Andrew, aged twenty-three and eighteen respectively, and Mrs Halleron's eighteen-month-old son Mark all died later. James Doyle's grief-stricken widow Lilian, aged fifty-two, who was rescued by firemen after perching on a window-ledge, said later that she wished that she, too, had died in the fire which claimed the lives of her husband, sons, daughter and grandson.

The attack had been the work of Thomas Campbell, a thirty-one-year-old gangster determined to take control of Glasgow's lucrative ice-cream trade, and one of his hench-men, a twenty-two-year-old petty thief named Joseph Steele. Campbell, who had already served a ten-year prison sentence, had been responsible for many attacks on drivers working for Marchetti Brothers, a well-established rival company, and was believed to have taken part in an attempt to burn down that company's premises.

Andrew Doyle, one of the drivers concerned, had actually been hired by Marchetti Brothers to protect two of their other vans rather than sell ice-cream. On one occasion he had been threatened and his van had been damaged with pickaxe handles; on another a man with a shotgun had fired through his windscreen. Then, a week after the second attack, a group of men had beaten him up in the street. But Andrew Doyle had refused to be intimi-dated by Campbell's men. It was because of this that the arson attack had taken place.

Though the police officers investigating the crime had little difficulty finding out what had happened, they hesi-tated to make arrests for fear that they would prove to be premature. A twenty-four-year-old man, William Love, was charged in connection with the shotgun attack and, while denying that he had committed the offence, agreed that he had been at the scene on the day in question; he afterwards made a statement claiming to have overheard Campbell and others planning to set fire to the Doyles' front door, as 'a frightener'. However, it was 12 May before the police took Campbell into custody and 1 June before they arrested Joseph Steele.

Eventually, on 3 September 1984, the case described as 'Scotland's biggest multiple murder trial' began in Glasgow, with Campbell, Steele and five other men appearing, each charged with offences in connection with the gang's activities. It lasted twenty-seven days, with one of the accused being released when the prosecution withdrew charges against him, and others being cleared on some charges because the judge found insufficient evidence against them.

But at the end of the trial Thomas Campbell and Joseph Steele were both given sentences of life imprisonment for murdering the six members of the Doyle family, the judge recommending that Campbell should serve twenty years, but making no recommendation in Steele's case. Campbell was also given ten years, to run concurrently, for taking part in the shotgun attack, and Steele received two shorter sentences, also to run concurrently, for conspiracy and damaging an ice-cream van.

Of the other accused, Thomas Gray, aged thirty-one, was sentenced to fourteen years for attempted murder; Thomas Lafferty, forty, was given three years for taking part in the shotgun attack; George Reid, thirty-three, received a total of three years for a knife assault and for damaging an ice-cream van, and John Campbell, twenty-one, was given a year for taking part in the attack on the ice-cream van and three years for taking part in the shotgun attack.

The jailing of Campbell and his fellow-accused did not bring Glasgow's 'ice-cream war' to an end, for others associated with them have continued to operate vans on the city's council estates and many further cases of assault and damage have been reported by drivers working for Marchetti Brothers. It is believed that, in spite of the length of his sentence, Campbell is still directing the activities of gang members who were not arrested from his prison cell.

Execution of Frederick Seddon, 1912

On 18 April 1912, Frederick Seddon, a forty-year-old insurance agent, was hanged at Pentonville Prison for the murder of Eliza Barrow, a lodger at his three-storey house in Tollington Park, north London. Miss Barrow, aged forty-nine, had died from arsenic poisoning on 14 September previously.

Seddon was a mean and calculating man, obsessed with making and saving money. He had worked for the same insurance company for over twenty years, but was constantly dealing in other things — anything which enabled him to make a profit, in fact — and even managed to make 2s 6d (12½p) commission out of his victim's funeral. He owned various properties in addition to the house at Tollington Park, where he and his family occupied the lower floors. His crime, needless to say, was committed for gain.

Eliza Barrow, who had moved into the house in July 1910, was shabby and dirty, and every bit as miserly as Seddon himself. She occupied the top floor, and had an orphan boy, the son of an earlier landlord and landlady, living with her.

At the beginning of her tenancy she had both property and money, but gradually her fortune passed into Seddon's hands, as she was impressed by his financial astuteness and thought he was helping her to take care of it. After her death he took over £400 in gold coins from her cash-box, and then arranged a pauper's burial for her, haggling with the undertaker over the cost of it.

Eliza Barrow's doctor, without seeing the body, made out a death certificate, giving the cause as 'epidemic diarrhoea'. But after complaints from her relatives, who were

116

suspicious of Seddon's evasive answers to their questions, an exhumation was authorized and a post-mortem carried out. On 4 December Seddon was arrested and charged with murder. His wife was similarly charged a few weeks later.

Frederick and Margaret Seddon were brought to trial at the Old Bailey on 4 March 1912, both pleading not guilty. The case lasted ten days, three of them being taken up by Seddon's own evidence; this was given in such an arrogant and self-assured manner that it served only to antagonize everyone. So, while his wife was acquitted, Seddon — against whom the case was no stronger — was convicted. When asked if he had anything to say before sentence was passed, he made a long speech protesting his innocence, during the course of which he raised his hand as though taking an oath of freemasonry.

The judge, who, like Seddon, was a freemason, said in reply: 'You and I know we belong to one brotherhood ... But our brotherhood does not encourage crime; on the contrary, it condemns it. I pray you again to make your peace with the Great Architect of the Universe. Mercy — pray for it, ask for it'. He was in tears as he pronounced sentence.

Seddon was the father of five children, the youngest of which had been born just a few months before the murder. Margaret Seddon remarried and moved to Liverpool a few months after her husband's execution. She made herself a lot of money out of a newspaper confession, stating that she had seen Frederick Seddon giving poison to Eliza Barrow on the night before her death. However, she published a second statement a fortnight afterwards, claiming that the first had been a lie. Eventually she emigrated to America.

Trial of David Greenwood, 1918

On 24 April 1918, David Greenwood, a twenty-one-year-old turner, was brought to trial at the Old Bailey, charged with the murder of Nellie Trew, aged sixteen, on 9 February previously. He denied the offence.

On the day of the murder the victim, a junior clerk working at Woolwich Arsenal, had left her home at Juno Terrace, Eltham Well Hall, to change a book at Plumstead Library. The following morning she was found raped and strangled on Eltham Common, about a quarter of a mile away. Her father had reported her missing when she failed to return home by midnight.

A replica of the badge of the Leicestershire Regiment and an overcoat button, which had been threaded with a piece of wire, were found trodden into the mud near the scene of the crime. The police had a photograph of both articles published in all the popular newspapers on the day after the body had been found.

David Greenwood, who worked for the Hewson Manufacturing Company near Oxford Street, normally wore a badge on the lapel of his overcoat. One of his workmates noticed that it was missing and remarked, pointing to the newspaper photograph, 'That looks uncommonly like the badge you were wearing.' Greenwood agreed, explaining that he had sold his badge two days earlier to a man he had met on a tram. It was then suggested to him that he should go to the police and 'clear the matter up'.

The same day, at lunch time, Greenwood went to the police station in Tottenham Court Road and told the same story. The police, learning that he lived in Eltham, took a particular interest in him, and the next day an inspector went to his place of work and took him back to Scotland Yard.

118

It was noticed that all the buttons had been removed from his overcoat, and that there was a little tear where one of them had been. The piece of wire which had been attached to the button discovered on Eltham Common was found to be part of a spring; the same type of spring was used at the Hewson works.

At his trial Greenwood's war record was revealed. Having enlisted at the beginning of the First World War, he had fought in the trenches and been buried alive at Ypres. He had then been discharged, suffering from neurasthenia, shell-shock and a weak heart. The defence suggested that he was not physically capable of committing the crime of which he stood accused.

The jury found the defendant guilty, adding a recommendation of mercy. His death sentence was commuted just before he was due to be executed, and he spent the next fifteen years in prison. At his release, in 1933, he was thirty-six years old.

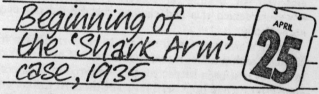

Beginning of the 'Shark Arm' case, 1935

APRIL 25

On 25 April 1935, a shark in an Australian aquarium began to vomit and, to the disgust of spectators, brought up a man's arm. When this was removed from the pool by police it was found to be so well preserved that a tattoo depicting two boxers was clearly visible on it. As there was also a length of rope tied tightly round the wrist, the police immediately suspected that a murder or suicide had taken place.

The shark had been caught by two fishermen off the beaches near Sydney a week earlier, when it became entangled in their lines. Not knowing what else to do with it, they had given it to the Coogee Beach aquarium. But it had not taken to captivity and its digestive system had failed to function normally. It died shortly afterwards.

No trace of any other part of the man's body was found in the shark's stomach or intestines, so an extensive search of the beaches and sea-bed was started in the area in which it had been caught. Though this was to be in vain, a study of missing-persons lists led to the man's identification. He was found to be James Smith, a forty-year-old former boxer who had worked as a marker in a billiard hall owned by Reginald Holmes, a wealthy boat-builder, prior to his disappearance. His wife and brother both identified the arm from its tattoo marks.

Smith had left his home on 8 April, telling his wife that he was going on a fishing holiday with a man named Patrick Brady, and that they would be staying in a rented cottage on the coast; she had heard nothing from him since. The police already knew Brady, a forty-two-year-old forger, and though he denied all knowledge of Smith's death, he was taken into custody. He then accused Smith's employer of dealing in forgeries. Reginald Holmes, however, denied this and claimed that he did not even know Brady.

Smith's arm was found to have been severed from his shoulder with a knife, rather than bitten off by the shark, as had at first been suspected; this appeared to have been done after he had been dead for some time. At the cottage on the coast a tin trunk, a mattress, three mats and a length of rope were found to be missing. It was therefore supposed that the body had been cut up there and pushed into the trunk, those parts for which there was insufficient room being tied to the outside. The trunk had then been taken out to sea and dumped, together with the mattress and mats, which were presumably bloodstained.

Three days after Brady's arrest Reginald Holmes, steering his speedboat in an erratic manner in Sydney Harbour, was pursued by a police launch. When the police caught up with him after a four-hour chase he was found to be suffering from a superficial bullet wound in his head and claimed that somebody had tried to kill him. He then admitted knowing Brady, and accused him of killing Smith and disposing of the body. On 17 May Brady was charged with murder.

However, on the night before the coroner's inquest Holmes, by now the most important witness, was shot dead in his car under Sydney Harbour Bridge, the sound of the shot being drowned by the noise of overhead traffic. Brady's lawyers then obtained an order from the Supreme Court to stop the inquest — after forty witnesses had been heard — on the grounds that Smith's severed arm was no proof of his death. Brady was released on bail, and at his trial in September for Smith's murder was acquitted for lack of evidence.

It was understood that both Smith and Brady had been involved in drug-trafficking and underworld intimidation, and that Holmes had been murdered in order to ensure his silence. But Brady, who died in 1965, maintained his innocence of Smith's murder to the end, and two other men who were tried for Holmes' murder were both acquitted.

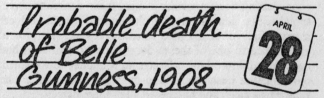

Probable death of Belle Gunness, 1908

APRIL 28

On 28 April 1908, a farm on the outskirts of La Porte, in Indiana, owned by a widow named Belle Gunness, was burnt to the ground. The fire, which had been started deliberately, led to the discovery of four bodies among the debris, and fourteen others which had been dismembered and buried. The four recovered from the debris were believed to be those of the widow and her three children. The other fourteen were found to be the remains of men who had been murdered by the widow for their money.

Belle Gunness, who was born in Norway in 1859, had had two husbands, both of whom had died; the death of the second had occurred in suspicious circumstances in La Porte in 1904. She had since managed the farm with the help of a local handyman, Ray Lamphere, who was also her lover. It was believed that Lamphere had killed her and then set fire to the farm in order to prevent the crime being discovered. However, the body believed to be hers was inexplicably headless. Those involved in the investigation had to point to the finding of her denture in order to prove that it *was* hers.

Almost immediately after Lamphere's arrest a stranger arrived in La Porte in search of his missing brother. Andrew Hegelein, of South Dakota, was known to have visited the farm, taking $1000 in cash, but nothing had been heard from him since; his brother, having written to Mrs Gunness, had now come to see her about it. Before long it was discovered that Andrew Hegelein was one of the men who had been murdered.

Mrs Gunness was found to have been in the practice of placing newspaper advertisements in other parts of America, each of them worded in the same way: 'Rich, good-looking woman, owner of a big farm, desires to correspond with a gentleman of wealth and refinement. Object matrimony.' All of the men whose bodies had been found had replied to one of these advertisements, and each had been duped into taking a large sum of money to the farm, thinking that he was about to meet his future wife. The widow had killed and butchered all of them herself.

Ray Lamphere was brought to trial for the widow's murder, but acquitted. At the same time, however, he was convicted of setting fire to her property and given a sentence of two to twenty-one years' imprisonment. He died of tuberculosis in the Indiana State Penitentiary.

He had, at some stage, made a claim that the widow's death had been faked, the headless corpse found after the fire being that of a drunken female tramp from Chicago. But, while this might explain why the head was missing, it also suggests that Mrs Gunness was responsible for the deaths of her own children, of whom she was very fond. It is therefore unlikely to be true.

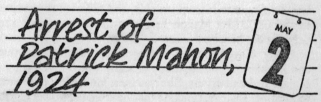

Arrest of Patrick Mahon, 1924

On the evening of 2 May 1924, Patrick Mahon, aged thirty-four, went to retrieve a Gladstone bag from the cloakroom at Waterloo Station, London. As he tried to leave the station afterwards he was approached by a police officer, who asked to be shown the bag's contents. Mahon said that he had not got the key, and was then taken to Kennington police station, where keys were found in his possession. Later, at Scotland Yard, the bag was opened and found to contain a cook's knife, a brown canvas bag with the initials E.B.K. and some bloodstained items of clothing.

Unable to account for these articles satisfactorily, Mahon was told that he would be held while inquiries were made. After much hesitation he finally made a statement which led to the discovery of human remains in a bungalow near Eastbourne the following morning. They were the remains of Mahon's mistress, Emily Kaye, who had been dead for over a fortnight and whose body had been dismembered. She had been pregnant at the time of her death.

Mahon, a soda-fountain salesman of Richmond, Surrey,

was a married man with one child. He had a criminal record, having been in trouble on one occasion for forgery, on another for embezzlement and on a third for robbery with violence; the third of these charges had been brought against him in 1916, when he was sent to prison for five years.

A day or two earlier Mahon's wife had found a cloakroom ticket in one of his pockets and asked a friend — a former railway policeman — to find out what had been left at Waterloo Station. The ex-policeman had inspected the bag, looking into it from the side, and reported the matter to the CID. Mrs Mahon had been asked to replace the ticket in her husband's suit.

Emily Kaye, a thirty-eight-year-old shorthand-typist and bookkeeper, was just one of many women with whom Mahon had had affairs. She had been induced to part with most of her savings, thinking that he intended taking her to South Africa — where he would set up home with her — and had joined Mahon in Eastbourne on 12 April, the bungalow having been rented for eight weeks. The exact date of her death was never established.

According to Mahon, who gave several different accounts during the course of the investigation, Emily Kaye had been accidentally killed as a result of a violent quarrel. Having dismembered her body, he had pushed the torso into a trunk — where the police found it — and burnt her head, legs and feet on the sitting-room fire; other parts were cut into small pieces and boiled in a pot or thrown from the window of a train. He had left the bag at Waterloo Station before going back to his home in Richmond.

While some parts of his story were undoubtedly true, others were clearly not — especially as he was found to have bought a cook's knife and a meat-saw in London before going to join the victim in Eastbourne. He was accordingly brought to trial in Lewes in July, with crowds of people mobbing the court-house.

Mahon denied the offence. He said that the victim had demanded that he should leave his wife in order to set up home with her, and that he had rented the bungalow as an 'experiment', in order to show her that this would be unwise. She had been killed, he said, when she hit her head against a coal-scuttle while he was defending himself against her. He was not believed.

On being found guilty, he protested about 'the bitterness and unfairness' of the judge's summing-up. He was, however, hanged at Wandsworth Prison on 9 September 1924.

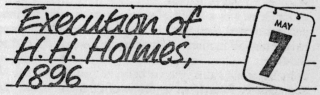

Execution of H.H. Holmes, 1896

MAY 7

H.H. Holmes, who was hanged at Philadelphia's Moya-mensing Prison on 7 May 1896, was a mass murderer. His victims included mistresses, employees and acquaintances, but how many of them there were altogether is not known. He was also an insurance swindler and a bigamist.

A native of Gilmanton, New Hampshire, Holmes was born on 16 May 1860; his real name was Hermann Webster Mudgett. He practised medicine in New York for a short while after obtaining a degree at the age of twenty-four, then moved to Chicago, where he worked in a drug-store owned by a Mrs Holden. Later he became the owner of the store, Mrs Holden having mysteriously disappeared.

Holmes had married at eighteen, but deserted his wife and son in 1886, changing his name when he went to Chicago. There he soon married again — it was the first of several such marriages — and he began to swindle one of his new 'wife's' uncles, causing a family quarrel in the process. He also had a succession of mistresses, some of whom disappeared as mysteriously as Mrs Holden.

125

With his business thriving, Holmes bought a vacant lot and began to build a hotel, with turrets, battlements and secret passages, which became known as 'Holmes's Castle'. When this was later investigated by police, it was found that there were air-tight rooms which could be filled with gas from hidden pipes operated from the office, and that the basement contained a kiln large enough to hold a human body.

Holmes sold the drugstore in 1892, after the completion of his hotel. During the following year he had a good many guests to accommodate as a result of the Chicago Exposition. But he was involved in petty crime as well, and received a term of imprisonment for fraud shortly afterwards. It was as a result of a conversation with a fellow prisoner named Hedgspeth in St Louis Prison that he was to find himself in more serious trouble towards the end of 1894.

In September that year a body alleged to be that of Benjamin F. Pitezel, an associate of Holmes' whose life had been insured for $10,000, was found in Philadelphia; he had evidently died as a result of an explosion. Holmes, among others, went to identify the body, and the insurance company paid the $10,000 to Pitezel's wife. On hearing of this, however, Hedgspeth wrote to the company, saying that Holmes had told him about a 'foolproof method' of insurance fraud, and warning them that the body was not that of Pitezel at all.

The company investigated the case and obtained evidence which appeared to substantiate Hedgspeth's allegation. Holmes, on being questioned, agreed that he had defrauded the company using a body which had been provided by a doctor; the real Pitezel, he said, had gone abroad, taking his three children. Mrs Pitezel also admitted fraud, but did not know her husband's whereabouts; she said that Holmes had taken her children to stay with a widow in Kentucky and that she had not seen them since.

Later, however, Holmes confessed that the body in Philadelphia *was* Pitezel's, and said that the dead man had committed suicide; the children were safe in England. But the bodies of two of the children were then found in a cellar in Toronto, and the remains of the third were recovered from a chimney in Irvington.

Holmes was eventually brought to trial on 28 October 1895, for the murder of Benjamin Pitezel, but the case against him included evidence that he had committed other murders, too. The witnesses included a Chicago car mechanic, who told the court that he had been employed by Holmes at the 'castle' to strip the flesh from three corpses which he believed to have been brought from the city mortuary. Holmes, he said, had paid him $36 for each of the bodies so treated.

While under sentence of death Holmes wrote his memoirs for a newspaper, claiming that he had killed twenty-seven people. He afterwards said that the confession was entirely false, and had been written for the sake of sensationalism. On the scaffold he said that he had been responsible for only two deaths and that these were both of women on whom he had performed illegal operations.

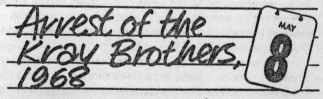

Arrest of the Kray Brothers, 1968
MAY 8

At 6 a.m. on 8 May 1968, teams of detectives raided homes in the East End of London and arrested seventeen members of a criminal gang led by the twin brothers Ronald and Reginald Kray. The gang ran a protection business and was responsible for many acts of brutality, including murder, and the arrests followed a long investigation which had been greatly hampered by the fear of witnesses to give information about them. But once the downfall of the gang seemed certain, these witnesses began to come forward of their own accord, and some of its members agreed to give evidence in return for their own freedom. It thus became possible to bring various charges against the gang leaders and nine other people.

These were all brought to trial together at the Old Bailey in January 1969, the most serious charges concerning the murder of George Cornell, a member of the rival Richardson Gang from south London, the murder of Jack McVitie, a small-time crook known as 'Jack the Hat', and the alleged murder of Frank Mitchell, a well-known escaped convict popularly called 'the Mad Axeman'. Among the witnesses called by the prosecution were the barmaid of a public house in which Cornell had been shot dead in March 1966, and Ronald Hart, a cousin of the Krays, who had been present when McVitie was stabbed to death in a basement flat in Stoke Newington in October 1967.

The trial lasted thirty-nine days, with many sensational disclosures being made, and ten of the prisoners were convicted. Ronald Kray and a henchman named John Barrie were both sentenced to life imprisonment for Cornell's murder, Reggie Kray being given ten years for being an accessory to the same crime. Both of the twins were given life sentences, with a recommendation that they serve at least thirty years, for the murder of Jack McVitie. Other members of the gang, including their older brother Charles, were given long sentences for crimes related to these murders, and some were given shorter sentences for lesser offences. The charges concerning the alleged murder of Frank Mitchell, whose body was never found, were not proved.

The Kray twins, aged thirty-five, were both former professional boxers. Outwardly they were respectable businessmen, owning clubs and restaurants, and had many celebrities among their friends. But, in fact, they enjoyed their reputation for violence and the power which it gave them. 'I saw beatings that were unnecessary even by

128

underworld standards and witnessed people slashed with a razor just for the hell of it,' said Ronald Hart, who had worked for them. On one occasion, after shooting somebody, Reggie Kray had said to him, 'You want to try it some time. It's a nice feeling.'

'We were well aware that many people thought we had bitten off more than we could chew in arresting a large number of known criminals without, at that time, having sufficient evidence to secure conviction,' Commander John du Rose later recorded. 'But we were convinced that once the Gang was in custody evidence would be forthcoming. Events proved us right but there was still a lot of work to be done verifying statements and digging up fresh facts. Nothing was left to chance and a vast team of detectives worked day and night.'

While serving an earlier sentence for grievous bodily harm Ronald Kray, a homosexual, was certified insane and transferred to a mental hospital in Surrey. In 1979 he was again found to be insane, and this time he was committed to Broadmoor.

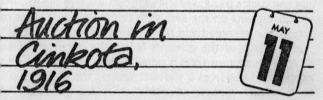

Auction in Cinkota, 1916

On 11 May 1916, a house with an adjoining workshop in the village of Cinkota, near Budapest, was sold by public auction. The owner was not present and his whereabouts were unknown; the sale had been ordered by the district court so that unpaid taxes on the property could be collected. It was bought by Istvan Molnar, a middle-aged blacksmith, who intended turning it into a smithy and general repair shop.

129

A week or so after Molnar and his family had moved into the house seven large tin barrels were discovered behind sheets of corrugated iron in the workshop; they were sealed and unexpectedly heavy. At first Molnar paid no attention to them, but when they were eventually opened each was found to contain the body of a naked woman.

The women, whose ages varied between thirty and fifty, had all been strangled, their deaths taking place over a period of two or three years; there was no means by which any of the bodies could be identified. Moreover, the property had previously been occupied by an unknown tenant who had rarely been seen by neighbours and who had left no personal belongings or papers which would have enabled the police to trace him.

After the investigation had dragged on for about three weeks without progress, Geza Bialokurszky, one of Budapest's most experienced detectives, was put in charge of it. Searching lists of missing persons, he came across an entry concerning a thirty-six-year-old spinster named Anna Novak who had disappeared five years earlier while employed as a cook by the widow of a Hussar colonel.

Bialokurszky questioned the widow and learnt that the missing cook's trunk was still in the attic where she had left it. Fingerprints on the lock were found to match those of one of the corpses from the Cinkota 'House of Horror', and a search of the contents led to the discovery of an advertisement torn from a popular daily newspaper. This purported to be from a widower seeking the acquaintance of a mature spinster or widow, with the possibility of marriage in mind. A post office box number was given for replies.

Bialokurszky made inquiries at the central post office in Budapest and found that the box-holder had given his name as Elemer Nagy; the address he gave was that of an empty plot of land in one of the suburbs. A search of back numbers of the newspaper revealed that the same box number had been used in over twenty advertisements of the same type during a period of less than two years. One of these had been paid for with a postal order, the advertiser using the same name but giving a false address in Cinkota. The others had been paid for in cash.

A facsimile of the signature on the postal order was published in the newspapers, and two days later a domestic servant named Rosa Diosi informed Bialokurszky that it was the handwriting of her former lover, Bela Kiss, who had been called up on the outbreak of war. She produced a postcard which he had sent her from a prisoner-of-war camp in October 1914, asking her to forward some underwear which had been left in her care; the handwriting had the same characteristics as the postal order signature, and Bialokurszky was certain that Bela Kiss was the 'Monster of Cinkota'.

Other women who had known him as a result of his advertisements came forward to provide further information, and finally a photograph was obtained. From this he was recognized as a frequent visitor to Budapest's red-light district.

Towards the end of the year five more bodies, all of naked women, were found under flowerbeds in Istvan Molnar's garden.

By this time it was known that, prior to committing his first murder Bela Kiss, a plumber by trade, had been in the practice of seducing middle-aged women, mainly servants, and coaxing them into parting with their savings. He had used the money to pay for the services of prostitutes, for which he appeared to have an almost insatiable need. He had started killing his victims after one of them had become too demanding for him.

Bela Kiss was never brought to justice, and what became of him is not known. Bialokurszky, who tried for years to trace him, became convinced that he had died in captivity after being wounded in battle. But his disappearance inevitably gave rise to a variety of legends, and some people claimed to have seen him in America long after the war ended.

On 12th May 1958, thirty-one-year-old Peter Manuel was brought to trial in Glasgow, charged with eight murders. The case lasted fourteen days, during the course of which the defendant dismissed his counsel and took over the defence himself. The evidence for the prosecution included Manuel's own confession, but he claimed that this had been made as a result of police threats to charge other members of his family in connection with the offences. The defendant was found guilty on all but one of the charges and sentenced to death. While awaiting execution he confessed to three other murders.

Manuel, a habitual criminal with a record of theft and rape, had been arrested following the discovery of a triple murder in Uddingston, south of Glasgow, at the beginning of the year. Peter Smart, a self-made businessman, his wife and their eleven-year-old son had been shot dead during a burglary at their home on 1 January, their bodies being found some days afterwards. Manuel, who lived with his parents, was suspected and housebreaking tools were found at his home. He and his father were both detained.

While in custody Manuel said that he would give the information which the police wanted on condition that his father was released. Later he admitted being responsible for the triple murder, and also said that he had killed seventeen-year-old Anne Kneilands in East Kilbride two years earlier, three members of a family living just outside East Kilbride in September 1956, and another seventeen-year-old girl, Isabelle Cooke, near her home in Mount Vernon a few days before the murder of Peter Smart and his family.

In the first triple murder case, as in the second, the

victims had all been shot during the course of a burglary. The two seventeen-year-old girls had both been the victims of sex murders, Anne Kneilands being found on a golf course with some items of clothing missing. Isabelle Cooke in a shallow grave, almost naked. It was in the case of Anne Kneilands that Manuel was acquitted for lack of evidence. In the case of Isabelle Cooke it was the murderer himself who showed police where the victim had been buried.

'This is the place,' he said. 'In fact, I think I'm standing on her now.'

Born in 1927, Manuel had been almost constantly in trouble from 1939 onwards. His first conviction was for burglary, for which he was put on probation. Soon afterwards he was sent to an approved school, from which he escaped eleven times, for housebreaking. He was then sent to Borstal for robbery and indecent assault — his first known sexual offence. Then, in 1946, he was jailed for housebreaking and rape, and served seven years before being released in 1953. He was again in prison between October 1956 and November 1957.

The three murders to which he confessed while under sentence of death were those of Helen Carlin, a prostitute found strangled in Pimlico in September 1954, Anne Steele, a fifty-five-year-old spinster who was battered to death in Glasgow in January 1956, and Ellen Petrie, who was stabbed, also in Glasgow, in June 1956.

On 8 December 1957, Sydney Dunn, a Newcastle taxi-driver, was found dead on the moors at Edmondbyers, County Durham; he had been shot in the head and his throat had been cut. A coroner's inquest found that he, too, had been killed by Peter Manuel.

Following the dismissal of his appeal, Manuel was hanged at Glasgow's Barlinnie Prison on 11 July 1958.

On 13 May 1983, workers digging in a Cheshire peat bog found a woman's skull which, though over 1500 years old, was so well preserved that it still contained parts of the brain, hair and ligaments. Because of its good condition, nobody at the time suspected its age, and a pathologist who examined it said that it was part of the body of a woman who had allegedly been murdered in the same area in 1960 or 1961. This mistake led to the conviction of Peter Reyn-Bardt, a fifty-seven-year-old former airline official, a few months later.

Reyn-Bardt, a homosexual, had married Malika Maria de Fernandez, a thirty-two-year-old part-time waitress, on 28 March 1959. At the time he was a BOAC executive at Manchester Ringway airport, fearing that discovery of his homosexuality would lead to prosecution and the loss of his job. He saw marriage as a means of acquiring an appearance of respectability. But when his wife realized this her attitude towards him changed, and she started to leave him for months at a time.

Reyn-Bardt set up home on his own in a cottage in Wilmslow, a suburb of Manchester, where his wife suddenly appeared some months later. After a bitter quarrel over money he strangled her, then hacked her body to pieces with an axe and buried the remains in his large wooded garden. In 1963 he moved to Portsmouth.

Twelve years later, still in Portsmouth, he met Paul Russell Corrigan, with whom he was arrested and sent to prison for abducting boys for sexual purposes. When Corrigan, following his release in January 1981, fell foul of the law again — this time he had tortured and killed a boy in Birmingham — he told the police how Reyn-Bardt had murdered his wife.

Now living in Knightsbridge, London, Reyn-Bardt was questioned about his wife's disappearance but denied having killed her. However, the discovery of the ancient skull 300 yards from the cottage in Wilmslow led to further questioning, and Reyn-Bardt, confronted with the 'evidence', then made a confession. In December 1983, after a three-day trial at Chester Crown Court, he was sentenced to life imprisonment.

By this time tests carried out at the radio-carbon dating laboratory at Oxford University had shown the skull from the peat bog to be that of a woman who had died, aged between thirty and fifty, about AD 410.

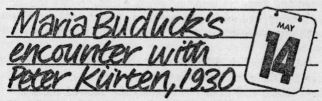

Maria Budlick's encounter with Peter Kürten, 1930

On 14 May 1930, Maria Budlick, a twenty-one-year-old domestic servant, left her home in Cologne to look for work in Düsseldorf, twenty miles away. Arriving at Düsseldorf station, she met a man who offered to show her the way to a hostel, and set off through the streets in his company. But when he tried to persuade her to go into the Volksgarten Park with him she refused.

At this time the city was being terrorized by the 'Monster of Düsseldorf', a brutal sadist responsible for many shocking crimes, and Maria Budlick was unwilling to go into the park with a stranger who, for all she knew, may have been 'the Monster' himself. However, her refusal led to an argument which continued until a second man intervened, asking 'Is everything all right?' The first man then took himself off.

The servant girl's rescuer was a soft-spoken, courteous man — the sort she could trust. Grateful for his help, she went with him to his one-room flat in Mettmännerstrasse, where he gave her a glass of milk and a sandwich. Afterwards they went by tram together to the edge of the city, Maria believing that she was being taken to a hostel, then got out to walk in the Grafenburg Woods. Suddenly the man stopped.

'Do you know now where you are?' he asked. 'I can tell you. You are alone with me in the middle of the woods. Now you scream as much as you like and nobody will hear you!'

At this, he seized her by the throat and tried to rape her. The terrified girl put up a struggle, but had almost lost consciousness when the man unexpectedly loosened his grip. 'Do you remember where I live, in case you're ever in need and want my help?' he asked. Maria, though she *did* remember, had the good sense to say that she did not. The man then released her and showed her the way out of the woods.

Maria Budlick did not report the attack, but when it came to the attention of the police (as a result of a letter of hers which had been misdirected) she showed them the building where she had been taken by her attacker. While they were there the man appeared; he entered his room after seeing the servant girl outside, then left a few minutes later. He was found to be Peter Kürten, a forty-seven-year-old married man with convictions for theft and assault, who had spent a total of over twenty years in prison. He was a factory worker and a keen trade unionist.

Though not questioned at the time, Kürten was arrested a week later after his wife had informed the police that he had confessed to being the 'Monster of Düsseldorf'. He admitted sixty-eight crimes, including the nine murders and seven attempted murders for which he was brought to trial in April the following year. It seems that after seeing Maria Budlick at the building in Mettmännerstrasse he had told his wife about his crimes so that she could claim a reward for his capture, knowing that he would soon be arrested anyway.

Kürten, described at his trial as 'the king of sexual delinquents', was stimulated to the point of orgasm by the sight of blood or fire. Unlike most other known sadists, he killed both men and women — and also children and animals. Moreover, to the spectators in the Düsseldorf courtroom it was evident that he derived pleasure from describing his crimes in detail.

Though a defence of insanity was made on his behalf, he was found guilty on all counts, and sentence of death was pronounced nine times. He was calm and courteous to the end, and before being executed by guillotine on 2 July 1931, said that it would give him much pleasure to hear the sound of his own blood gushing from his neck after the sentence had been carried out.

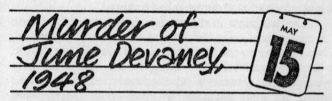

Murder of June Devaney, 1948

During the early hours of 15 May 1948, June Anne Devaney, aged three years and eleven months, was found to be missing from a ground-floor children's ward of the Queen's Park Hospital in Blackburn, Lancashire. The discovery was made by Staff Nurse Gwendoline Humphreys, who found the child's cot empty when she entered the ward just before 1 a.m. It appeared from a trail of footprints on the polished floor that she had been removed by an intruder.

Nurse Humphreys raised the alarm and a search of the hospital and its grounds was started. Just under two and a half hours later the missing child was found dead about

100 yards from the ward. She had been raped and then brutally murdered, her assailant holding her by the leg and dashing her head against one of the boundary walls.

The crime was such an atrocious one that the Chief Constable of Blackburn feared an outbreak of public disorder. He called on Scotland Yard for assistance without delay, hoping to bring the culprit to justice quickly, and within a few hours Detective Chief Inspector John Capstick and Detective Sergeant John Stoneman arrived to take charge of the investigation. But it was to take them three months to find the person responsible.

June Devaney, the daughter of a miner, had been admitted to hospital on 5 May suffering from mild pneumonia, but had made a good recovery and was due to be discharged on the morning of her murder. Though under four years of age, she was the oldest child in the ward and the only one who could talk. It would therefore not have been possible for any of the other five children, even if they had been awake at the time, to give the police any information about what had occurred.

The footprints in the ward had been made by a man wearing socks, who had entered by the door at one end, walked over to the cots, then moved towards the door at the other end before returning to the first door; those beside June Devaney's cot suggested that he had stood there for some moments. As these prints had not been made by any member of the hospital staff, it was assumed that they had been made by the murderer.

It seemed, too, that the person concerned had taken a Winchester bottle containing sterile water from a nearby trolley and placed it under June's cot, for Nurse Humphreys remembered that it had been in its usual place when she went into the ward prior to the child's disappearance. An examination of this bottle by a finger-print expert resulted in the discovery of several fresh prints which had also not been left by any of the staff. But when photographs of these were sent to Scotland Yard they were found not to match those of any known criminal.

138

Capstick believed that the murderer was a local man with a knowledge of the hospital; he therefore proposed that every male person in Blackburn between the ages of fourteen and ninety who was not bedridden should be fingerprinted. The Mayor of Blackburn made a public announcement about this, calling for co-operation from the town's 110,000 inhabitants and promising that all the fingerprints would be destroyed after they had been compared with those of June Devaney's murderer. He then set an example by becoming Capstick's first volunteer.

It was a tremendous undertaking, but Capstick was certain that it would eventually lead to the solution of the crime. Suddenly, on the afternoon of 12 August after 46,000 sets of prints had been checked, one of the experts scrutinizing the latest batch exclaimed, 'I've got him! It's here!'

That evening Peter Griffiths, a twenty-two-year-old former Guardsman working as a flour-mill packer, was arrested as he left his home in Birley Street, in one of the town's poorest districts. On being charged and cautioned, he admitted the offence, saying that he had had a number of drinks beforehand. He had abducted the child from the ward after removing his shoes, and had later beaten her head against the wall to stop her crying, he said.

The suit which he had worn on the night in question was examined and found to have been stained with June Devaney's blood; fibres taken from it were identical to others found on the dead girl's body. Though police suspected that Griffiths had also murdered an eleven-year-old boy in Farnworth earlier the same year, they were not able to obtain a second confession.

At his trial at the Lancashire Assizes, it was suggested that Griffiths, a solitary person who drank heavily, was suffering from a form of mental illness and was not responsible for his actions. But the jury took only twenty-three minutes to find him guilty and he was sentenced to death. He was hanged at Walton Prison on 19 November 1948.

Disappearance of Camille Holland, 1899

During the early evening of 19 May 1899, Miss Camille Holland, aged fifty-six, left her farmhouse near Saffron Walden in the company of her lover, fifty-three-year-old Samuel Dougal, telling their maid that she was going shopping and would not be long. Two hours later Dougal returned alone, saying that she had gone to London and would be back shortly. However, she did not return at all that day, and the following morning Dougal informed the maid that he had received a letter from Miss Holland, saying that she was going on a holiday. In fact, she was dead, but four years were to elapse before her body was discovered.

Miss Holland, a wealthy woman, had been living with Dougal as his wife for several months. She had bought the farm, which Dougal renamed Moat House Farm, in January, and they had moved into it on 27 April after staying in lodgings in Saffron Walden in the meantime. The day after her disappearance a younger woman moved in to take her place, bringing a little girl. Though Dougal began introducing this newcomer as his widowed daughter, it later turned out that she was his legal wife.

Dougal, an ex-soldier with a prison record for forgery, had been married three times; his first two wives had died in Nova Scotia, where he had served for ten years, and his third marriage had taken place in Dublin in 1892. He had had four children by his first wife and two by his third, in addition to an unknown number by other women. His third marriage ended in divorce in 1902 after Mrs Dougal had run away with an engine-driver. Dougal himself, whatever his marital state, was rarely without a mistress for long, and sometimes had several at the same time.

140

Soon after Miss Holland's disappearance he began to transfer money from her bank account to his own by means of forgery; he managed to become the owner of Moat House Farm in the same way. He was thus able to buy himself a car and spend much of his time hunting, shooting and drinking, as well as having affairs, without any financial difficulties. But Miss Holland's continued absence gave rise to rumours, and eventually one of the forgeries was discovered. A police investigation then became inevitable.

In March 1903 Dougal fled. He was arrested in London, with £563 in banknotes and gold and many valuables in his possession, and charged with forging a cheque. The following day he was taken to the police station in Saffron Walden, and a search of Moat House Farm was started.

Five weeks later Miss Holland's body was recovered from an old drainage ditch. She had been shot in the back of the head at close range, the bullet having been fired from a revolver owned by Dougal. The ex-soldier was charged with her murder on 30 April.

He was brought to trial in Chelmsford on 22 June. The following day, having given no evidence, he was convicted and sentenced to death. After an appeal had been dismissed, he wrote a long letter to the Home Secretary, claiming that he had shot Miss Holland by accident, but this was to no avail and he was hanged at Chelmsford Prison on 8 July 1903.

He admitted his guilt on the scaffold.

Murder of Bobby Franks, 1924

On 21 May 1924, Bobby Franks, fourteen-year-old son of a millionaire businessman, was abducted outside his school in the Chicago suburb of South Side Kenwood. The boy's mother received a telephone call, informing her that he had been kidnapped and that a ransom note would be sent through the post. The caller gave his name as Mr Johnson.

The following day a demand for $10,000 was received, the note stating that the missing boy was 'at present well and safe'. But before anything could be done about it the police informed Bobby Franks' father that a boy's body had been found in a culvert by the Pennsylvania railroad tracks.

In spite of facial disfiguration caused by hydrochloric acid, the body was quickly identified as Bobby Franks. His skull was fractured and he had been strangled.

A week later a pair of spectacles which had been found near the body were traced to Nathan Leopold Jr, a nineteen-year-old law student at Chicago University. Leopold, an amateur ornithologist, agreed that the spectacles were his and said that he must have dropped them in the culvert while bird-watching in the area some time previous to the murder. However, there were no weather marks on them, and this suggested that he was lying, as there had been a lot of rain prior to the date of the murder. Leopold was therefore regarded as a suspect.

Asked what he had been doing on the afternoon of 21 May, he said that he and his friend Richard Loeb, an eighteen-year-old fellow student, had been out with two girls, whose names were Mae and Edna. But, while Loeb corroborated this, neither he nor Leopold could give any information which enabled the police to trace these girls.

Moreover, specimens of Leopold's typing were found to match that of the ransom note. Leopold and Loeb who both, like Bobby Franks, had extremely wealthy parents and were accordingly questioned at length. Loeb eventually confessed; then Leopold confessed, too. They were brought to trial for murder and kidnapping in July the same year.

Besides being accustomed to wealth and luxury, the two defendants were both intellectually gifted, Leopold having an I.Q. of 200. But they were bored and had decided to commit a 'perfect' murder after failing to derive sufficient excitement from a series of petty thefts. Bobby Franks, a friend of Loeb's younger brother, had not been chosen as their victim because they disliked him; he had merely been an easy person to entice into a hired car. The crime, in the words of their lawyer, Clarence Darrow, had been a 'senseless, useless, purposeless, motiveless act of two boys'.

A plea that both defendants were mentally ill — Leopold being a paranoiac and Loeb a schizophrenic — probably saved their lives, for at the end of the trial each was sentenced to life imprisonment for murder and ninety-nine years for kidnapping. The failure of the judge to impose the death penalty, however, caused grave public disquiet and continued to be a contentious matter for years afterwards.

The case was brought back into the headlines in January 1936, when Richard Loeb was murdered by a fellow convict.

Nathan Leopold served thirty-three years, during which he ran educational rehabilitation courses for other prisoners and volunteered to take part in anti-malaria experiments. Following his release in 1958, he went to Puerto Rico, where he married in 1961. He died ten years later.

During the early hours of 22 May 1981, a police surveillance team on patrol near the Chattahoochee River in Atlanta, Georgia, heard the sound of a splash and saw a young black man driving away from the scene in a station-wagon. They stopped the man for questioning but afterwards let him go, as they appeared to have no cause to arrest him. However, they remained suspicious, and the man — Wayne Williams, a twenty-three-year-old music-talent promoter and freelance photographer — was placed under observation. Two days later, when the body of Nathaniel Cater, aged twenty-seven, was found floating in the river, Williams was suspected of murder.

Cater had been seen leaving a theatre with Williams just before his disappearance, the witness informing police that the two men had been holding hands. It was found, too, that dog hairs on Cater's body were similar to others found at Williams' home and inside his station-wagon. But by this time Williams was suspected not only of Cater's murder but also of twenty-seven others.

The twenty-seven other people who had been murdered were all young blacks, teenagers and children of both sexes whose bodies had been found in Atlanta during the previous two years. The crimes had been committed without apparent motive — except in the case of a girl who had been raped — and by a variety of means, including suffocation, strangulation, shooting and stabbing. They were believed by blacks to be the work of a white racist, and the police had been subjected to much criticism over their failure to catch him.

Their inquiries now established that Williams had been seen in the company of two of these other victims, and laboratory tests on fibres, as well as dog hairs, from his home showed that he had been connected with another eight. Though he was charged only with the murder of Nathaniel Cater and one other person — Jimmy Payne, the twenty-sixth victim — his arrest brought this long series of crimes to an end.

Wayne Williams, an intelligent and resourceful man, was a homosexual with a hatred of other blacks and a frustrated desire for instant personal success. The evidence against him was entirely circumstantial but at his trial, which began in January 1982, the prosecution was allowed to produce evidence relating to other murders besides those with which he was charged. This, together with the sudden cessation of the murders, weighed heavily against him, and he was convicted on both counts.

He was sentenced to two consecutive terms of life imprisonment.

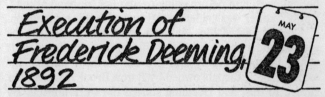

Execution of Frederick Deeming, 1892

On 23 May 1892, Frederick Deeming, a multiple murderer and confidence trickster aged about fifty, was hanged in Melbourne, Australia. A large number of officials and newspaper reporters were present, and the hangman and his assistant both wore false beards to prevent themselves being identified. A crowd of 10,000 people waited outside the prison while the execution was carried out.

Deeming, the youngest of seven children, had been born in Liverpool. A flamboyant and charming man, he travelled a great deal, committing many thefts and frauds with ease; women were generally fascinated by him. He married an English girl who bore him four children, but abandoned her twice — once in Australia and once in South Africa. It was because she pursued him that she was finally murdered.

In 1891 Deeming took up residence in Rainhill, to the east of Liverpool, claiming to be Mr Albert Williams, an Inspector of Regiments. He let it be known that he was looking for a house on behalf of Baron Brook, a personal friend, and went to look over a nearby villa which the owner, Mrs Mather, wanted to let furnished to a suitable tenant. Having reached an agreement with Mrs Mather, he was allowed to move into the property without paying any rent in advance, in order to prepare for the Baron's arrival. He then began to court Mrs Mather's daughter Emily, aged twenty-five, who believed him to be a bachelor.

Before long, however, Deeming's wife arrived unexpectedly, bringing their four children, and insisted on moving into the villa with him. When Emily Mather heard about this, Deeming told her that Mrs Deeming was his sister, and that she had brought her children to spend a short holiday with him before going to join her husband abroad. Emily Mather was evidently satisfied with this explanation.

Deeming asked Mrs Mather's permission to cement the ground under the floor of the villa so that the floorboards would lie more evenly and provide surfaces suitable for some valuable carpets owned by Baron Brook. Mrs Mather agreed to this, and Deeming started the work himself. By the time he had finished his wife and four children had been murdered and their bodies buried in the cement. He employed a local carpenter to re-lay the floorboards.

A short while after this Deeming told Mrs Mather that he had to go to Australia and that Baron Brook would not be moving into the villa after all. He then married Emily, and they set sail together, arriving in Melbourne in December 1891.

'Mrs Williams', however, was soon to be disposed of in the same way as Mrs Deeming and her children: about 20 December her body was buried in cement under the dining-room hearth of a small furnished house which the couple had rented in Andrew Street, Windsor. She had been struck on the head six times and her throat had been cut. But this time Deeming was more careless and the body was discovered by the owner of the house.

Deeming was arrested in Perth in March 1892, just in time to prevent him marrying an heiress named Kate Rounsevell. By the time he appeared for trial, charged with the murder of Emily Mather, the remains of his wife and children had been discovered and he had been accused in newspaper articles of both crimes, as well as many others.

He pleaded that he was insane, then, towards the end of the trial, made a long speech denying the allegations which had been made against him and describing the spectators in the courtroom as 'the ugliest race of people I have ever seen'.

He died unrepentant, smoking a cigar as he walked to the place of execution.

Death of Arthur Major, 1934

On 24 May 1934, Arthur Major, a forty-four-year-old lorry-driver of Kirkby-on-Bain, Lincolnshire, died in agony after a short illness. His wife Ethel, who was two years younger, told their doctor that her husband had died during the night after having 'another of his fits'. The doctor therefore put Major's death down to 'status epilepticus', and arrangements were made for the funeral. But the following day the local police received a remarkable anonymous letter, signed 'Fairplay'. It read:

'Have you ever heard of a wife poisoning her husband?

147

Look further into the death of Mr Major of Kirkby-on-Bain. Why did he complain of his food tasting nasty and throw it away to a neighbour's dog, which has since died? Ask the undertaker if he looked natural after death. Why did he stiffen so quickly? Why was he so jerky when dying? I myself have heard her threaten to poison him years ago. In the name of the law, I beg you to analyse the contents of his stomach.'

The police discovered that Arthur Major had been a drunken bully, whose fourteen-year-old son regularly slept at his grandfather's house, a mile away, to avoid him. Ethel Major, after being questioned, suddenly turned to the police officer concerned and asked: 'I'm not under suspicion, am I? I haven't done anything wrong!' The police officer gave a non-committal answer, then went to see the neighbour whose dog had died; the body was dug up so that its stomach contents could be examined. The next day Arthur Major's funeral was called off by order of the coroner, so that the contents of *his* stomach could be examined, too. Both the dog and the lorry-driver were found to have died from strychnine poisoning.

Further inquiries revealed that Arthur and Ethel Major had frequently quarrelled over the dead man's alleged affair with a neighbour's wife and his own wife's expenditure on clothes which he considered unnecessary. It was also discovered that Ethel's father, Tom Brown, was a retired gamekeeper, who had frequently killed vermin with poison.

When Ethel Major was asked if she knew about this, she replied, 'I didn't know where he kept his poisons. I never at any time had any poison in the house.' She then revealed that she knew more about the cause of her husband's death than had so far been made known to anyone except the police, for she added, 'I didn't know that my husband died of strychnine.'

Tom Brown showed the police a locked box which he kept in his bedroom; it contained a bottle of strychnine crystals. He informed them that his daughter knew the contents, but would not have been able to use them as the key to the box had been lost more than ten years previously and had not been replaced. The key was later found in Ethel Major's possession.

Ethel Major was brought to trial for her husband's murder at the Lincoln Assizes in November 1934, convicted and sentenced to death. Despite a strong recommendation of mercy from the jury, she was hanged at Hull Prison on 19 December the same year.

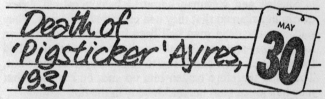

Death of 'Pigsticker' Ayres, 1931

On the night of 30 May 1931, Herbert Ayres, a forty-five-year-old casual labourer known as 'Pigsticker', was attacked and killed in an area of woodland and makeshift huts near Elstree, in Hertfordshire. The crime was committed by two other labourers and witnessed by a third, but nothing was reported until three days later, when the victim's charred body was found in a smouldering refuse tip at Scratchwood Sidings, half a mile away. It was then found that he had died as a result of a heavy blow on the head which had fractured his skull.

There were a large number of navvies in the area, all living in shacks and known to each other by nicknames. When the police began making inquiries, the one who had witnessed the crime — a fellow named Armstrong — told them what had happened, identifying the culprits as 'Moosh' and 'Tiggy', two men who shared a hut and kept three dogs to protect it. According to his account, Armstrong had been staying the night in this hut, and had been dozing on the floor when he heard a quarrel going on outside. He had then looked out and seen 'Moosh' and 'Tiggy' beating up 'Pigsticker'. Afterwards, he said, they took the body away in a sack, carrying it over a pole.

'Moosh' and 'Tiggy' were found to be William Shelley, aged fifty-seven, and Oliver Newman, sixty-one, both of whom had the reputation of being tough and disagreeable. To the police officers who went to arrest them, their dogs seemed tough and disagreeable as well, and the officers concerned waited outside the shack for some hours until its occupants gave themselves up. The arrests were followed by the discovery of a bloodstained axe under the floor of the hut.

Shelley and Newman admitted having caused Ayres' death, but claimed that they had only used their fists. They said that the dead man had been in the habit of stealing from them, and that on the night in question they had found some bacon and bread to be missing from their hut. They had therefore beaten him up and, on realizing that they had killed him, buried his body in the tip.

The two men were brought to trial at the Old Bailey, the case lasting two days. Both were convicted and sentenced to death, Shelley afterwards commenting that the sentence was twenty years late. They were hanged on 5 August 1931.

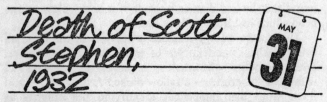

Death of Scott Stephen, 1932

MAY 31

During the early hours of 31 May 1932, Elvira Barney, a wealthy twenty-seven-year-old socialite, telephoned her doctor in a hysterical state and told him that there had been 'a terrible accident' at her home in Knightsbridge,

London. The doctor hurried to her address, 21, William's Mews, and found Michael Scott Stephen, her twenty-four-year-old lover, lying dead on the stairs. He had been shot in the chest at close range.

The police were called, and a Smith and Wesson revolver with two empty chambers was found near the body. Mrs Barney, who was separated from her husband, had been out to a party with Stephen earlier and, on returning, they had started to quarrel over another woman. According to her own statement, Mrs Barney had then threatened to commit suicide, using the gun which she kept at her bedside, and Stephen had been accidentally killed when he tried to take it away from her.

But neighbours who had been woken up by the quarrel told the police that Mrs Barney had actually threatened to shoot *him*, and that the threat had been followed by the shot or shots. On 3 June Mrs Barney was arrested and charged with murder.

At her trial at the Old Bailey the following month witnesses gave evidence that the accused and her lover had often quarrelled, and one — a chauffeur's wife — claimed that on an earlier occasion Mrs Barney had leant out of the window and fired at him while he was in the mews below.

The firearms expert, Robert Churchill, stated that the gun which had been used was one of the safest types in existence and that considerable pressure was needed to fire it. This evidence, however, was challenged by the defence counsel, Sir Patrick Hastings, who pointed out that there was no safety catch and proceeded to press the trigger several times without apparent difficulty. 'It doesn't seem to require any terrific muscular strength,' he remarked as he did so.

Mrs Barney stuck to her story that Stephen had been killed by accident. Her counsel, after asking for the gun to be placed on the edge of the witness-box, suddenly ordered her to pick it up. The fact that she automatically picked it up with her right hand served to cast doubt on the evidence of the chauffeur's wife, who had said that Mrs Barney had fired with her left hand on the earlier occasion.

The jury deliberated for an hour and fifty minutes before returning a verdict of not guilty. Mrs Barney then left the court and found herself applauded by a large crowd outside.

Four years later she was found dead in a hotel in Paris.

Mrs. Freeman Lee found murdered, 1948

JUNE 1

On 1 June 1948, a milkman on his delivery round in Maidenhead, Berkshire, called at the home of Mrs Freeman Lee, a ninety-four-year-old recluse, and found two full bottles still standing on the doorstep from previous days. He told a neighbour, who looked through the window of the downstairs room to which Mrs Lee normally confined herself night and day. As she was not there, the neighbour then peered through the letter-box.

He saw cushions lying on the floor of the hall and, beyond them, a black trunk with a woman's shoe beside it. As his eyes became accustomed to the light, he also saw a bunch of keys lying on the floor. He decided to inform the police.

A constable arrived soon afterwards, accompanied by a local solicitor who was a friend of the old lady. Unable to summon her to the door, they forced an entry and began to search the house. There were seventeen rooms altogether, and Mrs Lee was not in any of them; a search of the garden revealed that she was not there either. Finally, as the constable telephoned the police station to make a report, it occurred to the solicitor to open the trunk in the hall.

There, under a lot of old clothes, he found the body of

152

Mrs Lee. She had been battered over the head and also bound and gagged. It was later established that she had died from suffocation.

Mrs Lee had lived in the same house for about forty years, and was well-known in Maidenhead. It was generally believed that she was rich as, indeed, she had been in the distant past, but she had been very poor in recent years, existing on a small allowance from a legal benevolent society. Besides that, she had suffered a stroke which left her partially paralysed on one side. Her house was in a shocking state of disrepair and disorder; every part of it had been neglected.

Though the pathologist was unable to state with certainty when her death had occurred, it was found that the last person to see her alive — other than her murderer — had been an electrician who called at the house to install an electric boiling-ring during the early evening of 29 May. Clearly, she had been killed sometime between then and the following morning.

Two parts of a single fingerprint, discovered on the lid of a cardboard box, were identified at Scotland Yard; they had been left by George Russell, a housebreaker with a criminal record. When Russell was located in St Albans five days later a scarf which had belonged to the victim was found in his possession.

Russell denied ever having been inside the house, but when confronted with the fingerprint evidence he began to cry and said that he wanted to make a statement. In this, he inadvertently revealed that he knew Mrs Lee's true circumstances. He was therefore arrested and charged with her murder.

George Russell was brought to trial at the Berkshire Assizes, denying the offence. His counsel sought to discredit the prosecution witnesses, but to no avail; he was convicted and sentenced to death. Showing no emotion at this, the prisoner looked round the hushed courtroom, then tweaked his left ear before leaving the dock. His life of crime, which had lasted over twenty years, was brought to an abrupt end when he was hanged at Oxford Prison on 2 December 1948.

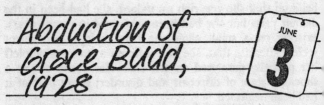

Abduction of Grace Budd, 1928

JUNE 3

On 3 June 1928, twelve-year-old Grace Budd left her home in New York City in the company of a harmless-looking old man who said that he was taking her to a children's party which was being given by his sister. When she had not returned by 10 p.m. her anxious parents reported the matter to the police. But it was six and a half years before they found out what had become of her — and then they were informed of it in a particularly cruel manner.

The harmless-looking old man, calling himself Frank Howard, had turned up at the home of Edward Budd and his wife on 1 June after seeing an advertisement asking for farm work which their son Paul, aged eighteen, had placed in a newspaper. He said that he owned a large farm in Farmingdale, Long Island, and promised the youth a job there. On the day of the abduction he had lunch with the family at noon, and said that he would take Paul back to Long Island with him when he and Grace returned from the party. The address at which he claimed that the party was being held proved to be non-existent, as did the old man's farm in Long Island.

The police obtained a sample of the man's handwriting from a telegram which he had sent to Paul from Yorkville, Manhattan, on 2 June. They also had an agate container in which he had given the family some cottage cheese; this was found to have been bought from a pedlar in the same vicinity, but provided no distinct fingerprints. There were

154

no other clues to the real identity of 'Frank Howard', and it was not until the morning of 11 November 1934, when Mrs Budd unexpectedly received a letter from him, that any further progress on the case was made.

In this letter, written solely for the purpose of causing further suffering to the missing girl's family, 'Frank Howard' stated that he had murdered Grace and 'feasted on her flesh for nine days'.

'I learned to like the taste of human flesh many years ago during a famine in China,' he said. 'I can't exactly describe the taste. It is something like veal, then again it resembles chicken, only it is tastier than either. The best flesh, that which is most tender, is to be had from children. Little girls have more flavour than little boys.'

The handwriting was identical to the sample which the police had obtained earlier, and the letter had been sent in an envelope which they were able to trace. On 13 December the culprit, whose real name was now known to be Albert Fish, was arrested in a shabby New York City boarding-house. He immediately made a confession, stating that he had originally intended to kill and eat Paul but had changed his mind after seeing Grace. Some hours later he led police to a patch of woodland in Westchester County, where the missing girl's remains had been buried.

The police dug into the frozen earth, working far into the night. Before daylight Grace Budd's skull and bones, together with her clothes, had been recovered.

Albert Fish, then aged sixty-four, was a house painter by trade and the father of six children. He had been arrested many times, and had been sent to prison for writing obscene letters, among other things. But while in custody he admitted to being responsible for numerous other crimes, and is now thought to have criminally assaulted over 100 girls and murdered at least fifteen of them.

He derived sexual pleasure from receiving pain as well as from inflicting it, and an X-ray photograph showed the presence of a large number of needles which he had inserted into his own body.

'There was no known perversion that he did not practise, and practise frequently,' a prison psychiatrist recorded.

Fish was brought to trial for the murder of Grace Budd in White Plains, New York, on 12 March 1935, the judge refusing to allow female spectators into the courtroom in view of the nature of the case. A plea of insanity was made on his behalf, but he was convicted and sentenced to death on 22 March.

'I thought he was insane, but I figured he should be electrocuted anyway,' one of the jurors said later.

Unperturbed by the prospect of his own death, Albert Fish was executed at Sing Sing Prison on 16 January 1936.

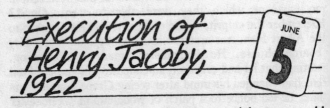

Execution of Henry Jacoby, 1922

JUNE 5

On 5 June 1922, Henry Jacoby, an eighteen-year-old pantry boy, was hanged at Pentonville Prison for the murder of Lady White, sixty-five-year-old widow of a former chairman of the London County Council. Though the crime had been a brutal one, the jury at his trial had made a recommendation of mercy on account of the prisoner's youth, and there had been a lot of agitation in favour of the sentence being commuted. When the execution was carried out within a few days of Ronald True being reprieved (See 6 March), the two cases together were seen by many people as proof of the existence of class privilege.

Lady White, on the morning of 14 March previously, had been found dying from head injuries in her bedroom at the Spencer Hotel in Portman Street, London. There were no signs of a struggle or a forced entry; the murder weapon had not been left at the scene, and nothing appeared to have been stolen. Jacoby, who had only been employed at the hotel for three weeks, was questioned by police and gave information about his background which was found to be false. He was searched and found to have two blood-stained handkerchiefs in his pockets. He finally made a confession of his own accord.

Jacoby said that while lying in bed in the early hours he had been aware of being in a hotel full of rich people, and suddenly decided to steal something from one of the rooms. He got up and took a hammer from a tool bag which some workmen had left in the basement — to 'use if necessary' — then started trying the doors. Finding one unlocked, he entered the room and shone a torch around.

When Lady White woke up and screamed he began to panic and struck her several times with the hammer. He later washed the hammer and wiped it dry with the handkerchiefs before returning it to the tool bag.

Jacoby was held on remand in Brixton Prison, where Ronald True greeted him with his customary joviality. 'Here's another for our Murderers' Club!' he said, slapping him on the back. 'We only accept those who kill them outright!'

Brought to trial at the Old Bailey on 28 April 1922, the prisoner pleaded not guilty. He said in his defence that he thought the person in Lady White's bedroom was an intruder and was afterwards frightened when he realized what he had done. The judge advised the jury that if blows were struck with the intention of inflicting grievous bodily harm and the victim died as a result of them, the assailant was guilty of murder.

When appeals for mercy were dismissed, requests were made for Henry Jacoby to be given a Christian burial. But these were similarly unsuccessful, and his body was interred inside the prison where the hanging took place.

Murder of Mrs. Paterson, 1927

JUNE 9

On the evening of 9 June 1927, William Paterson, of Riverton Avenue, Winnipeg, arrived home to find his wife missing. She had left no message for him and their two children did not know what had become of her. Some hours later, when she had still not appeared, he finished putting the children to bed and called the police to find out if any accidents had been reported. They were unable to help him.

Then, suddenly discovering that his suitcase had been forced open and some money stolen, Mr Paterson knelt at his bedside to pray. As he did so, he found his wife's body underneath the bed. Emily Paterson had been beaten to death with a hammer and then raped, her death occurring at approximately eleven o'clock in the morning. Some clothes had also been stolen from the house.

The crime led to the arrest, trial and execution of Earle Nelson, 'the Gorilla Murderer', who, at the age of thirty, had been responsible for many sex killings, mainly in the United States.

Nelson, a strange-looking man with a receding forehead and protruding lips, had hitch-hiked into Winnipeg on 8 June, taking a room in a boarding-house in Smith Street, where he told the landlady that he was 'a religious man of high ideals'. The same day he murdered a fourteen-year-old girl living in the same house and hid her body under the bed of an unoccupied room, where it was found four days later.

After the murder of Mrs Paterson he sold the stolen clothes to a second-hand shop, then went to a barber's to have a shave; the barber noticed that he had blood in his hair. He left Winnipeg in a hurry two days later, after his

158

description had been circulated by the police, and was arrested while hitch-hiking between Wakopa and Bannerman. His trial took place in Winnipeg in November 1927.

Nelson was born in America and brought up by an aunt, his mother having died of venereal disease contracted from his father, when he was nine months old. At the age of ten he was knocked down by a streetcar, receiving injuries which were to cause bouts of pain and dizziness for the rest of his life. In 1918 he was committed to an asylum after an assault on a child, but escaped several times and got married in 1919. His aunt and his wife both gave evidence at his trial, the defence being one of insanity.

Nelson's interest in religion was a genuine one; he had read the Bible avidly as a child, both before and after his accident, and is known to have talked about the subject a lot. But he was also an intensely jealous man — so much so that when his wife was in hospital he immediately began to accuse her of having affairs with the doctors. His marriage lasted only six months.

Of his twenty-two known victims, all but two were killed in America, the first in San Francisco in February 1926. Most were boarding-house landladies, some of them in their fifties or sixties; most were strangled and afterwards raped. The 'Gorilla Murderer' kept on the move and used false names in order to avoid capture. He showed no remorse for his crimes except at the place of execution, when he begged for forgiveness.

He was hanged in Winnipeg on 13 January 1928.

Murder in St. Lucia, 1971

During the early morning of 10 June 1971, an estate house in St Lucia, in the West Indies, was found to be on fire. The alarm was raised by neighbours, but by the time the fire was extinguished the building had been destroyed. The bodies of its two occupants, James and Majorie Etherington, who had been in the banana business, were then found among the debris of a ground-floor bedroom. They were buried on the neighbouring island of Barbados after being viewed, though hardly examined, by the Caribbean Government pathologist.

It was assumed that the fire had been started by accident, and the police at first gave it little attention. But a day or two later an insurance company investigator went to the site and found evidence of arson. A louvred window of the rear scullery, which the fire had not reached, had been broken from the outside, and footprints were found on the floor beneath it. A piece of plastic hose, smelling of petrol, led from the house to the garage, where a car was found with its petrol tank open.

When these discoveries were reported the police took the matter more seriously, and asked Scotland Yard to provide assistance. The local police commissioner, learning that a number of men had been seen hanging about near the Etheringtons' home on the evening before the fire, had three known criminals named Florius, Faucher and Charles held for questioning. 'If I get any real trouble on the island, I bring these three in,' he explained to Professor Keith Simpson, the Home Office Pathologist. 'If they haven't done it, they always know who has!'

Florius, the ringleader, had burn marks on his neck and arm, and he and Anthony Charles — 'who just does what he's told' — both had scratches which suggested that they had been involved in a struggle. The three men admitted having robbed the Etheringtons, and said that the couple had been tied up during the course of the crime. But they denied having used violence or starting the fire.

When the bodies were exhumed for a more thorough examination James Etherington's skull was found to have been smashed in with a blunt instrument, though he was still alive when the fire started. His wife had been gagged as well as bound, and she, too, had died in the fire.

Florius, Faucher and Charles were charged with murder, and brought to trial in Castries, the capital of St Lucia, three months later. The result was a foregone conclusion, and during a speech from the dock Faucher told the court that the victims had been burnt to death deliberately, as Florius had believed that electronic records could otherwise be made of their thoughts. All three were found guilty and subsequently hanged.

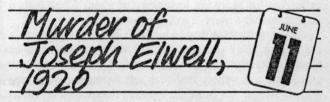

Murder of Joseph Elwell, 1920

JUNE 11

On the morning of 11 June 1920, Joseph Elwell, a well-known bridge expert, was found slumped in a chair in his New York home, with a bullet wound in his forehead. The discovery was made by his housekeeper when she arrived at the house about 8 a.m., at which time Elwell was still alive. He was immediately rushed to hospital, where he died a little while afterwards. The revelations which followed provided much entertainment for the general public, but did not help the New York police in their attempts to solve the crime.

Elwell, aged forty-five, was a rich man and a known philanderer. His two books, *Elwell on Bridge* and *Elwell's Advanced Bridge*, were widely read in the United States, and enabled him to move in high society. He was also thought to be handsome and young-looking, though this impression was due to his wigs and false teeth. At the time of the shooting he was not wearing either, so when his housekeeper arrived she saw him as a bald and toothless man whom she did not recognize. Joseph Elwell had been shot as he sat in his pyjamas, reading letters which had arrived in the morning's post.

Though married in 1904, Elwell had been separated from his wife for some years. Among his possessions police found a list of women's names and addresses, which the newspapers described as a 'love index'. A pile of women's underwear was also found, though the dead man was known to have been living on his own. His companion of the previous evening had been Viola Kraus, who had just been divorced; they had dined together and then been to a show before Elwell returned home in the early hours of the morning. He had afterwards made a number of telephone calls from his bedroom, including one about 6 a.m., when he tried to call a number in Garden City.

As the weapon with which Elwell had been shot was a .45 calibre army revolver, the culprit was thought to be almost certainly a man — and the fact that $400 in cash and items of jewellery had been left untouched suggested that theft had not been the motive. Police officers interviewed all of his known acquaintances, both male and female, and heard various rumours about lovers, husbands and fellow bridge-players, all motivated by jealousy. Yet no real suspect emerged, and nobody has since been able to provide us with one.

The murder of Joseph Elwell remains one of New York's most famous unsolved crimes.

Human remains left in the Bois de Boulogne, 1981

JUNE
13

On the evening of 13 June 1981, a man of Oriental appearance was seen leaving two large suitcases in the Bois de Boulogne before taking to his heels. The witnesses were suspicious and the police were immediately called to the scene. The suitcases were found to contain most of the remains of a young woman, whose body had been cut into pieces and wrapped in plastic rubbish sacks. A bullet was recovered from the base of her skull and traces of semen were found in her sex organs. There was, however, no evidence that she had been raped.

The remains were identified as those of Renée Hartevelt, a twenty-five-year-old Dutch student who had been doing post-graduate work at the Université Censier in Paris. They were found to have been left by Issei Sagawa, a Japanese student at the same college, who lived in the Rue Erlanger, in the sixteenth arrondissement. He had taken the two suitcases to the Bois de Boulogne by taxi on the evening in question, and when police searched his studio apartment they found not only the .22 calibre rifle with which the victim had been shot, but also some other parts of her body, which he had been keeping in his refrigerator.

Sagawa, aged thirty-two, made a confession. He said that Renée Hartevelt, with whom he shared an interest in literature, had visited his apartment on the afternoon of 11 June to help him with some difficult translations, as her French was better than his own. While she was there he asked her to have sexual intercourse with him, but she refused. It was as a result of this rebuff that the murder had taken place.

Sagawa explained, without remorse, that he had killed his fellow-student with a single shot in the back of the

163

neck, and had afterwards pulled off her clothes and had intercourse with the corpse. He had then cut the body into pieces, stopping every now and then to take photographs of it. Those parts which were not put into the suitcases for disposal were kept so that he could eat them, and some had already been consumed. He said that he had wanted to eat a girl's flesh for a long time.

Though all the known facts indicated that this account was true, Sagawa was not tried for the crime. He was, instead, placed under psychiatric observation and later declared to be unfit to stand trial by reason of insanity. He remained in a mental hospital in Paris until May 1984, when he returned to Japan as a result of an agreement between the two countries concerned. This agreement was reached about the same time as the Japanese company Kurita Water Industries, of which Sagawa's father was the president, signed a business deal with a French chemical conglomerate, Elf-Aquitaine.

In Japan, Issei Sagawa entered a mental hospital, where he remained until August 1985. He was then discharged on the hospital superintendent's orders because his 'examination and treatment were finished'. His discharge, however, had been opposed by the hospital's deputy superintendent, Dr Tsuguo Kaneko, who expressed the view that Sagawa was an untreatable psychotic who should have been in prison.

Sagawa, in the meantime, had written a book about the murder of Renée Hartevelt which quickly became a best-seller. Following his discharge from the hospital, he gave a magazine interview, saying that his act of cannibalism had been 'an expression of love', and that he still dreamed of eating a woman's flesh, though without murdering her and only with her consent. He was reported to be staying with his parents in Yokohama.

Housekeeper found dead in Belgravia, 1946

On 14 June 1946, Detective Inspector James Ball arrived at a house in the Belgravia district of London after being informed that the housekeeper, Miss Elizabeth McLindon, was missing. The house, in Chester Square, was shortly to become the home of the exiled King of Greece, and Miss McLindon, an attractive woman aged forty, had taken up residence there on her own some weeks earlier. It was the king's secretary who had reported her missing.

Miss McLindon's clothes and other belongings were still in the house, but it seemed from the supply of milk outside the back door that she had not been there for six days. However, the door of the library was locked and the key missing; it was therefore necessary for Ball to force it open. When he did so he found the housekeeper's dead body. Miss McLindon had been shot through the back of the neck as she sat at the telephone, evidently about to make a call — and from the condition of the body it appeared that she had been dead for five or six days.

A bullet recovered from the wall and a used cartridge found on the floor had both been fired from a Browning automatic pistol. But the door key was not found there, and there were no signs of a forced entry or a struggle. It seemed that the dead woman had let the culprit into the house herself, and that he had afterwards locked the library door and taken the key away with him.

A search of the housekeeper's bedroom resulted in the discovery of valuable jewellery and a box of letters from various men, all of whom appeared to have been her lovers — and generous ones at that. Two of the letters, both signed 'Arthur', were of particular interest: they had both been posted in Brighton — the first on 11 June, the second

165

the following day — and asked her why she had not been answering the telephone.

As they had both arrived after her death and yet been opened and placed in the bedroom with the others, it was suspected that the murderer had returned to the house in the hope of causing confusion over the date on which the crime had been committed.

Miss McLindon's sister Veronica told the police that 'Arthur' was the dead woman's fiancé, Arthur Boyce, a painter working on Brighton pier. On being questioned, Boyce claimed that he knew nothing of Miss McLindon's death — even though it had been reported in all the newspapers — and that he had been trying to contact her by telephone for several days. But it was learnt from his workmates that he had recently been in possession of a pistol, which he had told them he was going to throw into the sea.

It was also discovered that Arthur Boyce was a convicted bigamist who had served an eighteen-month prison sentence, and that he was wanted for passing dud cheques. One of these cheques — for £135 — had been used to pay for an engagement ring, which the jeweller concerned had recovered from Miss McLindon on 8 June, after the cheque had been returned to him. Boyce was arrested in connection with these offences.

Though Detective Inspector Ball was unable to find the gun with which the murder had been committed, he managed to trace a man named John Rowland, of Caernarvon, who had had a Browning automatic stolen from him while he was sharing lodgings with Boyce in Fulham some months previously.

Rowland was certain that Boyce had taken the gun, and had written to him to ask for it back, but received no reply. An empty cartridge case which had been fired from this gun was produced at Ball's request, and found to have markings indentical to those of the one which had been left in the house in Chester Square.

Arthur Boyce was then charged with murder and brought to trial shortly afterwards. It was believed that he had killed Miss McLindon because she was about to telephone the police after learning that he had paid for her engagement ring with a dud cheque, and that he had afterwards gone to great lengths to conceal his guilt. The jury was much impressed by the ballistics evidence, presented by the famous gunsmith, Robert Churchill, and the prisoner was convicted.

He was hanged on 12 November 1946.

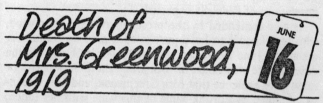

Death of Mrs. Greenwood, 1919 — JUNE 16

During the early hours of 16 June 1919, Mabel Greenwood, the wife of a solicitor, died at her home in Kidwelly, Carmarthenshire, after an agonizing illness which had started the previous afternoon. Her health had not been good beforehand and her doctor gave the cause of her death as valvular heart disease. But many people suspected that she had been poisoned.

Harold Greenwood, her forty-five-year-old husband, had a practice in nearby Llanelly, but relied upon his wife's private income for the comfort in which they and their four children lived. Unlike his wife, he was not liked in Kidwelly, and a nurse who had attended Mrs Greenwood maintained that there should have been a post-mortem.

Greenwood's marriage, four months later, to Gladys Jones, thirty-one-year-old daughter of one of the proprietors of the *Llanelly Mercury*, gave rise to further rumour and speculation, and the police informed him that they would probably want to have his first wife's body exhumed. He replied that he was agreeable to this, and on 16 April 1920, the exhumation took place.

A post-mortem then revealed that the rumours were justified, for there was no evidence of disease. Instead, arsenic was found in various parts of the body.

A coroner's jury in June found that the deceased had died of arsenic poisoning, and named her husband as the person who had administered the poison. This verdict was applauded by the spectators, and the following day Harold Greenwood was formally charged with murder.

He spent the next four and a half months in prison, and was brought to trial in Carmarthen on 2 November 1920. The case against him then proved to be weaker than the inhabitants of Kidwelly expected.

It was contended by the prosecution that Greenwood, who was known to have purchased a product containing arsenic in June 1917, had poisoned a bottle of wine on the day his wife was taken ill. But while the family's parlour maid gave evidence that Mrs Greenwood, and Mrs Greenwood alone, had drunk some of this wine with her lunch, Irene Greenwood, the defendant's twenty-one-year-old daughter, stated that she, too, had drunk some of it, not only at lunch, but also at supper.

Though another witness claimed that there had been no wine on the table at supper, Irene Greenwood's evidence was enough to raise doubts about the prisoner's guilt. Moreover, these doubts were reinforced by the defence counsel's suggestion that Mrs Greenwood's doctor, an extremely vague person, might have accidentally poisoned her himself.

Harold Greenwood, who had remained calm throughout the trial, was acquitted and left the court a free man. But his legal practice was ruined by the case and he was broken in spirit. He died nine years later, at the age of fifty-five.

Policeman murdered by Barry Prudom, 1982

On 17 June 1982, a policeman was shot dead by a motorist during the course of a routine traffic check near Harrogate in Yorkshire. There were no witnesses to the crime, and there was no apparent motive for it. But as he lay dying, PC David Haigh managed to write the registration number of the culprit's car in his notebook. The killer was then found to be Barry Peter Prudom, a thirty-seven-year-old man already wanted on a wounding charge. His car, a green Citroen, was found abandoned in a field near Leeds.

Prudom, formerly a stable and hard-working man, had had domestic problems for some years, and it seems that they had finally become too much for him. Towards the end of the seventeen-day manhunt which followed he told members of a family which he had taken prisoner: 'I told him (PC Haigh) I'd been sleeping out in the car, and that I didn't think that was an offence. But he said he was going to take me in and got stroppy, so I shot him.' He had, however, given a false name, probably because he feared being arrested for the earlier offence.

After abandoning the car Prudom made his way to Lincolnshire where he broke into a bungalow and robbed an elderly woman of £5, leaving her tied up but unharmed. He then went to Girton, near Newark-on-Trent, where he broke into the home of George Luckett and his wife Sylvia, in search of food and money. George Luckett was shot dead when he tried to defend himself with his own gun; his wife was shot in the head, but survived.

Prudom stole the Luckett's car and drove towards Dalby Forest in north Yorkshire, intending to lie low. But after another shooting, in which a policeman was injured, an intensive search for him was begun. Before long there

169

was a third encounter; this time an unarmed police sergeant was shot three times, the last shot being fired as he lay helpless on the ground.

The search received a great deal of publicity, with much being made of the large number of policemen who were armed and the fact that Prudom had once had SAS training. Another unusual feature of the manhunt was the part played by Eddie McGee, a survival expert called in by the police to track the fugitive.

The taking of the prisoners occurred on the evening of 3 July when Prudom broke into a house in Malton; the victims were Maurice Johnson and his wife, both in their seventies, and their son Brian, aged forty-three. They were held at gunpoint at first, then tied up until Prudom felt that it was safe for him to release them.

He ate and rested in their house, threatening to kill them unless they did as they were told; he also watched television news bulletins and made a voluntary confession of his crimes. When they tried to persuade him to give himself up he refused.

'I'll never let the police take me,' he said. 'I'll kill myself first.'

Early the following morning he left the house and hid in a shelter which he had made by putting wooden boards against a wall. A few hours later Eddie McGee found him and the police started to close in. Prudom immediately began shooting at them. 'Come and get me, you bastards!' he shouted. 'I'll take some of you to hell with me!'

He remained in the shelter as police armed with a variety of weapons took up positions nearby. At 9.30 that Sunday morning an assault was made, with stun-grenades being hurled and rifle-shots fired. Just before 9.40 a.m. Prudom was killed by a bullet which, according to evidence given at the subsequent inquest, was 'almost certainly' fired from his own gun.

He was later found to have sustained twenty-two other injuries during that short series of exchanges which brought Britain's biggest manhunt to an end.

On the afternoon of 19 June 1928, a Chinese couple spending part of their honeymoon in the Lake District village of Grange-in-Borrowdale, left their hotel to go for a walk. Chung Yi Miao, a twenty-eight-year-old doctor of law, and his wealthy twenty-nine-year-old wife had arrived in Grange the previous day after being married in New York a little over a month earlier. They seemed to be happy together.

Some hours later Chung returned for dinner alone, saying that his wife had gone shopping in the nearby town of Keswick. He then remained at the hotel, keeping himself to himself, until finally he began to express anxiety about the lateness of the hour. His wife had still not returned when he decided to go to bed.

Suddenly, at eleven o'clock that night, a police officer called to tell him that his wife was dead.

Mrs Chung's body had been discovered beside a bathing pool a short distance from the hotel; she had been strangled. Her skirt had been pushed up round her waist, and she was lying in such a way as to give the impression that she had been raped or sexually assaulted, though this was later found to have been simulated. Articles of jewellery which had apparently been stolen were discovered — without Chung's knowledge — during a search of the couple's bedroom. They had been deliberately concealed.

Chung Yi Miao was taken into custody on suspicion of murder. At Keswick police station the following morning, having been told nothing about the apparent sex offence and robbery, he convinced the police of his guilt by remarking, 'It is terrible — my wife assaulted, robbed and murdered!' Despite uncertainty about his motive for the crime, he was formally charged and brought to trial at the Carlisle Assizes in November the same year.

Chung denied the offence, and the trial lasted three days. The evidence offered by the prosecution was entirely circumstantial — the defendant's knowledge of the state in which the body had been found, the jewellery hidden in the hotel bedroom, the fact that the cord used to murder Mrs Chung was of the same type as used in the hotel, and so on. The motive now suggested was thwarted sexual desire.

In his defence it was stated that two unknown men of Oriental appearance had been following the couple, the suggestion being that *they* could have murdered Mrs Chung after the defendant had left her. An attempt was also made to show that Chung's accent had caused misunderstandings. For example, he denied that in referring to his wife's body, on the night that he was informed of her death, he had asked, 'Had she knickers on?' What he had really asked, he said, was, 'Had she necklace on?'

The jury was not impressed by all this and found the case proved; Chung was sentenced to death. Following an unsuccessful appeal, which he conducted himself, he was hanged at Strangeways Prison, Manchester, on 6 December 1928.

It was afterwards suggested that the real reason for the murder was Chung's discovery, just after their marriage, that his wife would not be able to have children.

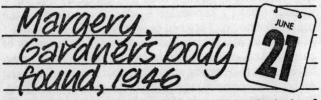

Margery Gardner's body found, 1946

During the early afternoon of 21 June 1946, the body of Margery Gardner, aged thirty-two, was found in a hotel bedroom in the Notting Hill district of London. She had died from suffocation, though only after being subjected to a number of sadistic acts: while alive, she had been whipped, her nipples almost bitten off and a rough instrument rotated in her vagina, causing much bleeding. After washing blood from her face, her murderer had covered her body up to the neck with bedclothes. He had left the curtains drawn.

Margery Gardner was a married woman, separated from her husband; she spent much of her time drinking and dancing and occasionally worked as a film extra. On the night of 20 June she had been to the Panama Club in South Kensington in the company of Neville Heath, a twenty-nine-year-old former RAF officer with a criminal record for housebreaking, theft and fraud. He had afterwards taken her to the hotel by taxi.

The police were certain that Heath was the person responsible for the murder, and released his name and description to the press, saying that they wanted him 'to assist them with their inquiries'. On 24 June they received a letter from him, posted in Worthing, in which he claimed to be innocent of the crime.

'I booked in at the hotel last Sunday, but not with Mrs Gardner, whom I met for the first time during the week,' he wrote. 'I had drinks with her on Friday evening, and whilst I was with her she met an acquaintance with whom she was obliged to sleep. The reasons, as I understand them, were mainly financial.

'It was then that Mrs Gardner asked if she could use my hotel room until two o'clock and intimated that, if I returned after that, I might spend the remainder of the night with her. I gave her my keys and told her to leave the hotel door open.

'It must have been almost 3 a.m. when I returned to the hotel and found her in the condition of which you are aware. I realised I was in an invidious position, and rather than notify the police I packed my belongings and left.'

He said that he was using a false name, but could be

contacted through the personal column of the *Daily Telegraph*. He also said that he had the instrument with which Mrs Gardner had been beaten and would be forwarding it to them. It never arrived.

The police continued their search for him, circulating copies of a photograph to every force in the country. On 6 July he went to Bournemouth police station, calling himself Group Captain Rupert Brooke, in connection with the disappearance of twenty-one-year-old Doreen Marshall, who was believed to have had dinner with him on the evening of 3 July. He was recognized and held for questioning by officers of the Metropolitan Police. On 8 July he was taken by car to London, where he was later charged with the murder of Margery Gardner.

About the time the charge was made the body of Doreen Marshall was found in Branksome Chine, a wooded valley about a mile from the hotel in which Heath had been staying in Bournemouth. Like Margery Gardner, she was naked and had various injuries. In this case, however, the victim had died as a result of deep knife-wounds in her throat, and had been mutilated afterwards.

Though Heath was charged with this second murder, his trial, which began at the Old Bailey on 24 September, concerned only the first. A defence of insanity was made on his behalf, his counsel seeking to establish that his long history of petty crime was proof of instability. Heath, however, appeared indifferent to it all. On being found guilty, he had nothing to say; on being sentenced to death, he made no appeal. He showed no sign of remorse and made no confession.

'My only regret at leaving the world is that I have been damned unworthy of you both,' he wrote to his parents.

Neville Heath was hanged at Pentonville Prison on 26 October 1946.

Murder of Mrs. Parker, 1954

On the afternoon of 22 June 1954, Mrs Honora Parker, a middle-aged woman, was beaten to death in a park in Canterbury, New Zealand, by two teenage girls, one of whom was her own daughter. The girls attacked her with a brick wrapped in a stocking, striking forty-five blows — twenty-four of them to their victim's head and face — before running to a nearby teashop to raise the alarm. But nobody was taken in by their story that Mrs Parker had been killed when she slipped and fell on the pavement, and soon they admitted the truth. Pauline Parker, aged sixteen, and her friend Juliet Hulme, fifteen, were therefore charged with murder.

The two girls were found to have had a lesbian relationship which had been a matter of concern to the parents of both. Mrs Parker had been determined to put a stop to it, but had failed to do so. Then, early in 1954, Mr Hulme decided to take Juliet to South Africa. Pauline declared that she would go, too, regardless of the opposition of her own parents. The idea of murdering her mother seems to have occurred to her about the same time. 'Why could not mother die?' she wrote in her diary on 13 February. 'Dozens of people, thousands of people, are dying every day. So why not mother, and father too?'

A later entry, written two days before the crime took place, showed that both girls had given the idea a lot of thought. 'We discussed our plans for moidering mother and made them a little clearer,' Pauline recorded. 'I want it to appear either a natural or an accidental death.'

Pauline Parker and Juliet Hulme were brought to trial in Christchurch, both apparently unrepentant. The court was given details of their sex life and various fantasies in which they had jointly indulged, the defence contending that their crime had been the result of 'paranoia of the exalted type', and that they were both certifiably mad. To the prosecution, however, they were 'highly intelligent and perfectly sane, but precocious and dirty-minded girls', who had committed a 'callously planned and premeditated murder'.

The jury agreed with the prosecution, and the prisoners were found guilty and sentenced to be detained during Her Majesty's pleasure. But this proved not to be a very harsh sentence, for they were both released in 1958.

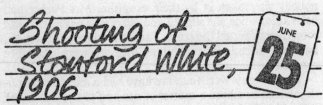

Shooting of Stanford White, 1906

On 25 June 1906, Stanford White, a distinguished architect aged fifty-two, became the victim of a sensational shooting during the first performance of a new farce at the Madison Square Roof Garden Theatre in New York. In the middle of the play he was suddenly shot dead by Harry Thaw, a thirty-four-year-old millionaire playboy. He fell to the floor and died instantly, one of Thaw's three bullets having entered his brain.

Thaw, on being arrested, admitted responsibility for White's death, but claimed that it had been a justified act. He said that his wife, a former model and chorus girl, had been seduced by the victim some years earlier, and that in such a case an 'unwritten law' allowed the husband to avenge the wrong which his wife had suffered. He was charged with murder.

Thaw was the son of a railroad magnate. Born in Pennsylvania, he had inherited his father's wealth while

Right: George Joseph Smith, the Brides in the Bath murderer.
(SYNDICATION INTERNATIONAL)

Below: Eight of the Boston Strangler's victims.
(POPPERFOTO)

Right: Lesley Whittle's killer Donald Neilson after his arrest. He was attacked by members of the public as police struggled with him. (SYNDICATION INTERNATIONAL)

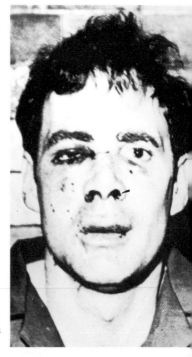

Below: Lesley Whittle's body is carried in a coffin from the drain where it was found.
(SYNDICATION INTERNATIONAL)

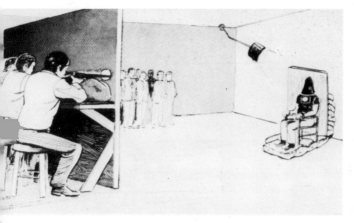

Above: Artist's impression based on eye-witness accounts of the execution of Gary Gilmore. (POPPERFOTO)

Below: A group of newsmen examine and photograph the chair in which Gary Gilmore faced the firing squad. (POPPERFOTO)

Above: A reconstruction of the place where Marcel Pétiot's victims met their death. (POPPERFOTO)

Below: Police search the grounds of the 'factory' at Crawley, Sussex, scene of the acid bath murders committed by John George Haigh. (SYNDICATION INTERNATIONAL)

R

In replying to this letter, please write on the envelope:—

Number 9656 Name R. Ellis

H.M. PRISON HOLLOWAY. N.7. ...Prison

2. 6. 55

Dear Alex,

Sorry to be so long in answering your letter of April 24. Thank you for offering to help me, but there is not a thing any one can do.

So you are once again at Skindles. How are things going with you? I hope your son is well, give him my best regards. to him

I am quite well, just waiting patiently to get into court. This place is not bad as one may think, on the outside.

You should come and do some sketching here?

Well Alex. if you see Jackie, tell her I am sorry I could not see her when she came.

Bye for now, and than-

Yours
Ruth Ellis

NO. 244   (21441—3-11-42)

letter to 'Alex' from Ruth Ellis while she
is in Holloway Prison. (inset) Ruth Ellis.
(SYNDICATION INTERNATIONAL)

Special Notice

MURDER

M.P. (FH). It is desired to trace the after-described for interview respecting the dea[th] of **MARGERY GARDNER**, during the night of 20th-21st inst. **NEVILLE GEORGE CLEVE[LY]** **HEATH**, alias **ARMSTRONG, BLYTH, DENVERS** and **GRAHAM**, C.R.O. No. 28142-[ ]b. 1917, 5ft. 11½in., c. fresh, e. blue, believed small fair moustache, h. and eyebrows fair, squa[re] face, broad forehead and nose, firm chin, good teeth, military gait ; dress, lt. grey d.b. s[uit] with pin stripe, dk. brown trilby, brown suede shoes, cream shirt with collar attached [ ] fawn and white check sports jacket and grey flannel trousers. Nat. Reg. No. **CNP 21471[ ]**

Has récent conviction for posing as Lt.-Col. of South African Air Force. A pilot a[nd] believed to possess an "A" licence, has stated his intention of going abroad and m[ay] endeavour to secure passage on ship or plane as passenger or pilot. May stay at hote[l] accompanied by woman.

Enquiries are also requested to trace the owner of gent's white handkerchief with bro[wn] check border, bearing "L. Kearns" in black ink on hem and stitched with large "K" in bl[ue] cotton in centre.

The poster issued by the police during their search for Neville Heath.
(SYNDICATION INTERNATIONAL)

Above: The burnt-out car in the Rouse murder case. (SYNDICATION INTERNATIONAL)

Below: The car belonging to the Drummond family, murdered while on holiday in France, being prepared to go on show at Blackpool in a reconstruction of the crime for holidaymakers. (POPPERFOTO)

Above: Police searching Norman Thorn's farm for the body of his victim (SYNDICATION INTERNATIONAL)

Police dogs on Wimbledon Common hunting for clues to the disappearance of Muriel McKay (POPPERFOTO) (inset) Muriel McKay. (SYNDICATION INTERNATIONAL)

still in his twenties, and was well-known for his extravagance and gambling. In April 1905 he married twenty-year-old Evelyn Nesbit, with whom he had been in love for the previous four years. But he was a jealous man and, on learning that his wife had been Stanford White's mistress, became enraged and decided upon the shooting.

He was brought to trial in January 1907, his wife appearing as a witness in support of his claim that he had a moral right to kill Stanford White. His lawyers pleaded that he had suffered a temporary aberration which absolved him of responsibility for what had happened. The District Attorney, however, claimed that the shooting had been a 'cruel, deliberate, malicious, premeditated taking of human life', and that the concept of the 'unwritten law' had been devised solely to prevent his conviction. The jury deliberated for two days, but was unable to reach agreement.

The prisoner was brought to trial again in January 1908, his lawyers this time making a plea of insanity and producing evidence to show that he was a manic-depressive. The plea was successful and Thaw, on being found guilty but insane, was committed to an asylum in Matteawan.

During the next four years a number of appeals were made for his release, but all were dismissed. Then, in August 1913, he escaped from the asylum and went to Canada. Though deported and taken back to New York, he managed to obtain a retrial which resulted in his acquittal; he was accordingly set free in June 1915. He then began divorce proceedings, his wife having given birth to a child which could not have been his in 1913.

As a result of the murder case many disclosures had been made about Thaw's private life: he had been revealed not only as a libertine but also as a sadist who enjoyed whipping members of the opposite sex, including his wife. But eighteen months after his release he was indicted for kidnapping and whipping a nineteen-year-old youth. Once again he was declared insane and committed to Matteawan, where he remained until 1922, when the verdict was reversed.

After that he roamed the world, always living in style. He managed to keep out of further trouble for the rest of his life, but sometimes showed signs of madness. He died, aged seventy-four, in 1947.

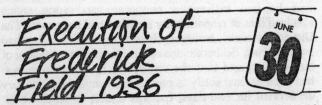

Execution of Frederick Field, 1936

On 30 June 1936, Frederick Field, a thirty-two-year-old deserter from the Royal Air Force, was hanged for the murder of Beatrice Sutton, a middle-aged widow and prostitute, in her flat in Clapham, London, the previous April. The crime had been committed for no real reason. Field, in a confession which he later retracted, stating; 'I was just browned off. I don't even know who the woman was.'

It was not the first time he had been involved in a murder case; he had been 'browned off' before. On the morning of 2 October 1931, the body of another prostitute, twenty-year-old Norah Upchurch, was found in an empty building in Shaftesbury Avenue, where Field, then employed by a signfitter, had been working. She, too, had been strangled, and on that occasion Field aroused suspicion by claiming to have given the key to the premises to a person he believed to be a prospective purchaser; as a result, the door had to be forced.

His conduct at the inquest on Norah Upchurch was also suspicious for, having described the person to whom he had given the key as a 'man in plus fours, with gold fillings', he identified one of the other men present as the person concerned. The coroner and his jury together inspected the man's teeth and found that 'there was not a gold tooth in his head'. Field was afterwards said by the coroner to be a compulsive liar.

Though no charge had been made against him in connection with that crime, Field approached a newspaper in July 1933 and offered the editor an exclusive confession on the understanding that his defence costs would be paid in the event of him being brought to trial. He was then serving in the RAF.

As a result of this confession, Field was charged with the murder and brought to trial at the Old Bailey. He had by now retracted the confession, and said that he had wanted to be tried in order to prove his innocence. As his account of the murder differed from the findings of the police, the jury was directed to acquit him. But in view of what subsequently occurred, it is accepted that he was, in fact, guilty.

Three years later, after being arrested as an RAF deserter, Field confessed to the murder of Beatrice Sutton — expecting, no doubt, that if he withdrew *this* confession his second trial would have the same result as the first. But this time he made the mistake of including information which only the murderer could have known. The jury took only fifteen minutes to find him guilty.

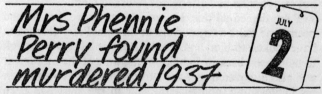

Mrs Phennie Perry found murdered, 1937

JULY 2

On the morning of 2 July 1937, Mrs Phennie Perry, aged twenty, was found murdered on a pathway in the Jamaica district of Queens County, New York, with her two-year-old daughter lying unhurt beside her. The crime had been committed about 10.30 the previous night, and the victim's screams had been heard by a night-watchman at a nearby junk-yard. But the watchman had been drunk at the time and the police had not taken his report seriously. They had therefore failed to make a proper investigation.

Mrs Perry, of 153rd Street, Jamaica, was the wife of an employee of a steel construction corporation. She had been battered over the head with a piece of concrete which the person responsible had left at the scene. Besides the murder weapon, the police found a number of other items, including a man's shoe, a strip of material torn from a shirt, and some letters and bills addressed to Ulysses Palm, a Deacon of the Amity Baptist Church, who lived in a flat below the one occupied by Mrs Perry and her husband.

Palm, a married man aged thirty-nine, worked in a chain store. The police went to his flat in his absence and found a shoe from the same pair as the one left at the scene of the crime, and also the shirt from which the strip of material had been torn. When Palm was questioned he admitted owning some of the articles found near the body, but said that he had given the pair of shoes to Arthur Perry, the dead woman's husband.

Perry, aged twenty-two, said that Palm had written a suggestive letter to his wife and had tried to break into her bedroom the previous morning, as a result of which there had been a confrontation between the two men later in the day. He agreed that Palm had given him the pair of shoes, but said that he had afterwards returned them.

Palm denied all this. He was able to prove that he had been some miles away at work at the time Perry claimed to have spoken to him, and that he had not left early enough to have been back in Jamaica at the time of the murder. It was also discovered that the letter to Mrs Perry was not in his handwriting, and that the tear in the shirt had been started with a cut.

When police made inquiries at a theatre where Mrs Perry had played bingo on the evening in question they learnt that Perry had been seen there, in the company of a woman and a child, about 10 p.m. Moreover, an examination of Perry's clothes revealed a bloodstain on one of his socks, corresponding with a hole in the shoe found at the scene of the crime. It was therefore clear that Perry was the culprit, and that in murdering his wife he had sought to divert suspicion from himself to Ulysses Palm.

While in jail awaiting trial, Arthur Perry admitted his guilt to a detective who was posing as one of his fellow prisoners. 'I don't know why I did it,' he said.

Perry was tried in November 1937, found guilty and sentenced to death. The conviction was quashed on appeal, as the judge had allowed hearsay evidence to be introduced. But a second trial in 1938 had the same result as the first, and the condemned man was executed in the electric chair on 3 August 1939.

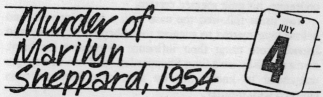

Murder of Marilyn Sheppard, 1954

During the early hours of 4 July 1954, a brutal murder was committed in one of the bedrooms of a luxurious house overlooking Lake Erie, in Cuyhoga County, Ohio. Marilyn Sheppard, the wife of a young neuro-surgeon working at Cleveland's Bay View Hospital, had gone to bed alone two or three hours earlier, her husband having fallen asleep on a couch downstairs. She was later found to have been struck thirty-five times over the head with a blunt instrument.

Dr Samuel Sheppard, aged thirty, claimed that he had been woken up by his wife's screams and that he was knocked unconcious from behind when he rushed up to the bedroom. On regaining his senses, he heard a noise downstairs and went down in time to see an unknown man leaving the house. Pursuing him in the direction of the lake, he managed to catch hold of him, only to be knocked unconscious again. This time, when he came to, he was lying on the edge of the lake, his body partly in the water. He then struggled back to the house and telephoned a neighbour to ask for help.

The police were sceptical about Sheppard's story. So, too, was Dr Samuel Gerber, the coroner, who arrived on the scene soon after them. A burglary appeared to have been simulated. There was no sand in Sheppard's hair, as there should have been if he had really been lying unconscious on the edge of the lake. A bloody imprint, which the coroner believed to be that of a surgical instrument, was found on the victim's pillow. And Sheppard's wrist-watch, speckled with blood, was found among other items in a canvas bag near the house. Later, when it was discovered that he had been having an affair with a young female colleague, his guilt seemed certain.

The press followed the case with a keen interest, and before long started to suggest that Sheppard's family and friends were using their influence to prevent his being arrested. 'Why isn't Sam Sheppard in jail?' one newspaper demanded to know. Shortly after this Sheppard was charged with murder.

His highly-publicized trial at the Cuyhoga County criminal court lasted from 18 October to 21 December 1954. At the end of it he was found guilty and sentenced to life imprisonment.

Despite several attempts to secure a retrial, Sheppard spent the next twelve years in jail. But a retrial was eventually granted, and began at the same court on 24 October 1966. The course which this one took was very different from that of the first trial.

In the first place, the police officer who had originally accused him of the crime had to admit that he had not made inquiries to ascertain whether injuries which the prisoner had received could have been self-inflicted; he had merely assumed that they *had* been.

Dr Gerber, whose evidence about the bloodstained imprint of a 'surgical instrument' had made such an impression at the first trial, had to admit that he had never seen an instrument of the sort he had in mind, though he had since looked for one all over the United States.

The speckles found on Sheppard's wrist-watch, according to the prosecution, could only have been caused by 'flying blood' during the course of the attack. However, Sheppard's lawyer drew attention to blood particles on the inside of the watch band, arguing that this proved that his client's watch had been removed from his wrist *before* the attack had taken place.

The trial ended on 16 November 1966, the prisoner being found not guilty of the murder for which he had already spent so long in prison; he was therefore released. Although he managed to get himself reinstated on the medical register, Sheppard was widely mistrusted and eventually forced out of the profession. He then turned to professional wrestling as a means of earning a living.

His private life gave him further cause for unhappiness. His second wife, a German divorcée whom he had married while still a prisoner, sued him for divorce, claiming that he carried offensive weapons and had threatened her with violence. A third marriage followed, but his health began to deteriorate soon afterwards.

A sad, rejected figure, Dr Samuel Sheppard died on 6 April 1970. His few remaining friends believed that his death had been caused by his failure to regain his position in society.

JULY
5

On the evening of 5 July 1919, Bella Wright, a twenty-one-year-old factory worker, left her home in the village of Stoughton, in Leicestershire, by bicycle to visit her uncle in the nearby hamlet of Gaulby. She arrived at her uncle's home in the company of another cyclist, a man whom she described as a stranger, but who waited outside the house until it was time for her to return home. Bella then joined him again, and after stopping to speak briefly to her uncle and his son-in-law at the garden gate, they rode off together. It was the last time that Bella was seen alive.

Later the same evening her body was discovered on the Gartree road, about two miles from Gaulby. Her head was covered in blood, but she was fully dressed and her bicycle lay beside her. It therefore seemed that she had died from injuries received as a result of falling off the bicycle. However, the following morning the local policeman found a bullet embedded in the surface of the road about seventeen feet from the place where the body had lain. An examination of the body then revealed that Bella Wright had been shot in the face.

The bullet had struck her below the left eye, then — according to the doctor who carried out the post-mortem — travelled 'upwards, inwards and backwards', finally leaving an exit wound which had been hidden by her hair. A gunsmith who examined the bullet was unable to say for certain whether it had been fired from a revolver or a rifle. And as there was no evidence of robbery or sexual assault, there was no apparent motive for her murder.

From Bella's relatives in Gaulby the police obtained a description of the stranger who had accompanied her to and from the house, and also learnt that he had been riding a green bicycle. All attempts to trace him, however, were unsuccessful until suddenly, on 23 February 1920, the frame of a green bicycle with the front wheel still attached to it was brought to the surface of the Leicester Canal after becoming entangled with the tow-rope of a barge.

Dredging of the canal bed then resulted in the discovery of a revolver holster containing live cartridges of the type which had caused the death of Bella Wright, together with other parts of the same bicycle.

Though the frame number of the bicycle had been removed by filing, a secret identification number on the handlebar bracket enabled police to trace it to Ronald Light, a thirty-four-year-old Leicester man now employed as mathematics master at a school in Cheltenham, Gloucestershire. Light, a former Army officer, had been living with his widowed mother in Leicester at the time of the girl's death. On being questioned about his bicycle, he at first denied having owned one and then claimed to have sold it to somebody whose name he could not remember. He was arrested and charged with Bella Wright's murder.

At his trial, which began at the Leicester Castle Courthouse on 10 June 1920, the evidence against him appeared to be overwhelming. But Light, who had been educated at Rugby, proved to be an impressive witness. He admitted having met Bella while cycling in the Leicestershire countryside and again outside her uncle's house, but claimed that he had not gone as far as the Gartree road with her.

Afterwards, on reading newspaper reports of her death, he had realized that he was suspected and feared that he might be accused of her murder. The disposal of the bicycle, and also the holster and ammunition for his old service revolver, had resulted from this fear, he told the court. The revolver itself had been taken from him when he left the Army, suffering from shell-shock.

Sir Edward Marshall Hall, defending, suggested that Bella Wright had not, in fact, been murdered, but accidentally hit by a stray rifle bullet fired from a distance. He then went on to stress that the prisoner, who had not known her before the day of her death, had had no motive for killing her. After considering the case for three hours, the jury returned a verdict of not guilty, and Light was released to the cheers of the spectators and the crowds outside.

What became of him afterwards is not known.

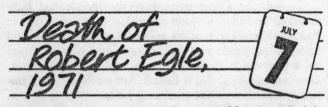

Death of Robert Egle, 1971

JULY 7

On 7 July 1971, Robert Egle, aged fifty-nine, died in hospital in St Albans, Hertfordshire, after eight days of intense pain. His death was put down to broncho-pneumonia and polyneuritis, and no inquest was thought necessary. His body was cremated.

Egle had worked for a firm which produced photographic equipment in the village of Bovingdon, near Hemel Hempstead; he was the head of its storeroom. He had been taken ill at the beginning of June with a severe attack of diarrhoea, but after three days at home was well enough to return to work. At the end of the month, when he became ill again, he suffered from nausea, a violent backache and numbness at the tips of his fingers.

In the meantime another of the firm's employees, forty-one-year-old Ronald Hewitt, had been repeatedly ill with diarrhoea, vomiting and stomach pains over a period of four weeks. He continued to feel 'a bit shaky' until he left the job two days after Egle's death.

Two months earlier, on 10 May, a smart young man named Graham Young had started working for the firm as an assistant storeman. As such, he had been in close contact with the dead man and had been in the practice of fetching tea for the storeroom employees. Ron Hewitt was later to recall that he had often left his tea after just a sip or two because it tasted bitter, and that on those occasions Bob Egle had finished it for him after drinking his own.

Young was absent-minded and unpredictable. He had a keen interest in chemistry and pharmacy; he also talked about Hitler a lot. At Bob Egle's funeral he impressed his managing director by showing a detailed knowledge of the illness from which the deceased had suffered. He was afterwards put in charge of the storeroom for a probationary period.

In September the same year another of the firm's employees, Frederick Biggs, sixty-year-old head of the Work-In-Progress department, was taken ill with stomach pains and vomiting. Later the same month Peter Buck, the import-export manager, was similarly ill.

Then, in October, David Tilson, a clerk in Buck's department, and Jethro Batt, assistant storeman, both began to suffer from a variety of symptoms, including stomach pains, vomiting and pains or numbness in their legs. Both became worse, Tilson being admitted to hospital; both started losing their hair. Another employee, Mrs Diana Smart, also began suffering from stomach and leg pains, vomiting and other symptoms.

Tilson, having been discharged from hospital on 28 October, was readmitted four days later; he was by then almost bald and completely impotent. Fred Biggs was admitted to hospital on 4 November with pains in his chest and feet. Batt was admitted on 5 November, by which time he was completely bald, impotent and suicidal. Mrs Smart, after returning to work, became ill again.

These illnesses alarmed the rest of the firm's staff, and gave rise to rumours that the water supply had been contaminated. The area medical officer carried out a thorough examination of the premises, but could find no explanation. Then, on 19 November, Fred Biggs died. At this, several members of the staff announced that they were leaving.

A local doctor was called in to give a talk to the entire staff at a meeting in the firm's canteen, to assure them that there was no cause for alarm. Graham Young, as if determined to draw attention to himself, questioned him at length. It was as a result of this that he was suddenly suspected of being responsible for what had happened, and a police investigation was instigated.

Young was then found to have been released from Broadmoor only six months earlier, having spent nine years there for poisoning his father, his sister and a schoolfriend.

He was immediately arrested on suspicion, and a search of his bedsitter in Hemel Hempstead resulted in the discovery of various poisons, together with a diary containing incriminating evidence.

Fred Biggs was found to have died of thallium poisoning; Bob Egle, whose ashes were exhumed for analysis, was then found to have died from the same cause.

While in custody Young boasted that he had poisoned his stepmother, whose death in 1962 — when he was fourteen years old — had been put down to natural causes. A further case of administering poison was also revealed. In July 1972 he was brought to trial at St Albans for the murders of Robert Egle and Frederick Biggs and several lesser crimes. He pleaded not guilty.

Throughout the trial he conducted himself with remarkable calmness. He claimed that a partial confession had been made in return for food, clothes, access to a solicitor and an opportunity to sleep, and that his diary entries were merely notes for a novel which he had intended to write.

To the jury, however, it was clear that he was a psychopath who had used his victims for the purpose of scientific experiment. He was found guilty on both charges of murder, two of attempted murder and two of administering poison.

After sentencing Graham Young, aged twenty-four, to life imprisonment, the judge allowed the foreman of the jury to read a statement expressing concern about the sale of poisons to the public.

Sir Harry Oakes found murdered 1943

On the morning of 8 July 1943, Sir Harry Oakes, a self-made millionaire, was found brutally murdered at his home in the Bahamas. He had been struck four times over the head with a blunt instrument and his body had been doused with insecticide and set on fire while he was still alive. This horrifying crime had been committed in the victim's bedroom during the course of the previous night, while his wife and son were away from home. As nothing had been stolen, it was assumed that robbery had not been the motive for it.

Sir Harry Oakes, aged sixty-nine, was American by birth, but had become a Canadian citizen in 1939; he had made his fortune out of Canadian gold mines. He lived in style in the Bahamas, but there were many people there who disliked him, and it was clear that narrowing down the list of suspects was not going to be easy. The Duke of Windsor, who was governor of the islands and a friend of Sir Harry's, took personal charge of the investigation, calling in two Miami police captains to find the culprit. Within a few days the victim's son-in-law, Count Alfred de Marigny, was charged with the murder.

De Marigny, an adventurer from Mauritius, had married the victim's daughter Nancy in secret in May 1942, a few days after her eighteenth birthday; the ceremony had taken place in New York. While some members of the family found the Count a likeable man, Sir Harry was convinced that he had only married Nancy for the sake of her inheritance, and repeatedly told him that she would be left nothing; there had been frequent quarrels between the two men, some of them in public. By the time the thirty-three-year-old de Marigny was brought to trial in

189

October few doubted that he was guilty, and there were even suggestions that a lynch mob might be formed.

But Nancy de Marigny was certain of her husband's innocence, and hired a New York private detective named Raymond Campbell Schindler to collect evidence for his defence. Schindler, finding that the prosecution's case depended on the evidence of a single fingerprint which had allegedly been found on a Chinese screen beside Sir Harry's bed, brought in Maurice O'Neill, a fingerprint expert from the New Orleans Police Department, to examine it. His findings led to a courtroom sensation.

The fingerprint had not been photographed on the screen: it had, according to the prosecution, been dusted with fingerprint powder, then removed from the surface with a piece of transparent tape, so that its outline remained intact. As this was not in accordance with established police procedure, O'Neill viewed it with suspicion and photographed the screen himself, using highly sensitive equipment. He found no evidence of the fingerprint ever having been there.

Moreover, the fingerprint produced by the prosecution was found to have a background of circles, which appeared to be moisture marks. There was nothing on the Chinese screen which could have caused these; the only possible explanation for them was that the fingerprint had not been taken from the screen at all, but from a wet glass. As one of the investigating officers was known to have asked de Marigny at the beginning of the investigation to pour him a glass of water, it was claimed by the defence that the evidence had been fabricated.

Alfred de Marigny was found not guilty and carried from the courthouse in triumph. His marriage ended six years later.

Schindler one of the greatest of America's private detectives, was not entirely satisfied with the outcome of his investigation: he wanted to bring the real culprit to justice. However, he was denied the co-operation of the Bahamas authorities, and so was unable to make any further progress. The following year, when he asked for the case to be reopened, the Duke of Windsor would not hear of it.

Attempts by other investigators to solve the mystery were similarly thwarted.

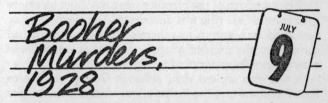

Booher Murders, 1928

On the evening of 9 July 1928, Henry Booher's farm near the village of Mannville, in Alberta, was the scene of a multiple murder. Henry was some miles away, working on another farm, when it took place, and his two teenage daughters had gone into Mannville to watch a game of basketball. The other members of the family — his wife, Eunice, and his two sons, Fred, aged twenty-four, and Vernon, twenty — had remained at home.

Between 8 and 9 p.m. Vernon ran to the home of their nearest neighbour to raise the alarm. He had been getting the cows in from the pasture for the night, he said breathlessly, and on returning to the house had found his mother and brother dead. He had to telephone Mannville for a doctor.

An examination revealed that Mrs Booher had been shot in the back of the head while she sat at the living-room table. Fred was lying on the kitchen floor, having been shot through the mouth and neck; he had apparently rushed into the kitchen on hearing the shot which killed his mother. There was another body, that of Gabriel Goromby, a Hungarian hired hand, in the nearby bunkhouse; he had been shot twice through the head and once through the breast. Dr J.D. Heaslip, who was also the coroner, insisted that nothing should be disturbed until the police arrived.

Soon afterwards Henry Booher arrived home and learnt what had happened. He and Vernon went outside together, Vernon returning a few minutes later to say that a fourth person had been killed. Wasyl Rosyak, another hired hand, had been shot in the face and stomach as he was about to feed some pigs which the family kept in a barn.

When a search of the premises was carried out an empty shell from a .303 rifle was discovered. The Booher family owned no such gun; it was therefore assumed that it had come from the murder weapon. The other empty shells must all have been removed by the murderer.

It was also noticed that, although Vernon claimed to have found the first two bodies after getting the cows in for the night, there were no cows in the corral until the following morning, when they brought themselves back from the pasture. So while the 'Mannville tragedy' was generally supposed to have been the work of an unknown maniac, Vernon Booher was, in fact, regarded by the police as a suspect right from the start.

Charles Stevenson, another neighbour, informed the police that *he* owned a .303 sporting rifle and that it had been taken from his house, together with a box of shells, without his knowledge; he had last seen it on 8 July, a Sunday, before he and his family went to church. This rifle had often been lent to members of the Booher family. Moreover, it was discovered that on that Sunday morning Vernon Booher had been seen riding towards Stevenson's farm.

By 17 July it was considered that there was enough circumstantial evidence to bring charges against Vernon, who was already being held as a 'material witness'. The preliminary hearing was held in Mannville the following day, the proceedings being watched by Dr Adolph Maximilian Langsner, a Viennese criminologist with psychic powers, who had been asked to assist the police in their search for the murder weapon. On 20 July Langsner located the missing gun in a patch of brush 135 yards from the Boohers' house.

Two days later Vernon made a confession. He had been in love with a nurse whom his mother and brother had tried to prevent him seeing, he explained; that was why he had killed them. The two hired hands had been killed a little while afterwards in order to mislead the police.

When Vernon Booher was brought to trial in Edmonton on 24 September he surprised the spectators by pleading not guilty to the charges when everybody knew that he had confessed. The judge ruled that the confession should not be admitted as evidence after a defence claim that it had been obtained as a result of hypnotic influence exercised by Langsner. However, the crown was able to present evidence of three partial confessions, as well as a good deal of circumstantial evidence, and the accused was convicted on all four charges. He was sentenced to death.

On 4 December the conviction was quashed on appeal, a second trial beginning on 21 January the following year. By this time Vernon Booher was unwell; he was suffering from nervous strain and close to a breakdown. Convicted again on all charges, he was hanged at Fort Saskatchewan jail on 24 April 1929.

None of his surviving relatives was at the jail when the execution took place, and there was nobody to claim his remains. His body was buried in the prison grounds.

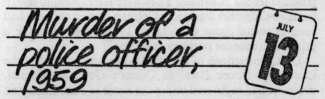

Murder of a police officer, 1959

JULY 13

On the afternoon of 13 July 1959, Mrs Verne Schiffman, a thirty-year-old model occupying a flat in South Kensington, London, received a telephone call from a man who was trying to blackmail her. It was not the first time that he had been in contact with her, and Mrs Schiffman's telephone was being tapped by the police; the call was quickly traced to a kiosk at South Kensington underground station. Mrs Schiffman kept the man talking for fifteen minutes while Detective Sergeant Raymond Purdy and Detective Sergeant John Sandford went to arrest him.

Pulling the culprit from the telephone box, the two police officers took him up the stairs towards the exit, but he managed to break away from them. Chasing him along Sydney Place, they cornered him in a block of flats in Onslow Square, about 100 yards from the station, and questioned him briefly before Sandford went to ring the caretaker's bell, to ask him to assist them. Purdy was thus left to guard the prisoner on his own.

The ringing of the bell brought no response, and Sandford called out to his colleague across the hall, saying that the caretaker must have gone out. At that moment the prisoner suddenly pulled out a gun and shot Purdy through the heart. He then ran out into the street and made good his escape while Sandford hesitated to leave his dying colleague.

The gunman, who had called himself Mr Fisher when he spoke to Mrs Schiffman, was described by Sandford as being about thirty years old and 5 feet 10 inches tall, with a slim build and brown hair; he spoke with an American accent. His fingerprints, taken from the scene of the murder, enabled the police to discover that he had no criminal record in Britain. They were later found to match those of Guenther Podola, a German immigrant who had been deported from Canada in 1958, after receiving a prison sentence for burglary and theft.

On the afternoon of 16 July Podola was arrested at the Claremont House Hotel in Queen's Gate, Kensington, where he had registered under the name of Paul Camay on 25 June. The manager, having reported that 'Mr Camay' was acting 'very strangely' — he had been hiding in his room ever since the shooting — was shown a photograph of Podola provided by the Royal Canadian Mounted Police, and said he believed it to be the same man. A small party of police officers then broke into the room and overpowered him, Podola being struck in the face by the door handle as the door flew open. His gun was found hidden in the hotel attic.

At Chelsea police station Podola was found to be 'dazed, frightened and exhausted', and suffering from a number of minor injuries, the worst of which was a bruise under his left eye. The following day he was taken to St Stephen's Hospital, where he was handcuffed to a bed in a public ward and kept under guard by two policemen. He appeared to be in a state of shock and seemed hardly aware of his surroundings. He was later to claim that he could remember little of what had happened to him before his arrival at the hospital.

On 20 July he was charged with the murder of Detective Sergeant Purdy, then taken to Brixton Prison to await trial. During the weeks that followed he continued to maintain that he was suffering from loss of memory, and several doctors examined him to try to determine whether this was really true. When he appeared at the Old Bailey on 10 September with the bruise under his eye still visible, a jury was empanelled to decide the matter, his counsel arguing that he was unfit to stand trial.

The jury, having listened to the evidence for nine days, decided that Podola was *not* suffering from a genuine loss of memory. He was therefore brought to trial before a different jury, but the same judge, on 24 September. The main prosecution witness was Detective Sergeant Sandford.

In his own defence, Podola made a statement from the dock, declaring that he did not know whether he was guilty or not because he could not remember the crime. However, the jury took only a little over half an hour to find the charge proved, and he was sentenced to death.

Guenther Podola was hanged at Wandsworth Prison on 5 November 1959.

Eight Chicago nurses found murdered, 1966

Just after 6 a.m. on 14 July 1966, two patrolmen arrived at a nurses' residence in Chicago's South Side and found a young woman standing on a window ledge above the sidewalk, screaming hysterically. Corazon Amurao, a twenty-three-year-old Filipino, was the sole survivor of a massacre which had taken place during the course of the preceding night. The eight other nurses in the building had all been strangled or stabbed to death.

All these murders were the work of a man who had forced his way into the residence, armed with a gun and a knife, about seven hours earlier, telling the nurses that he wanted their money. Miss Amurao said that he was about twenty-five years old, with short, brownish hair, and had worn a dark jacket and trousers with a white T-shirt. He had smelled of alcohol.

He made all the nurses lie on the floor of one of the bedrooms while he tied and gagged them with strips of bed linen, then went through the house searching for money. He then took them out of the room one at a time, at intervals of about twenty minutes, and murdered them in other parts of the building.

Though he had told them repeatedly that he would not harm them, Miss Amurao had not believed this, and had taken advantage of one of his absences to conceal herself under a bunk bed, where she remained unnoticed. Having thus saved her own life, she had gone on lying there until she felt it was safe to move.

An examination of the bodies revealed that several of the victims had been strangled *and* stabbed, but that none had been sexually assaulted. It also revealed that the culprit was skilled at tying knots, which led police to

196

suspect that he was a seaman. They therefore made inquiries at a nearby branch of the National Maritime Union, and found that a man answering the killer's description had been there to seek work during the previous few days.

The man had filled in an application form, giving his name as Richard F. Speck and providing the statutory photograph to accompany it. As no work had been found for him so far, he was expected to call at the union again. A trap was set to ensure that he was arrested when he did so.

At the same time copies of the photograph were distributed to all the detectives in Chicago's South Side, and visits were made to bars and boarding-houses during an intensive search for him. He was soon found to be registered at a flop-house called the Raleigh Hotel, where freshly-laundered clothes fitting Miss Amurao's description of those which the killer had been wearing were discovered in his room.

Though Speck failed to return to the Raleigh that night, fingerprints found in the room matched those left at the nurses' residence, and police were left in no doubt that he was the killer. On the morning of 16 July a press conference was called, Speck being named as the main suspect in the case and his photograph released for publication. Late at night on the same day an ambulance was called to the Starr Hotel, in Chicago's North Side, where a man who had registered under a different name had slashed his wrists with a broken bottle. It was found to be Richard Speck.

The suspect was identified by Corazon Amurao, and brought to trial for first-degree murder in April 1967. Found guilty, he was sentenced to death, the sentence being later commuted to terms of imprisonment totalling 400 years.

Chicago's worst case of multiple murder, described as the 'most bestial crime in the city's history', had effectively been solved in a record sixty-seven hours.

Execution of Charlotte Bryant 1936

On 15 July 1936, Charlotte Bryant, a thirty-three-year-old Irish woman with five children, was hanged at Exeter Prison for the murder of her husband. The crime had been committed at the couple's home near Sherborne, Dorset, the previous December, the victim being poisoned with weed-killer. It was not the first time that an attempt had been made on his life.

Frederick Bryant, aged thirty-nine was a former corporal in the military police. He had met his wife while serving in Ireland during 'the Troubles' of 1920-1 and brought her back to England with him. He had since worked as a farm labourer, living with his family in tied cottages. One of the farms on which he had been employed was at Over Compton, near Yeovil. He had remained there for eight or nine years before moving to the Sherborne area early in 1934.

Charlotte, an illiterate woman, was unkempt and almost toothless. She had had a long succession of affairs with other men, taking money in return for her favours whenever it was forthcoming. Her reputation in Over Compton was so bad that her husband had lost his job over it. However, Frederick Bryant made no complaint about his wife's behaviour, and was even pleased that she was able to bring home money to supplement his wages.

'Four pound a week is better than thirty bob,' he said to a neighbour. 'I don't care a damn what she does.'

Shortly before Bryant lost his job Leonard Parsons, a gypsy pedlar and horse-dealer, began staying with them as an occasional lodger, sleeping on a couch in the kitchen. He and Charlotte became lovers, resuming their affair each time he returned to the cottage. But she became more attached to him than he was to her, and it was as a result of this attachment that she started trying to poison her husband.

In October 1935, after two unsuccessful attempts had been made on Bryant's life — his illness, in each case, was diagnosed as gastro-enteritis — Parsons left, saying that he would not be coming back. A few weeks afterwards Charlotte set out in pursuit of him, having made a third unsuccessful attempt to kill her husband in the meantime, but returned home after an encounter with his 'natural wife', Priscilla Loveridge, at a gypsy camp near Weston-super-Mare. Three days after that, on 22 December, Frederick Bryant died in agony.

Arsenic was found not only in his body but also in household dust taken from the cottage. An empty tin, containing traces of the poison, was found among some rubbish a short distance away.

At Charlotte's trial at the Dorset Assizes in May 1936, Parsons gave evidence against her, telling the court that some months before her husband's death the prisoner had told him that she would soon be a widow and that he and she could then get married. An elderly woman, who had also been a lodger at the cottage, said that on the night of 21 December Charlotte had coaxed her husband into drinking some Oxo, and that on another occasion she had disposed of a tin of weed-killer. Charlotte ate caramels in the dock and appeared to be unaware of the gravity of her situation.

While in the condemned cell she refused to see her children, saying that she did not want to cause them any further distress, and on the day of the execution she went to the scaffold bravely.

'Her last moments were truly edifying,' said the priest who attended her.

Murder of Herman Rosenthal, 1912

During the early hours of 16 July 1912, Herman Rosenthal, a professional gambler, was shot dead outside the Hotel Metropole in New York by a number of men who left the scene in a car. The murder was followed by the arrest of Lieutenant Charles Becker, forty-two-year-old head of New York City's Gambling Squad, whose subsequent conviction was hailed by the press as a blow against organized crime.

Prior to his downfall Becker had run a protection racket, taking a percentage of the profits of New York's gambling salons in return for allowing them to operate without hindrance from his own men. Rosenthal had accepted him as a business partner following the enforced closure of one establishment and frequent police raids on another, but when a dispute about money led to further interference he swore an affidavit giving details of Becker's activities.

On the evening of 15 July District Attorney Charles Whitman, who was determined to bring police corruption in the city to an end, interviewed Rosenthal at length. Later, on hearing of the murder, he was convinced that the police chief had instigated it. He then offered immunity from prosecution to anyone who helped him to bring Becker to justice.

Before long the offer was accepted by Jack Rose, the man who had hired the killers on Becker's behalf. Rose made a thirty-eight-page confession and agreed to appear as a prosecution witness. Becker was therefore brought to trial, with six others, in October the same year, Rose's evidence helping to ensure his conviction. He was sentenced to death for first-degree murder.

A fresh trial was granted in April 1914, the defence suggesting that prosecution witnesses had been offered rewards for giving evidence against him. He was nonetheless found guilty again, and once more sentenced to death.

An appeal for clemency was made to Charles Whitman, who had since been elected State Governor, but this was turned down and Becker was executed in the electric chair on 30 July 1915. A silver plate was attached to his coffin, stating that he had been murdered by Governor Whitman, but this was removed when Becker's widow realized that she could be prosecuted for criminal libel.

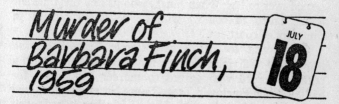

Murder of Barbara Finch, 1959

On the night of 18 July 1959, Mrs Barbara Finch, the second wife of a rich medical practitioner, was shot dead in the driveway of her home in a Los Angeles suburb. Her estranged husband, Dr Raymond Bernard Finch, and his young mistress, Carole Tregoff, were both involved in the incident, and to the police officers who investigated the affair it appeared to be a clear case of premeditated murder.

Dr Finch and his wife, who were both members of the Los Angeles Tennis Club, had married in 1951, each having been divorced by previous partners as a result of their association. Mrs Finch, then aged twenty-six, already had a daughter from her first marriage and bore her new husband a son two years later. By 1957, however, their marriage was merely a façade that they kept up for the sake of the children.

Finch, who was seven years older than his wife, rented

an apartment in the name of George Evans. Carole Tregoff, a twenty-year-old model who worked as his secretary, regularly met him there, and later divorced her own husband. She then moved into another apartment, calling herself Mrs George Evans. But not long afterwards Mrs Finch announced that she was going to begin divorce proceedings, citing Carole as co-respondent. The financial settlement which she sought would be so great that her husband would be left almost penniless.

Bitter quarrels, acts of violence and threats of murder followed, Finch becoming desperate. But eventually, in May 1959, Mrs Finch filed for divorce and her lawyer obtained a court order for her husband's income to be turned over to her. When Finch, who had by this time left home, failed to comply with it, he found himself in contempt of court.

On a visit to Las Vegas, Carole Tregoff became acquainted with John Cody, a thirty-year-old man with a criminal record who agreed to murder Mrs Finch for $1400. When Finch and Tregoff were later brought to trial Cody gave evidence against them, saying that he had taken their money but made no attempt on Mrs Finch's life. He even quoted Finch as saying on one occasion, 'When you shoot her, let her know what she's getting it for. Tell her, "This is from Bernie!"'

On the night of 18 July Marie Anne Lidholm, a Swedish *au pair* who lived in the doctor's house, was watching television in the company of Mrs Finch's twelve-year-old daughter. Mrs Finch was out at the time, but her car was heard in the garage shortly before midnight. A few seconds later she was heard screaming for help, and the *au pair* ran out to see what was happening.

Mrs Finch, who had been lying on the floor of the garage in her husband's presence, managed to get away and ran out across the lawn. Marie Anne then ran back to the house to call the police, hearing the sound of a shot as she did so. Barbara Finch was afterwards found with a bullet in her back and two skull fractures which could have been caused by the butt of a gun.

A leather dispatch-case, identified as the property of 'Bernie' Finch, had been left in the garage. It contained an assortment of articles, including drugs, hypodermic syringes, a large carving knife and two coils of clothes-line, later described as a 'do-it-yourself murder kit'. The gun, a .38 revolver, was not found.

Finch claimed that he had been trying to obtain evidence which he could use against his wife at the divorce hearing, and that it was for this purpose that he had hired Cody. He said that he and Carole Tregoff had confronted her in the garage, and that it was Mrs Finch who had produced the gun. Carole had fled at the sight of it, but he, during the course of a struggle, had managed to get hold of it and throw it into some bushes. The gun had discharged the shot which killed his wife as it hit the ground.

Carole Tregoff likewise declared that they were innocent, denying that she had been involved in a conspiracy to kill Mrs Finch or that she had intended her any harm on the night in question. However, they were both charged with murder and conspiracy to murder, and brought to trial in December the same year.

The case was sensational, and various well-known people, including film actresses, attended as 'guest reporters'. But on 12 March 1960, after deliberating for nine days, the jury was unable to reach agreement and the judge declared a mistrial. Three months later, on 27 June, a second trial started before a different judge. This lasted until 7 November, making it the longest murder trial in Californian history, but ended the same way. Finally, on 27 March 1961, the jury at a third trial found Finch guilty of first-degree murder, Tregoff of second-degree murder and both of conspiracy to murder. They were both given sentences of life imprisonment.

Carole Tregoff remained in jail until 1969, when she was released on parole, having refused to answer any letters from Finch in the meantime. Her lover served another two years before he, too, was released.

Murder of Adele Kohr, 1970

JULY 20

On the night of 20 July 1970, Adele Kohr, a nurse in her early twenties, was driving towards her home in the village of East Islip, Long Island, when she found herself being followed by the driver of another car. Sensing that she was in danger, she tried to pull away from him, but could not do so. The man brought his car up alongside hers and appeared determined to force her to stop.

Fearing for her safety, Adele drove on, but used only her left hand to steer the car. With her other hand she scrawled notes haphazardly across the pages of a spiral-bound notebook which she normally used to record gasoline purchases and mileages. She wrote:

'A man in a car pulled alongside me ... on the Sagtikos ... he wants me to stop ... he is following me in the same lane and I can't pull away ... doing 65 ... he is alongside again ... beard ... glasses ... long hair ... hippy type ... blue shirt ... the car is a Tempest ... light green ... T-37 ...'

The man finally forced her to a halt within a quarter of a mile of her home, then quickly reversed his own car up to hers so that she could not drive off again. As he got out of the car and came towards her, she noted one last detail — 'dark pants ...' Then the man smashed her windscreen with a jack and reached in to open the door.

Adele Kohr's car was found abandoned by a patrolman not long afterwards, its headlights still switched on, its engine turning over in neutral — and the spiral-bound notebook lying on one of the seats. Her naked body was found the following morning in a small wood about twenty miles away; she had been savagely beaten, raped, murdered and then run over by her killer's car. Her death had been caused by strangulation.

Detectives of the Suffolk County Homicide Squad found Adele's notes to be of very great assistance to them in their search for the person responsible. Checking the county automobile records, they made a list of eighteen people owning Pontiac Tempests which were either green or might have appeared green in the sodium vapour light of the Sagtikos State Parkway, along which the frightened nurse had been driving. They then started to interview them in the hope that one would be found to match the dead girl's description of the killer.

One of the car-owners was found to be Linda Meyer, of Hawthorne Street, Central Islip, whose husband, a tall young man, had long hair, a beard and glasses. When asked by police officers to accompany them to headquarters, he walked out to their waiting car without a word. By the time they arrived at the Suffolk County Police Headquarters he was utterly despondent. 'I'm sick,' he said helplessly. 'I'm very sick. I need help ...'

It was found that he had already been tried three times for attacks on women, and that each charge had been more serious than the one before. He was also found to have kidnapped, robbed and raped a twenty-three-year-old woman from Huntingdon, Long Island, just a few weeks previously.

Brought to trial on a number of serious charges, Robert Meyer pleaded temporary insanity. He was found guilty of second-degree murder and sentenced to twenty-five years' or life imprisonment. His wife afterwards thanked the Homicide Squad detectives for the way in which they had dealt with the case. 'My husband is a sick man, and I don't believe he has any business being free,' she said.

Murder of Archibald Brown, 1943

On the afternoon of 23 July 1943, Archibald Brown, a forty-seven-year-old invalid of Rayleigh in Essex, was taken out in his wheelchair, as usual, by Nurse Mitchell, his family's resident help. After they had gone some distance along one of his favourite walks they stopped so that he could have a cigarette and the nurse could tidy his blankets. Suddenly there was a loud explosion, the invalid being blown to pieces and Nurse Mitchell thrown to the ground. An anti-tank mine, known as a Hawkins No. 75 Grenade Mine, had been attached to the seat of the wheelchair.

Nurse Mitchell, who suffered only minor injuries, told the police that the wheelchair was kept in an airraid shelter next to the victim's house in London Road when it was not in use, and that Mr Brown's nineteen-year-old son Eric had been busy inside the shelter, with the door bolted, earlier in the day. Eric, a bank clerk, was currently serving in the army, and was found to have attended lectures on the type of mine which had been used. It was also found that a store of these mines was kept at his company headquarters.

Archibald Brown had been a constant bully, and had made life difficult for the whole family. Some years earlier he had been involved in a motor-cycle accident, as a result of which he had gradually developed paralysis of the spine; since then his conduct towards his wife had been insufferable. When Eric, the elder of two sons, was questioned he admitted attaching the mine to the wheelchair, saying that he had resented the way in which his mother was treated.

'My father is now out of his suffering, and I earnestly hope that my mother will now live a much happier and normal life,' he said.

Eric Brown had difficulty accepting the fact that he was a murderer, and while in custody made an unsuccessful attempt to take his own life. At his trial in Chelmsford, in November 1943, the defence produced evidence that he was suffering from schizophrenia and the jury returned a verdict of guilty but insane.

On 27 July 1889, a Paris court bailiff named Gouffé was reported missing by his brother-in-law. The police did not take the matter too seriously at first, for the forty-nine-year-old widower was known to have had affairs with at least twenty women and may well have started another. But three days later, when there was still no sign of him, Marie-François Goron, Chief of the Sûreté, decided to look into the matter himself. He had a feeling that Gouffé was in trouble.

Going to the bailiff's office in the Rue Montmartre, he found eighteen used matches on the floor near the safe. He also learnt from the concierge that on the night of 26 July an unknown man had let himself into the office, leaving shortly afterwards. It therefore seemed that this man had obtained Gouffé's keys and attempted to open the safe. Though nothing was known to have been stolen, Goron was sure that the case was important enough to justify a full-scale investigation.

He examined the bailiff's financial affairs and sent detectives to interview his mistresses. At the same time he circulated Gouffé's description to all the police forces in France, and set several clerks the task of checking provincial newspapers for reports of bodies found anywhere in the country. It was thus that he found out about the discovery of an unidentified male corpse in the village of Millery, near Lyons.

The corpse had been found in a sack on the bank of the Rhône on 13 August after villagers had reported noticing an unpleasant smell in the vicinity. The man had been strangled, and the remains of a wooden trunk in which he had evidently been confined were discovered some distance away.

There were no real grounds for Goron to believe that this was the body of the missing bailiff, especially as a local physician estimated that the man had been dead for about a year. In any case, Gouffé's brother-in-law, who was taken to see the corpse, said that it could not be Gouffé because it was the body of a black-haired man; Gouffé's hair was chestnut, he said. But Goron's instinct told him that it *was* Gouffé, and he refused to believe otherwise.

Some months afterwards, when he wrote to the Lyons police to ask what progress had been made on the case, Goron was sent some labels which had been removed from the broken trunk. Taking these to the Gare de Lyon, he found that the trunk had been transported from Paris by train on the very day that Gouffé had been reported missing.

This discovery led to an exhumation of the body, a fresh post-mortem being carried out by Professor Alexandre Lacassagne at the University of Lyons. Lacassagne found that the earlier examination had been carried out incompetently and that many of its reported findings were incorrect. The body *was* that of the missing bailiff; the hair had changed colour as a result of confinement in the trunk. To prove his point, Lacassagne washed the hair and beard with soap and water until their colour changed back to chestnut.

Goron had already discovered that a couple named Michel Eyraud and Gabrielle Bompard had disappeared from Paris on 27 July. Eyraud, a middle-aged professional swindler, and his companion, a young woman from a middle-class home who was known to have resorted to prostitution, had both been seen in Gouffé's company two days earlier, and further inquiries revealed that they had purchased a wooden trunk in London on 11 June.

Determined to trace them, Goron circulated their descriptions, together with a photograph of Eyraud, and these were published in French, British and American newspapers. As a result, on 16 January 1890, he received the first of three letters from Eyraud, all protesting his innocence and all posted in New York. Then, on 22 January Gabrielle Bompard arrived at Goron's office in the company of another man, to blame Eyraud and a stranger for the murder and claim that she had personally had no part in it. She was arrested and interrogated unmercifully for a fortnight before she finally made a confession.

She then revealed that on the night of 26 July previously she had received Gouffé in her apartment in the Rue Tronson-Ducoudray, ostensibly for the purpose of making love, while Eyraud was concealed in an alcove behind the divan. Eyraud had strangled Gouffé by hand after an elaborate attempt to hang him had failed. He had then taken the bailiff's keys and tried, also unsuccessfully, to open his safe by the light of matches. The following day the couple had taken the body to Millery and disposed of it.

Michel Eyraud remained at large until 20 May 1890, when he was arrested as he left a brothel in Havana. He was then returned to Paris where he and Gabrielle Bompard stood trial at the Seine Assize Court in December.

He was executed by guillotine in February 1891, his former companion receiving twenty years' imprisonment.

Besides being a personal triumph for Goron, the case is nowadays seen as a milestone in the history of forensic science.

Murder of Hella Christofi, 1954

On the evening of 29 July 1954, Hella Christofi, a thirty-six-year-old German woman married to a Cypriot waiter, was murdered at the couple's home in South Hill Park, Hampstead. The crime was committed by the victim's mother-in-law, Styllou Christofi, a fifty-three-year-old peasant who could speak little English, and appears to have been motivated by obsessive jealousy.

Hella and her husband Stavros had been married for fifteen years and had three children. Stavros worked at a West End restaurant, and Hella in a fashion shop. Styllou Christofi had lived with them since her arrival in London a year earlier, but it had been decided that she should return to Cyprus as she and her daughter-in-law could not get on together.

On the evening in question Styllou Christofi struck Hella with an ash-plate, fracturing her skull, and then strangled her. Shortly before midnight a neighbour walking his dog saw her trying to burn the body with newspaper in the backyard. But as the body was almost naked he assumed that it was a tailor's dummy and took no further notice.

An hour later Mrs Christofi spoke to a couple in a car near Hampstead station. 'Please come!' she said excitedly. 'Fire burning! Children sleeping!'

When the police were called the body was found to be charred and smelling of paraffin. The victim's wedding ring was discovered in her mother-in-law's bedroom.

Styllou Christofi was brought to trial at the Old Bailey. Though the prison doctor at Holloway believed her to be insane, she refused to allow a plea of insanity to be made on her behalf and so, on being found guilty, was sentenced to death. Three other doctors examined her afterwards and found her to be sane.

It was not the first time that she had been tried for murder. A similar charge had been brought against her in Cyprus in 1925, after her own mother-in-law had died as a result of having a burning torch rammed down her throat. On that occasion she had been acquitted.

Following the dismissal of her appeal, Styllou Christofi was hanged at Holloway on 13 December 1954.

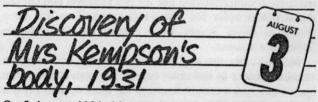

Discovery of Mrs Kempson's body, 1931

AUGUST
3

On 3 August 1931, Mrs Annie Louisa Kempson, a widow in her fifties, was found murdered at her home in St Clement's Street, Oxford. Her killer had battered her over the head with a hammer in the entrance hall and then, after moving her to the dining-room, had driven a sharp instrument through her neck, severing an artery. By the time her body was discovered Mrs Kempson had been dead for two days.

The house had been ransacked and a small sum of money stolen, but a much larger amount hidden in the bedroom had not been found. It appeared that the victim had known the person responsible, for there were no signs of a forced entry and the first blow had been struck from behind. However, there were no fingerprints and the weapons used had not been left at the scene. There were no clues to the murderer's identity at all.

The police began routine inquiries in the neighbourhood, but made no progress until nine days later, when another widow, Mrs Alice Mary Andrews, was interviewed.

Mrs Andrews, who lived about ten minutes' walk from the victim's home, revealed that on the evening of 31 July a salesman named Seymour, from whom she had earlier purchased a vacuum cleaner, had called at her own house, claiming to have been robbed of all his money while he was bathing in the Thames.

Mrs Andrews had lent him 4s 6d (22½ p), but he had returned to the house later the same day, asking if she could put him up for the night as he had missed his last bus home. She had agreed to do this and the following morning, before he left, noticed that he had a hammer and chisel wrapped in brown paper. She had afterwards received a letter from him, thanking her for her kindness and enclosing a postal order for 10s 6d (52½p). This had been posted in Hove, Sussex, on 5 August but did not give Seymour's address.

Mrs Andrews also said that Mrs Kempson had bought a vacuum cleaner of the same type as her own at about the same time, and a receipt found at the dead woman's home confirmed this. Moreover, it was soon learnt from other inquiries that the salesman in question, after borrowing the 4s 6d from Mrs Andrews, had bought the hammer and chisel at a local ironmonger's shop for 4s (20p). The remainder had been spent on a shave before he and Mrs Andrews had breakfast together the following morning.

Henry Daniel Seymour turned out to be a fifty-year-old man with a long record of serious crime. He lived by housebreaking and fraud, using his job as a salesman as a means of discovering suitable victims to rob. Only a year earlier he had been in trouble for assaulting a woman during the course of one of his demonstrations.

It was learnt, too, that Seymour had left a hotel in Aylesbury, Buckinghamshire, on 31 July without paying his bill and returned surreptitiously the following afternoon (after the murder) to collect his personal belongings. On being seen by the landlord, he had then promised to pay the bill later. But the landlord had insisted on keeping his suitcase until he did so — and still had it, as Seymour had not been back since.

Inside the suitcase the police found a hammer which matched the identations in Mrs Kempson's skull. It had been soaked, and the maker's label had been removed — only to be discovered in tiny fragments when the case was subjected to closer examination.

Seymour was traced to Brighton, where he was living in lodgings. He admitted having bought the hammer and chisel on 31 July, saying that he had hoped to get a job as a carpenter, but denied all knowledge of the crime. He was unable to give a satisfactory account of his movements on the morning of 1 August, as the witnesses he named could not corroborate his story. He was charged with murder.

Brought to trial in Oxford in October the same year, he pleaded not guilty. Though there was no proof that he had been to the victim's house on the morning of the crime, there was a considerable amount of circumstantial evidence against him, and he gave a poor impression of himself when he entered the witness box. He was accordingly found guilty and sentenced to death.

His execution took place at Oxford Prison on 10 December 1931.

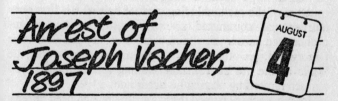

Arrest of Joseph Vacher, 1897

AUGUST 4

On 4 August 1897, a tramp attacked a woman gathering pine cones in a wood near Tournon, in southern France. The woman called to her husband, who was close at hand, and between them they overpowered the offender and took him to a nearby inn where he was forced to await the arrival of the police. Joseph Vacher, a man with a history of mental instability, was later sentenced to three months' imprisonment for an offence against public decency. But he was also questioned in connection with a series of far more serious crimes.

During the previous three and a half years no fewer than eleven sex murders had been committed in country regions in the south-east of France. The victims — seven women and four youths — had all died from strangulation or stabbing, and had afterwards been raped, mutilated or disembowelled. Though witnesses failed to identify Vacher as the person responsible for these crimes, he eventually confessed to all of them. He had committed them 'in moments of frenzy', he declared.

Born in 1869, Vacher was a member of a large peasant family; his parents had fourteen other children. While serving in the army he tried to commit suicide by cutting his throat with a razor because his expected promotion was delayed. On another occasion he shot himself with a pistol after shooting a girl in a fit of jealousy. This second attempt on his own life left him scarred and partially paralysed in the face as well as damaging one of his eyes.

After periods of confinement in two different lunatic asylums he was discharged on 1 April 1894, and began roaming the countryside, begging food from farms. He carried a large sack, a cudgel and an accordion, the contents of the sack including a set of knives. His first sex murder was committed six weeks after he had been pronounced cured, the victim being a twenty-one-year-old factory girl; his other victims were mainly farm workers. While at the inn at Tournon, waiting for the police, he amused himself by playing his accordion.

Joseph Vacher claimed that as a child he had been bitten by a mad dog, and said that he believed this to be the cause of his own madness. However, he was examined by Professor Alexandre Lacassagne and other doctors, who declared him sane. He was brought to trial at the Ain Assizes in October 1898, charged with the murder of a shepherd three years earlier, and found guilty after further speculation about his sanity.

The 'Ripper of the South-East' was executed by guillotine, at the age of twenty-nine, on 31 December 1898.

Drummond family found murdered, 1952

AUGUST 5

On the morning of 5 August 1952, French police were called to the scene of a triple murder on a riverbank near the village of Lurs in Provence. The victims — Sir Jack Drummond, a distinguished British biochemist aged sixty-one, his forty-six-year-old wife and their eleven-year-old daughter Elizabeth — had been on holiday in France and had camped at the site the previous evening. Sir Jack and Lady Drummond had both been shot; their daughter had been battered to death. The nearest house was about 150 yards away, on a farm owned by a seventy-five-year-old peasant named Gaston Dominici.

It was Dominici's thirty-three-year-old son Gustave, who lived and worked on the farm, who had raised the alarm. According to his statement, he had heard shots being fired about one o'clock in the morning, but had been too frightened to go out and investigate them. The matter had been reported after his discovery of the girl's body about 5.30 a.m. The weapon with which Sir Jack and Lady Drummond had been murdered was later recovered from the river a short distance away, its position indicating that the murderer was somebody who knew the area well. It was a carbine of a type issued to American troops during the Second World War.

Though a search of the farmhouse revealed nothing, the

police suspected that its inhabitants — Gaston Dominici, his son and his daughter-in-law — knew more about the crime than had so far been admitted. Little progress was made for some weeks until it was learnt from a railway worker that Elizabeth Drummond had still been alive when Gustave Dominici found her. When Gustave confirmed this, he was arrested for failing to give aid to a person who was in danger of dying. He was sentenced to two months' imprisonment, but this was afterwards quashed on appeal.

For the next twelve months Commissaire Edmond Sebeille, who was in charge of the case, persisted with his inquiries, questioning not only the inhabitants of the farmhouse but also their many relatives throughout the region. He was constantly hampered by lying, the people responsible being apparently indifferent to whether their stories sounded plausible. But eventually Gustave Dominici and his brother Clovis, aged forty-nine, admitted that their father was the murderer. The old man, cursing his sons' treachery, made a confession a few days later.

Gaston Dominici, carrying his carbine, as he always did at night, had been discovered in the act of watching Sir Jack and Lady Drummond as they undressed for the night. He had shot Sir Jack during the course of a struggle and had then killed the other two members of the family to prevent them having him arrested. Elizabeth Drummond had been attacked with the butt of the carbine as she tried to escape.

The prisoner later retracted his confession and went on to make and retract several others before being brought to trial at the Digne Assize Court in November 1954. At one point he made a counter-accusation against Gustave, and Gustave withdrew his accusation against his father and accused somebody else. On another occasion, during a reconstruction of the crime, the prisoner attempted to commit suicide by jumping from a railway bridge.

After an eleven-day trial, Gaston Dominici was found guilty and sentenced to death, the sentence being commuted to life imprisonment on account of his advanced

216

age. He was pardoned and released on 14 July 1960, at the age of eighty-three, and died five years later.

Body found in Scottish cemetery, 1967

AUGUST 7

On the morning of 7 August 1967, the body of fifteen-year-old Linda Peacock was found in a cemetery a short distance from her home in Biggar, between Edinburgh and Glasgow. She had died as a result of head injuries and strangulation and, although no attempt had been made to rape her, there were bite-marks on one of her breasts. These marks were quite distinct, indicating that they had been made a few minutes before the girl's death. Had she lived longer, their outlines would have been masked by the spread of bruising.

Linda had been reported missing from home the previous night. The autopsy report stated that she had probably died between 10 and 11 p.m., and it was learnt that screams had been heard coming from the cemetery at 10.20 p.m. Chief Superintendent William Muncie, Head of the Lanarkshire CID, soon began to suspect that a teenager at a nearby approved school was the person responsible.

Gordon Hay, aged seventeen, had been seen lying in his bed by one of the school's masters at 10.30 p.m.; another of the masters had seen him in the dining-room just over half an hour earlier. But the school was only a few minutes' walk from the scene of the crime, and it was discovered that Hay had entered the dormitory in a dirty and dishevelled state just before 10.30 p.m. He was also found to have spoken to the victim at a fair on 5 August and to have in his possession a boat hook which could have caused her head injuries.

However, the evidence against him was insufficient to justify an arrest until Dr Warren Harvey, a consultant at the Glasgow Dental Hospital, and Detective Inspector Osborne Butler of the Identification Bureau of the Glasgow Police managed to identify him from the bite-marks on his victim's breast. This took many weeks' work of a largely experimental nature, in a branch of forensic science which was relatively new. But when Hay was finally brought to trial in Edinburgh the following year the evidence was impressive enough to satisfy the court that he was guilty.

Gordon Hay thus became the first murderer to be identified by this method in Scotland and, having been under the age of eighteen when the crime was committed, was sentenced to be detained during Her Majesty's pleasure. An appeal was subsequently heard by a panel of five judges, who upheld his conviction.

Mabel Tattershaw's body revealed, 1951

AUGUST 9

On 9 August 1951, a young man telephoned the offices of the *News of the World* in London, claiming to have found the body of a woman who had been strangled. He said that he was speaking from Nottingham and had not yet informed the police of his discovery. He offered the newspaper an exclusive story about it for £250.

While one reporter tried to get further information out of the man, another telephoned the Nottingham police. It turned out that the caller was speaking from a public call-box and when his time was up he had to give its number so that he could be recalled. The number was immediately passed to the Nottingham police, with the result that an officer arrived at the kiosk while the call was still in progress. He took the man away for questioning.

Herbert Leonard Mills, an unemployed clerk aged nineteen, then informed the police that he had found a woman's body in an orchard in Sherwood Vale, on the outskirts of Nottingham, the previous day. He said that he liked to read and write poetry, and often went to the orchard for this purpose. He afterwards led police to the place in question.

The body was found to be that of Mrs. Mabel Tattershaw, aged forty-eight of Longmead Drive, Nottingham, who had disappeared from her home on 3 August. Mrs. Tattershaw at first appeared to have died as a result of being battered with a blunt instrument; it was only when a post-mortem was carried out that strangulation was established as the cause of her death. She had not been robbed or sexually assaulted.

Herbert Mills, who said that he had not known Mrs. Tattershaw, was not regarded as a suspect and so was allowed to go free. He wrote his own account of the discovery of the body for the *News of the World,* and this was published, together with his photograph. He was, however, rebuked at the coroner's inquest for failing to tell the police about the body immediately after finding it.

For a few days the police made no real progress with the case; there seemed to have been no motive for the murder, and suggestions that Mrs. Tattershaw had had a lover proved to be unfounded. Then, suddenly, certain questions were asked about Herbert Mills and his various statements. Why had he told Norman Rae, crime reporter for the *News of the World,* that he had found the body of a woman who had been strangled when the cause of her death was not apparent at a preliminary examination by a pathologist? And why had he described her face as white and pale in his newspaper article when it had not been white and pale at all?

219

These doubts were confided to Norman Rae, who agreed to raise them with Mills himself. When he did so Mills began to change his story, saying that he had actually discovered the body some days earlier than he had previously claimed. The victim's face *had* been white then and the marks on her neck had been apparent, he said. Even so, the questions served to unnerve him, and at a subsequent meeting, on 24 August he admitted that *he* had been Mrs. Tattershaw's murderer.

In a fresh account of what had happened, which Rae obtained from him in writing, Mills said that he had met Mrs. Tattershaw at a cinema on 2 August while he was preoccupied with the idea of committing a 'perfect' murder. He had then met her again the following day by arrangement, and taken her to the orchard where the crime was committed. He had afterwards become impatient for the body to be discovered, so that he could gloat over the inability of the police to bring him to justice.

Mills' confession was handed to the police, and he was arrested and charged with murder. He was brought to trial at the Nottingham Assizes in November, convicted and sentenced to death. He was hanged on 11 December 1951.

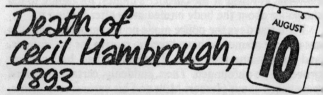

Death of Cecil Hambrough, 1893

On 10 August 1893, Cecil Hambrough, a twenty-year-old lieutenant in the Yorkshire Militia, was mysteriously killed while out shooting with two other men on an estate at Ardlamont in Argyllshire. It was at first accepted that he had shot himself by accident while climbing over a dyke, but later the police learnt that the same man had almost been drowned in another 'accident' the previous day. Further inquiries then resulted in one of Hambrough's companions, Alfred John Monson, being charged not only with murder but also with attempted murder. The trial which followed attracted a great deal of attention.

Monson, an undischarged bankrupt involved in crooked financial dealings, lived in style; he had rented the estate at Ardlamont, and pretended that he was about to buy it, but in fact he had no money at all. Cecil Hambrough, the son of an impoverished landowner who had mortgaged a life interest in his own estates, lived with Monson and his family; he was completely dominated by Monson, who had originally been engaged as his tutor, and his life had been insured for £20,000, with Mrs. Monson as beneficiary in the event of his death.

Edward Sweeney, the other man present at the shooting, was a bookmaker's clerk from London, also known as Edward Davis and — in this case — Edward Scott. An associate of Monson's, he had arrived at Ardlamont on 8 August, Monson having travelled to Glasgow to meet him, and was introduced to Hambrough as 'a marine engineer'. He had disappeared almost immediately after the tragedy of 10 August and as the police could not trace him and he failed to return of his own accord, he was declared an outlaw.

Monson had earlier devised a scheme to enable him to purchase the life interest which Hambrough's father had mortgaged, but had failed in this particular venture. On moving to Ardlamont, he had arranged the insurance on the young man's life himself, using money obtained by false pretences to pay a premium of nearly £200, also on 8 August.

In the first 'accident' on 9 August, he and Hambrough, who could not swim, were fishing in Ardlamont Bay when their boat sank. The boat was found to have had a plug-hole cut into it a few hours before, apparently by Sweeney, but no cork seemed to have been provided for it. Monson, in a statement about what had happened, claimed to have left Hambrough sitting on a rock while he went for a second boat in order to rescue him. But local fishermen did not know of any rocks in Ardlamont Bay.

As for the shot with which Hambrough had been killed, three experts declared that this had been fired from a distance of nine feet. It was therefore impossible for him to have killed himself by accident, as Monson maintained.

When the accused man was brought to trial in Edinburgh, in December 1893, he was thought to have no chance. However, the case proved to be far from clear-cut, for evidence about the shooting was contradictory, and the financial transactions in which Monson had been involved were baffling. The judge accordingly summed up in Monson's favour, remarking that it was the business of the Crown to prove the case, and not for the defence to prove innocence. The jury then adjourned for seventy-three minutes before returning a verdict of not proven.

Not long afterwards Edward Sweeney returned to Scotland to stand trial. But when the case was called nobody appeared for the prosecution; Sweeney was therefore released.

Monson went back to his old ways, and in 1898 was sentenced to five years' penal servitude for conspiring with two others to defraud the Norwich Union Life Assurance Society. He remained an undischarged bankrupt for the rest of his life.

Murder of three police officers, 1966

On the afternoon of 12 August 1966, the crew of a police patrol car stopped three men in a blue Vanguard shooting-brake in Braybrook Street, near Wormwood Scrubs Prison in London. Detective Sergeant Christopher Head and Detective Constable David Wombwell, got out to question the driver and found that he had no tax disc and that his insurance had expired. Head left Wombwell to write down the particulars while he went to inspect the rear of the car. Suddenly there was a shot and the young detective constable fell to the ground, fatally injured. He had been shot in the left eye.

Two of the three men got out of the Vanguard, both armed with guns. Head ran to the patrol car to take cover, but was shot in the back and fell in front of it. One of the gunmen then ran over and fired three shots at Police Constable Geoffrey Fox, who was still in his driving-seat with the engine running — too shocked to know what to do. As one of the bullets entered his left temple, his foot pushed down on the accelerator and the patrol car lurched forward. Head, who was dying, was trapped underneath it. Police Constable Fox lay dead at the wheel.

The two gunmen returned to the Vanguard, which was then driven in reverse along Braybrook Street. A moment later, it turned and sped away. But its licence number had already been noted by a married couple in another car, who suspected that a jail-break had just taken place. It was as a result of this that the culprits were quickly identified.

The owner of the car was found to be John Witney, a thirty-six-year-old unemployed man with ten convictions for petty theft. He lived with his wife in a basement flat in Fernhead Road, Paddington, where two police officers called to see him within six hours of the murder of their three colleagues. Witney, who was trembling and sweating, claimed that he had sold the car to a stranger for £15. The two police officers took him to Shepherd's Bush police station, where he was detained.

Though a search of his flat revealed no incriminating evidence, the Vanguard was found the following day in a garage rented by Witney in a railway arch at Vauxhall; used cartridges and car-theft equipment were found inside it. On 14 August, when charged with the three murders, Witney admitted that he had been the driver on the day in question and named two other men as the gunmen. The three men, who had committed various robberies together, had been afraid that Head and Wombwell would search the Vanguard and find their guns.

The men Witney named were Harry Roberts, a thirty-year-old man with convictions for attempted store-breaking, larceny and robbery with violence, and John Duddy, aged thirty-seven, a long-distance lorry-driver who had been in trouble several times for theft in his youth. Both were found to be missing from their homes.

Duddy, a Scotsman, was arrested in Glasgow on 16 August. In a statement, which he afterwards denied having made, he said, 'It was Roberts who started the shooting. He shot two who got out of the car and shouted to me to shoot. I just grabbed a gun and ran to the police car and shot the driver through the window. I must have been mad.'

The search for Roberts intensified, with a reward of £1000 being offered for information leading to his capture. Yet he remained at large until 15 November, when he was found asleep in a barn at the edge of Nathan's Wood, in Hertfordshire. Taken to Bishop's Stortford police station, he then confessed his part in the 'Massacre of Braybrook Street'. He was committed for trial.

Witney and Duddy had already been brought to trial at the Old Bailey on 14 November, but when news of Roberts' capture was received the trial was adjourned so that the three prisoners could appear together. The following month they were all convicted of murder and possessing firearms, and the judge, in passing sentences of life imprisonment on each of them, recommended that they should serve at least thirty years.

John Duddy died in Parkhurst Prison, at the age of fifty-two, in February 1981.

Execution of Arthur Devereux, 1905

AUGUST 15

Arthur Devereux, who was hanged at Pentonville Prison on 15 August 1905, was a twenty-four-year-old chemist's assistant who had murdered his wife and their twin sons by poisoning them with morphine. The bodies of his victims had been discovered in a tin trunk in a furniture depository in Harrow, Middlesex, the previous April. The top of the trunk had been coated with a mixture of glue and boric acid to make it airtight.

Arthur and Beatrice Devereux had been living in a back street in Kilburn, London, when the twins were born. They had an older son, Stanley, of whom Devereux was extremely fond. However, his wages were low and his wife was already under-nourished; he knew that he would be unable to support a larger family. In January 1905, having decided to murder Beatrice and the two younger children, Devereux acquired a trunk and a bottle of poison.

He induced his wife to drink some of the poison, and also to give some of it to the twins, by telling her that it was cough medicine. He afterwards had the trunk — with the three bodies inside it — removed to the furniture depository, claiming that it was 'filled with domestic articles', and moved with six-year-old Stanley to another part of London. He managed to find Stanley a place in a private school.

When his mother-in-law asked what had become of Beatrice, Devereux answered evasively. She, becoming suspicious, made inquiries among the couple's former neighbours in Kilburn and learnt of the trunk being taken away in a Harrow company's van. Having located the company, she obtained authority to have the trunk opened, and then her fears were confirmed. Inspector Pollard of

Scotland Yard was put in charge of the case.

Devereux, in the meantime, had moved to Coventry, where he was working in a similar job to the one he had had before. When visited by Pollard, he did not even wait to be told the purpose of the inspector's visit before stammering, 'You have made a mistake. I don't know anything about a tin trunk.'

At his trial at the Old Bailey, in July 1905, he claimed that his wife had poisoned the twins and then herself, and that he, fearing that he would be suspected of murdering them all, had panicked and hidden the bodies. But it was pointed out by the prosecution that Devereux, in applying for a new job while his wife was still alive, had described himself as a widower.

This was seen as evidence of premeditated murder on his part, and he was convicted and sentenced to death.

Execution of Thomas Allaway, 1922

AUGUST 19

On 19 August 1922, Thomas Henry Allaway, a thirty-six-year-old private chauffeur, was hanged for the murder of Irene Wilkins, following a five-day-trial at Winchester the previous month. The crime had been committed on 22 December 1921, the victim's body being found on waste ground on the outskirts of Bournemouth the following morning. She had been killed by blows with a heavy car spanner after an unsuccessful attempt at rape.

Irene Wilkins, aged thirty-one, was the daughter of a barrister; she was unmarried and lived in Streatham, London. On the day of her death she had an advertisement published in the *Morning Post*, seeking employment as a cook, and within hours had received a telegram asking her to travel to Bournemouth to meet a prospective employer. She left Waterloo the same afternoon and arrived in Bournemouth about 7 p.m. The murder took place a short while afterwards.

A car designer informed police that he had seen the victim being driven from Bournemouth Central Station in a Mercedes and was even able to give the car's licence number. But for some reason his statement was overlooked during the early part of the investigation, the police believing that their only clues were tyre marks found at the scene of the crime and the telegram message in the murderer's handwriting. The investigation thus took considerably longer than necessary.

It was discovered that two other telegrams of the same type had been sent from the same area during the previous few days in reply to similar advertisements; both had been ignored by their recipients. The postal clerks concerned in each case could only vaguely remember the person who had handed in the message, though one said she believed it to have been a chauffeur 'with a rough voice'.

Eventually the police began to suspect Allaway, who was employed by one of the residents of nearby Boscombe. And it was at this point that the car designer's statement came to light, the licence number which he had given proving to be that of the car owned by Allaway's employer. The police then started trying to find a sample of Allaway's handwriting, to compare with that of the telegram messages.

Allaway, on learning that he was under suspicion, suddenly fled from Bournemouth, having stolen some of his employer's cheques and passed them off with forged signatures on local tradesmen. He was arrested at his wife's home in Reading on 28 April with betting slips in his pocket which bore the same handwriting as the telegram. Further samples of his handwriting were found at his lodgings in Boscombe, and the car designer and another witness identified him as the man who had been at

Bournemouth Central Station in a car on the evening in question.

At his trial Allaway claimed to have been alone at his lodgings reading a newspaper for part of that evening, and tried to give himself an alibi by saying that he had spoken to his landlord about the time of the murder. His landlord, however, said that Allaway had never spent the evening alone in his lodgings; he had always gone out about 6.30 p.m. and stayed out the whole evening. Allaway, in fact, gave a very poor impression of himself under cross-examination, and so was found guilty. It has since been revealed that he confessed to the crime on the night before his execution.

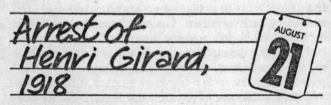

Arrest of Henri Girard, 1918

On 21 August 1918, Henri Girard, a French swindler, was arrested in Paris following an insurance company's investigation of the death of Mme Monin, a war widow who had collapsed and died at a Métro station. A policy had been taken out on her life by one of Girard's mistresses, and it was discovered that Mme Monin had visited Girard's apartment just before her death and been given an apéritif there. Her death was found to have been caused by bacterial poisoning.

Girard, who called himself a bookmaker, already had a criminal record as a result of a fraudulent company which he had set up nine years earlier. But he had lived by fraud ever since his dishonourable discharge from the Tenth Hussars in 1897, and his suspended prison sentence and 1000 franc fine on that occasion had not caused him to change his ways. Indeed, it was discovered that since that time he had made other attempts at poisoning as a means of financing his extravagant lifestyle, though he had only succeeded once.

In that case, in 1912, he had done well for himself. His victim, an insurance broker named Louis Pernotte, had admired Girard so much that in 1910 he had given him power of attorney over his estate. Girard had Pernotte's life insured for over 300,000 francs (using several different companies), and in August 1912, just before the broker and his family left on a trip to Royan, poured typhoid bacilli into a water carafe on their lunch table.

Pernotte, his wife and their two children were all taken ill, and when they returned to Paris some months later the broker had still not fully recovered. Girard was therefore allowed to give him a daily injection, as a result of which he died shortly afterwards. Then, having murdered her husband, Girard somehow convinced Mme Pernotte that she owed him 200,000 francs.

Whatever doubts she may have had about it, she paid him that sum, and the crime remained undetected for the next six years.

Girard had a laboratory in an apartment in the Avenue de Neuilly, where he also kept one of his other two mistresses. There, some years after the death of Pernotte, he experimented with poisonous mushrooms, having taken out insurance policies on the lives of two other unsuspecting people. However, both of these intended victims survived the attempts on their lives, neither of them realizing that Girard was responsible for the illnesses which they suffered.

Following his arrest, Girard remained in prison for nearly three years while the police made extensive inquiries about his activities, and built up a case which they hoped would send him to the guillotine. Finally, in May 1921, while still waiting to be brought to trial, he killed himself by swallowing a germ culture which he had managed to acquire. He was forty-six years old.

Christine Darby found murdered, 1967

On 22 August 1967, the body of seven-year-old Christine Darby, who had been abducted from outside her home in Walsall, Staffordshire, three days earlier, was found on Cannock Chase, fourteen miles away; she had been sexually assaulted and suffocated. Tyre marks were discovered nearby, and Identikit pictures were issued of a man who had been seen driving a grey Austin car in the area on the day of the child's disappearance. He did not come forward.

During the investigation which followed the owners of over 23,000 grey Austins were interviewed and extensive house-to-house inquiries carried out. But the suspect was not traced until November 1968, when a woman in Walsall saw a man trying to entice a girl of ten into a car.

The girl resisted and the man, realizing that he was being watched, drove off. But the witness, having made a note of his car number, reported the incident to the police.

The car-owner was found to be Raymond Leslie Morris, a thirty-nine-year-old foreman engineer who lived with his second wife in the same town. It was discovered that Morris, in 1966, had been accused of interfering with little girls, and that at the time of Christine Darby's murder he had owned a grey Austin. He was later identified as the man who had been seen on Cannock Chase on the day of Christine's disappearance. His arrest took place on 15 November 1968.

Raymond Morris was found to be a well-liked man with both charm and intelligence. But his first wife, whom he had divorced, revealed that at the time of their marriage he had been a fantasist whose sexual demands exhausted her. At his home police found pornographic films and indecent

230

photographs of a small girl.

Morris's second wife had at first given him an alibi, claiming that he had been out shopping with her on the day of Christine Darby's abduction. However, she had afterwards changed her mind about this, saying that she had been mistaken.

At his trial at the Staffordshire Assizes, in February 1969, Raymond Morris was convicted and sentenced to life imprisonment. The murders of two other little girls, whose bodies had also been found on Cannock Chase, have never been solved.

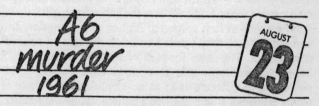

A6 murder 1961

During the early hours of 23 August 1961, a shooting took place in a lay-by on the A6 in Bedfordshire which has since been the subject of much controversy. The victims were Michael Gregsten, a young research scientist who was shot dead, and his girlfriend Valerie Storie, who was also shot but managed to survive. The crime led to the execution of James Hanratty, a twenty-five-year-old petty criminal whose guilt has been disputed in at least three books on the case.

On the night of 22 August the two lovers, according to Valerie Storie's account, were sitting in a parked car near Windsor when they were held up by a man with a gun. The man got into the back seat of the car and forced Gregsten to drive at gunpoint until they reached the isolated stretch of the A6 known as Deadman's Hill, near Clophill. There he ordered him to pull into the lay-by, saying that he wanted to sleep but had first to tie them up.

Having tied Miss Storie's hands, he told Gregsten to

pass him a duffle bag. But as Gregsten moved to do so the gunman fired two bullets into his head, killing him instantly; he said the victim had moved too quickly and frightened him. A few minutes later he raped Valerie Storie, then made her help him to move the dead man's body out on to the ground. Finally, he shot her five times at close range and made off in the car on his own.

Valerie Storie lay on the ground, paralysed in both legs and semi-conscious, until a farm worker found her about 6.30 a.m. The car was found abandoned in Ilford, the murder weapon on a London bus. Two cartridge cases from the same gun were later found in a London hotel room which had been occupied by Hanratty — using a different name — on the night before the murder, and by a man named Peter Louis Alphon the following night.

The police at first suspected Alphon of the murder, and announced that they wanted to interview him in connection with it. He came forward of his own accord on 22 September and was held in custody until Valerie Storie picked out a different man at an identification parade at Guy's Hospital, where she was a patient, on 24 September. He was then released, the police turning their attention to Hanratty, who was later arrested in Blackpool.

Three weeks after the first identification parade Miss Storie was asked to attend another; this time she asked if she could hear the men speak. She was wheeled along the line several times, asking each man in turn to say, as the gunman had said after shooting Gregsten: 'Be quiet, will you? I'm thinking.' This time she identified Hanratty.

Hanratty's trial at the Bedford Assizes was the longest murder trial in English history, lasting twenty-one days. The defence made much of the fact that Valerie Storie had picked out a different man at the first identification parade, and also the Identikit picture constructed from her description, which bore a greater resemblance to the clerk of the court, who had to hold it up, than to the prisoner.

The prosecution, however, was helped when Hanratty, after claiming to have been in Liverpool at the time of the murder, suddenly changed his story and said that he was in Rhyl. Even so, it took the jury nine and a half hours to bring in a verdict of guilty.

Following Hanratty's execution, which took place at Bedford on 4 April 1962, witnesses were found who said that they thought they had seen him in Rhyl about the time of the murder, and Peter Alphon made a written statement declaring that *he* was the A6 murderer.

While these developments have helped to convince many people that Hanratty was the victim of a miscarriage of justice, many others have remained unshaken in their belief that he was guilty.

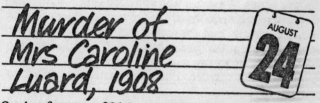

Murder of Mrs Caroline Luard, 1908

On the afternoon of 24 August 1908, Mrs. Caroline Luard, fifty-eight-year-old wife of a retired army officer, was shot dead in a summer-house close to the couple's home at Ightham, near Sevenoaks, Kent. The murder took place at 3.15 p.m., the shots being heard by others in the vicinity. The body was discovered by the victim's husband, Major-General Charles Luard, when he went to look for her during the early evening.

The Luards had left their home together at 2.30 that afternoon, the General, who was sixty-nine years old, intending to walk to his golf club at Godden Green, three miles away. Mrs. Luard accompanied him to a nearby village on her way to the unoccupied summer-house at Fish Ponds Woods. On his return to Ightham at 4.30 p.m., the General was surprised to find that she was not back because they had invited a friend to tea. Later, after entertaining the visitor, the General went to the summer-house on his own, and found his wife's body on the verandah.

Mrs. Luard had been shot twice through the head. Some valuable rings had been taken from the fingers of her left hand and her purse was also missing. Though there were no clues to the identity of the murderer, and the victim had had no known enemies, the Reverend R.B. Cotton, a friend of the Luards, told the coroner's inquest that he had seen a 'sandy-haired tramp' emerging from the woods about the time of her death. But it had been established at the post-mortem that Mrs. Luard had been dead for some time before her rings were removed.

Following the adjournment of the inquest, General Luard, already grief-stricken by the loss of his wife, became the main suspect in the case and began to receive abusive letters. Witnesses who appeared later testified that they had seen him on the day of the murder, their evidence showing clearly that he could not have been at the summer-house at the time of Mrs. Luard's death. Even the coroner saw fit to say that the General could not have committed the murder. But these statements failed to alleviate his distress.

Putting his home up for sale, General Luard went to stay with a friend. Not long afterwards he threw himself under a train, leaving a note saying that he had gone to join his wife.

Two years later, when John Alexander Dickman was convicted of the murder of John Nisbet, a colliery wages clerk, it seems to have been believed in some circles that he was also the murderer of Mrs. Luard. Dickman, it was said, had met Mrs. Luard at the summer-house after she had written to him about a cheque which he had forged on her account, and had killed her in order to conceal the crime.

However, an account of the case published by ex-Superintendent Percy Savage in 1938 states: 'It remains an unsolved mystery. All our work was in vain. The murderer was never caught, as not a scrap of evidence was forthcoming on which we could justify an arrest, and to this day, I frankly admit that I have no idea who the criminal was.'

Crime of Dr. Geza de Kaplany, 1962

On 28 August 1962, a young married woman in San José, California, was admitted to hospital with third-degree burns covering sixty per cent of her body. Her breasts and genitals had been particularly badly burnt and her eyes were in such a frightful state that the pupils could not be seen. Hajna de Kaplany, twenty-year-old wife of a hospital anaesthetist, was writhing in agony when police arrived at her apartment, and ambulance men burnt their hands on her body when they moved her. She had been soaked in acid.

The police had been called to the apartment block by other residents, who reported hearing a horrifying wail against background sounds of loud classical music and running water. They found, in the couple's apartment, disintegrating, acid-soaked bedclothes, a large hole in the bedroom carpet, a leather carrying-case containing bottles of sulphuric, hydrochloric and nitric acids — the last of these only one-third full — a pair of rubber gloves and a medical prescription form on which a note had been written.

The note read: 'If you want to live — do not shout; do what I tell you; or else you will die.'

Dr Geza de Kaplany, aged thirty-six, was a Hungarian refugee working at one of the San José hospitals; he and his wife, a former model, had been married for only five weeks. He admitted responsibility for his wife's injuries,

235

telling police that he had soaked her in acid in order to deprive her of her beauty and warn her against adultery. When his wife died, after thirty-six days of intense suffering, he was charged with her murder.

De Kaplany, the 'Acid Doctor', was brought to trial in San José on 7 January 1963. He faced the court calmly at first, but became hysterical when photographic evidence of the crime was produced. Having already pleaded not guilty and not guilty by reason of insanity, he then declared that he was guilty. The reason given for the terrible way in which he had treated his wife was that his love for her had been rejected.

The jury reached a verdict of guilty on 1 March, the trial having lasted thirty-five days, and de Kaplany was sentenced to life imprisonment. He was released on parole in 1976, and went to work in Taiwan as a missionary.

Nancy Chadwick found murdered, 1948

AUGUST
29

On 29 August 1948, the body of Nancy Chadwick, an eccentric sixty-eight-year-old widow who worked as a housekeeper, was found at a roadside in Rawtenstall, Lancashire. She appeared at first to have been the victim of a hit-and-run accident, but on examination was found to have been battered over the head. The body was found by a bus driver near a house occupied by Margaret Allen, a forty-two-year-old lesbian, early in the morning.

Margaret Allen, a former bus conductress who called herself 'Bill', took a keen interest in the investigation which followed, and it was she who drew a constable's attention to the dead woman's empty handbag, which was lying in a river behind her home. During the two days which followed the discovery of the body she spoke to newspaper reporters — as well as anyone else who was willing to listen to her — in a local public house, suggesting reasons for the murder. Mrs. Chadwick had been an old fool to sit on a roadside bench counting her money, she said on one occasion.

Margaret Allen was a short, sturdy woman with cropped hair; she wore men's clothes and was generally unkempt. The twentieth of twenty-two children, she lived alone, smoking heavily and neglecting the need for proper meals. She was known to have a violent temper, and it was not long before her interest in Mrs. Chadwick's murder began to arouse suspicion. On 31 August she was interviewed by police officers, and the following day her home was searched. When bloodstains were found there she confessed to the crime.

Mrs. Chadwick, she said, had turned up at her house and asked to be allowed inside. Margaret Allen had not wanted to let her in, but the old woman 'seemed to insist' on it. A hammer was lying in the kitchen at the time, and Allen hit her with it on the spur of the moment. At this, '... she gave a shout and that seemed to start me off more, and I hit her a few times — I don't know how many ...' The body was hidden in the coal-house before being taken out and placed at the roadside after dark.

At her trial, which lasted only five hours, a plea of insanity was made on Margaret Allen's behalf, and her only close friend, Mrs. Annie Cook, gave evidence of the prisoner's history of depression and headaches. The accused did not give evidence herself, and the jury took just fifteen minutes to find her guilty. She was sentenced to death.

Mrs. Cook afterwards organized a petition in favour of a reprieve, but such was the prisoner's reputation that only 152 of the town's 26,000 inhabitants signed it. Ill-tempered to the end, Margaret Allen was hanged at Strangeways Prison on 12 January 1949. She was the first woman to be executed in Britain for twelve years.

Arrest of John and Janet Armstrong, 1956

On 1 September 1956, John Armstrong, a naval sickberth attendant, and his wife Janet were arrested for the murder of their five-month-old son Terence, who had died from barbiturate poisoning at their home in Gosport, near Portsmouth, on 22 July the previous year.

John Armstrong, at the time of the child's death, was twenty-five-years old and his wife nineteen. Their eldest child, Pamela, who was three, had been ill two months earlier, but had recovered in hospital; their second, a boy, had died at the age of three months in 1954. The illness, in each case, seemed to follow the same course.

Terence was at first thought to have died as a result of eating poisonous berries from the couple's garden, for the pathologist who carried out the postmortem found what appeared to be red skins in his stomach and throat.

But it was later found that these 'red skins' were, in fact, gelatine capsules which had contained Seconal, a powerful sleep-inducing drug. When the child's body was exhumed for re-examination, he was found to have swallowed enough of these capsules to cause his death in less than an hour.

Neither of the parents appeared grief-stricken over the loss of the child, and, though both denied that there had ever been any Seconal in the house, it was discovered that fifty capsules of it had been stolen in February 1955 from the hospital where John Armstrong worked. However, it was considered that there was not enough evidence to prove that either John or Janet Armstrong was guilty of murder, so neither was arrested at that time.

A year later, on 24 July 1956, Janet Armstrong applied to the Gosport magistrates for a separation order and

238

maintenance, alleging that her husband had repeatedly used violence against her, but the order was refused.

As she left the court in tears, a senior police officer approached her and asked whether she had anything she wanted to tell him. She then said that her husband had had Seconal in the house at the time of Terence's death, and that she had afterwards disposed of it at his request. She made a written statement giving the same information, and this additional piece of evidence led to a reconsideration of whether murder charges could be justified.

As both parents had been in the house at the time the capsules were swallowed, and as it appeared from other evidence that an unsuccessful attempt had been made to poison the child the previous day — at a time when the father was not there — it was decided that John and Janet Armstrong should be jointly charged.

They were brought to trial together in Winchester in December 1956, both pleading not guilty and accusing each other of the crime. John Armstrong was convicted, his death sentence being afterwards commuted to life imprisonment; his wife was acquitted. A month later Janet Armstrong admitted that she had given the child a capsule of Seconal to help him sleep.

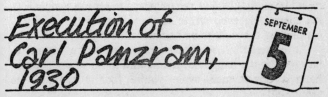

Execution of Carl Panzram, 1930

SEPTEMBER 5

The American murderer Carl Panzram, who was hanged on 5 September 1930, was a native of Warren, Minnesota; his parents were Prussian immigrants. Born in 1891, he turned to crime at an early age; he committed robberies at eleven, and was sent to a reform school, which he burnt down, at twelve. He never changed, except for the worse: he lived by robbery and burglary for the rest of his life — at least, when he was not in prison — and also committed many sex crimes, including murders.

'In my lifetime, I have murdered twenty-one human beings,' he declared in his autobiography. 'I have committed thousands of burglaries, robberies, larcenies, arsons and last but not least, I have committed sodomy on more than 1000 male human beings.'

The various accounts of his life, taken together, suggest that he actually killed rather more than twenty-one people; it is said, for example, that he killed ten people in one year alone. But it is impossible to say whether these claims are really true. Panzram was contemptuous of the rest of society and boasted about his crimes for the sake of being offensive. It is by no means inconceivable that he exaggerated for the same reason.

Panzram, at any rate, was arrested in Washington in 1928 for burglary and murder, and given a long term of imprisonment in Fort Leavenworth. 'I'll kill the first man who bothers me!' he threatened. On 20 June 1929, he killed Robert Warnke, the prison laundry superintendent. It was for this that he was sentenced to death.

He showed no remorse for his crimes and scoffed at opponents of the death penalty who tried to get him reprieved. 'I wish you all had one neck, and I had my hands on it,' he said. 'I believe the only way to reform people is to kill them.' He even wrote to President Herbert Hoover, demanding the right to be hanged without delay.

At his execution, which took place at Fort Leavenworth, he swore at the hangman, telling him to hurry up. 'I could hang a dozen men while you're fooling around!' he remarked.

His autobiography was published forty years later.

On the morning of 6 September 1949, Howard Unruh, a twenty-eight-year-old recluse, entered a shoemaker's shop a few doors from his home in Camden, New Jersey, armed with a Luger pistol and shot the shoemaker dead. Immediately afterwards he went to the barber's shop next door and killed the barber and a six-year-old boy whose hair he had been cutting. He then went to a drugstore next to the building in which he lived and, having shot a customer who was about to enter, killed the druggist, his wife and his mother.

Having thus murdered seven people in under six minutes, Unruh, who hated all his neighbours, began walking about outside, firing at anyone who could not take cover quickly enough. A man getting out of a delivery truck was shot dead; a youth crossing the road was wounded in the thigh and ankle; a young married woman was killed in her husband's cleaning shop, and a child of two was shot dead at the window of his parents' home.

By this time the street was almost deserted. Shopkeepers were locking and barricading their shops; urgent calls were being made for police, ambulances and doctors. The proprietor of a cafe shot the gunman from behind, causing a wound which made him limp. But he went on looking for more victims, and when a car stopped at the street corner, waiting for the traffic light to change, he killed its three occupants — a woman driver, her sixty-seven-year-old mother and her nine-year-old son. He then turned the corner and entered a house.

A woman screamed; her seventeen-year-old son tried to tackle him. But Unruh struck the youth over the head with his pistol and shot him in the arm. The woman was shot in the shoulder.

When he finally ran out of ammunition the gunman returned to the flat where he and his mother lived and barricaded himself in his bedroom. Having more ammunition there, he started firing from the window. But when the police closed in on him and hurled tear-gas into the room he gave himself up. He had killed thirteen people in fifteen minutes, and was later found to have a bullet from the cafe proprietor's gun lodged in his spine.

The police found other weapons in the basement of the building, where Unruh had set up a shooting range. They also learnt that before going out into the street that morning he had attempted to kill his mother.

Howard Unruh had no criminal record. He had served as a tank machine-gunner in Italy and France during the Second World War and, on returning to the United States, started to study pharmacy. However, he was seething with resentment towards his neighbours, seeing himself as a victim of frequent insults and irritations.

'I knew that some day I would kill them all,' he told the District Attorney, showing no remorse for his crimes.

Unruh was observed for a month by four psychiatrists, who found him to be mentally ill. Instead of being brought to trial, he was committed to the Trenton State Hospital for the Insane.

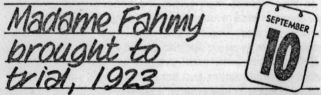

Madame Fahmy brought to trial, 1923

SEPTEMBER 10

On 10 September 1923, Marie-Marguerite Fahmy, a beautiful Frenchwoman of thirty-two, was brought to trial at the Old Bailey for the murder of her playboy husband,

Prince Ali Kamel Fahmy Bey, a wealthy Egyptian ten years her junior. Prince Fahmy had been shot and fatally wounded at London's Savoy Hotel, where the couple had occupied a luxury suite, in the early hours of 10 July previously, and the coroner's inquest had concluded with a verdict of wilful murder against his wife. When Mme Fahmy pleaded not guilty to the charge, the prosecuting counsel outlined the case.

It was explained that Fahmy Bey, the son of an engineer, had inherited his wealth from his father. He had met the prisoner, a divorcée, in Paris in May the previous year, and they had married a few months later, after she had become a Muslim. However, they had not been happy together and appeared to be incompatible.

Arriving in London at the beginning of July 1923, they had had a disagreement over an operation which the prisoner was to have, and at supper in the hotel restaurant on 9 July Mme Fahmy had allegedly threatened to smash a bottle over her husband's head. Later, after they had returned to their suite, a luggage porter heard three shots and arrived in time to see Mme Fahmy throwing down a pistol. Her husband, who was lying on the floor, was bleeding from the head. He died in hospital soon afterwards.

Seid Enani, who had been Prince Fahmy's secretary, was called as a witness and gave details of his late master's life and marriage. Cross-examined by Sir Edward Marshall Hall, he denied that Fahmy Bey had treated his wife 'with persistent cruelty', but acknowledged that he had been 'a bit unkind' to her. He was then obliged to admit that on one occasion Fahmy had struck the prisoner on the chin and dislocated her jaw.

'They were always quarrelling,' said Seid Enani.

The gun which had been used on the night of Fahmy's death was a .32 Browning automatic, capable of holding eight cartridges. Though it loaded automatically, the trigger had to be pressed for each shot. However, the prosecution's expert witness, Robert Churchill, conceded that when the gun was gripped tightly little pressure was needed to fire it.

A doctor who had been called to the scene of the tragedy said that he had been shown marks on Mme Fahmy's neck which, under cross-examination, he agreed could have been caused by a hand clutching her throat. Asked about the complaint for which an operation had been thought necessary, he said that it was a painful complaint which could have been caused by her husband, whose sexual demands were alleged by the defence to have been abnormal.

Called to give evidence in her own defence, the prisoner, speaking through an interpreter, said that her husband's black valet had followed her around continually and had been in the practice of entering her room when she was dressing. When she complained to her husband, he replied that the valet had the right to do this. 'He does not count,' said Fahmy. 'He is nobody.'

She went on to say that on one occasion, in Paris, her husband had seized her by the throat and threatened her with a horse-whip, and that on another he had sworn on the Koran that he would kill her. On a further occasion, she said, he had held her prisoner aboard his yacht for three days. 'Every time I threatened to leave him, he cried and promised to mend his ways,' said Mme Fahmy.

Asked about the night of his death, she said that she had picked up the revolver, which he had given her himself, when her husband advanced on her in a threatening manner during the course of a quarrel. She claimed that, having already fired one bullet out of the window, by accident, she had not realized that it was in a condition to be fired again.

'He seized me suddenly and brutally by the throat with his left hand,' she continued. 'His thumb was on my windpipe and his fingers were pressing on my neck. I pushed him away, but he crouched to spring on me, and said, "I will kill you."

'I lifted my arm in front of me and, without looking, pulled the trigger. The next moment I saw him on the ground before me without realizing what had happened. I do not know how many times the revolver went off. I did not know what had happened.'

Under cross-examination she said that she had not wanted to kill her husband. 'I only wanted to prevent him killing me,' she maintained. 'I thought the sight of the pistol might frighten him.'

The prisoner's sister, maid and chauffeur all corroborated her claims of ill-treatment at her husband's hands, and on the fifth day of the trial, after a moving speech by Marshall Hall which held the spectators spellbound, the jury returned a verdict of not guilty. At this, there were loud cheers and the judge ordered the court to be cleared.

'Oh, I am so happy, I am so thankful,' said Mme Fahmy as she was helped from the dock. 'It is terrible to have killed Ali, but I spoke the truth. I spoke the truth.'

The trial prompted an editorial in the *Daily Mirror*, stating that marriages between Oriental men and Western women were ridiculous and unseemly.

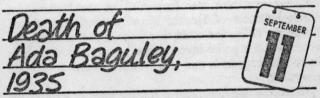

Death of Ada Baguley, 1935

SEPTEMBER 11

During the early hours of 11 September 1935, Ada Baguley, a bedridden fifty-year-old spinster weighing seventeen stone, died at a 'nursing home for aged and chronic cases' in Devon Drive, Nottingham, run by Dorothea Waddingham, an unqualified nurse aged thirty-six, and her thirty-nine-year-old lover, Ronald Sullivan. Her death was at first thought to have been caused by a cerebral haemorrhage, but a post-mortem revealed the presence of morphine in her body. The morphine had not been prescribed by the home physician.

Miss Baguley, who suffered from disseminated sclerosis, had been placed in the home in the company of her eighty-nine-year-old mother by the County Nursing Association the previous January. There was only one other patient there at the time — a Mrs. Kemp, who died shortly afterwards. But the new arrivals were satisfied with the care they received and, after a trial period lasting three weeks, agreed to remain there.

In May 1935 Ada Baguley, who owned a small business, made a will leaving her property to 'Nurse' Waddingham and her lover, in return for a promise that she and her mother would be looked after for the rest of their lives. But her mother's health began to decline almost immediately afterwards, and she died a few days later.

When Ada Baguley died Dorothea Waddingham sent the home physician a note which her patient had evidently signed a few days earlier. The note, which had been written by Sullivan, read: 'I desire to be cremated at my death, for health's sake and it is my wish to remain with Nurse and my last wish is my Relatives shall not know of my Death.' Sullivan had signed it himself as a witness.

When this note was forwarded to the Nottingham Medical Officer of Health, whose consent was needed before the cremation could take place, a post-mortem was ordered and a police investigation began. Mrs. Baguley's body was exhumed, and this was also found to contain morphine.

Dorothea Waddingham, a former ward orderly at the Burton-on-Trent workhouse, had a criminal record for theft and fraud. She had been married to a man named Thomas Leech, but reverted to her maiden name after his death. She was brought to trial at the Nottingham Assizes in February 1936, charged with Ada Baguley's murder.

Ronald Sullivan, who had won the Military Medal for gallantry during the First World War, was also brought to trial, but he was soon released as there was no direct evidence of his involvement in the crime.

Dorothea Waddingham denied responsiblity for Ada

Baguley's death, claiming that she had only given her morphine in accordance with her doctor's instructions. But the doctor told the court that he had never prescribed the drug and the prisoner was convicted. Despite a recommendation of mercy from the jury, she was hanged at Winson Green Prison, Birmingham, on 16 April 1936, shortly after writing a letter to Sullivan in which she asked him not to be afraid for her.

Budapest-Vienna Express blown up, 1931

SEPTEMBER 12

About midnight on 12 September 1931, the Budapest-Vienna night express train was blown up by a device placed on the Bia-Torbagy Viaduct in eastern Hungary. Twenty-two people were killed and fourteen others taken to a hospital in Budapest, seriously injured. A letter found near the scene suggested that the explosion had been caused by political extremists, and the Hungarian police suspected that it was the work of the same person or group of people who had blown up the Basle-Berlin Express at Jüterbog — causing many other casualties — on 8 August the same year.

Among the journalists who hurried to the scene during the next few hours was Hans Habe who, at twenty, was chief reporter for two Viennese newspapers. Speaking to survivors, he found several of them too shocked to be able to give him any information about the disaster. So, when a burly man of about forty with a military haircut introduced himself and began to give details of his own accord, Habe naturally took an interest in him, and later gave him a lift back to Vienna.

The man, Sylvester Matuska, was a Hungarian businessman living in Vienna with his wife and daughter; he said that he had been staying in Budapest on business. Far from being in a state of shock, he described the accident at length and gave the impression of being pleased to be the centre of attention. Later, in Vienna, he provided Habe with drawings of the wreckage and photographs of himself. The newspaper reports which resulted from this caused a sensation.

Having drawn so much attention to himself, however, Matuska was regarded with suspicion by both the Austrian and the Hungarian police. It was found that none of the other passengers could remember seeing him on the train; it was also discovered that he had secretly acquired large quantities of explosive from two different munitions factories prior to the crime. The police officers concerned therefore suspected that, although Matuska had bought a ticket for the journey to Vienna, he had actually travelled to the viaduct by car and arrived there in time to place the explosive on the track.

Arrested in October, Matuska was questioned not only about that particular explosion, but also about the one at Jüterbog, together with an earlier attempt at a similar crime at Anzbach in Lower Austria. He made a confession, and was brought to trial in Vienna on 15 June 1932.

Matuska, a former officer in the Sixth Honved Regiment, claimed that under the influence of a man named Bergmann, or the spirit of the same man, he had decided to found a Communist party which was in favour of the Christian religion, and it was for this reason that he had started wrecking trains. But his explanation was too confused to be taken seriously as a political motive, and it was also known that he had had an orgasm at the moment the disaster occurred. He was therefore considered to be a sadist.

Having been sentenced to six years' hard labour for attempting to cause an explosion at Anzbach, Matuska was returned to Hungary, where he was sentenced to death for the Bia-Torbagy crime. This sentence was automatically commuted to life imprisonment as the death penalty did not exist in the country from which he had been extradited. It appears that he remained in prison until Hungary was overrun by the Russians, and was then set free, but what finally became of him is unknown.

A report that he was captured by the Americans during the Korean War is unlikely to be true.

Minister and Sexton's wife found murdered, 1922

SEPTEMBER
16

On the morning of 16 September 1922, a courting couple found two bodies under a crab-apple tree off a quiet road on the outskirts of New Brunswick, a small town in New Jersey. The Reverend Edward Hall, rector of St John's Episcopal Church, and Mrs. Eleanor Mills, the church sexton's wife, had been murdered about thirty-six hours previously.

Both had been shot, the minister once and Mrs. Mills three times; Mrs. Mills, who sang in the church choir, had also had her throat cut and her tongue and vocal chords removed. Some passionate love letters which the rector had received from Mrs. Mills were found on the grass near the bodies.

It was already well known in New Brunswick that the couple had been having an affair, and there was even reason to suppose that they had been planning to elope together. So when murder charges were eventually brought against the rector's wife and her two brothers, after a lapse of four years, the case naturally excited much public interest.

The trial began in Somerville, New Jersey, early in

November 1926, the prosecution alleging that Mrs. Frances Hall had overheard her husband arranging to meet Mrs. Mills on the evening of 14 September 1922, and that she and her brothers, Henry and William Stevens, had planned to catch them in a compromising situation. The murders, according to the prosecutor, had followed a quarrel witnessed by Mrs. Jane Gibson, a fifty-four year-old widow who lived nearby.

The sexton, James Mills, appeared as a prosecution witness. He told the court that Mrs. Hall had called on him before the bodies were found, and that when he suggested to her that her husband and his wife had eloped she told him that they were dead. He admitted that he had read some of the rector's letters to his wife — which he had earlier denied — before selling them to a newspaper company.

Louise Geist, a former parlourmaid employed by the Halls, was also called to give evidence but denied having any evidence to give. Her own husband, in a petition for annulment of marriage, had accused her of having taken part in, or been an accessory to, the crime; it was this which had caused the case to be reopened after a grand jury had found that there was insufficient evidence to warrant a trial. But the maid claimed to have had no part in it and said that she did not know who was responsible for the deaths of the rector and the sexton's wife.

Mrs. Gibson, who became famous as a result of this case, was suffering from a kidney complaint and had to be brought into court on a stretcher. She gave evidence from a hospital bed, attended by a doctor and a nurse; as she kept pigs, the press called her 'the Pig Woman'.

On the night of the murders, she said, she had been roused by her dog. As she had had two rows of Indian corn stolen a few nights earlier, she went outside, hoping to catch the thief returning for more. But instead she witnessed a quarrel in the lane where the bodies were afterwards found, and then a struggle, which was followed by a scream and four shots.

Mrs. Gibson identified Mrs. Hall and William Stevens as two of the people concerned. However, she did not give the impression of being a trustworthy witness, and it was suspected that she had made up the whole story for the sake of publicity. This, at any rate, was the view of her elderly mother who, sitting close to her daughter's bed, repeatedly interrupted her testimony. 'She's a liar, a liar, a liar!' the Pig Woman's mother kept saying. 'That's what she is, and what she's always been!'

Mrs. Hall denied having taken part in the crime and said that her husband's behaviour had never given her cause to be suspicious. She said that on the night of the murders she had gone to the church, in the company of her brother William, to see if he had fallen asleep there. The next morning, she telephoned the police, to find out if any accidents had been reported. William Stevens corroborated her account.

On 3 December 1926, after a trial lasting a month, the defendants were all acquitted. Mrs. Hall's cousin, Henry Carpender, who had been awaiting trial on a charge of complicity in the murders, was released at the same time. The case remains unsolved, the only plausible solution which has so far been put forward being that the murders had been carried out by the Ku Klux Klan, which was active in New Jersey at that time, as a warning against adultery.

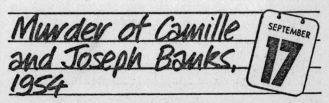

Murder of Camille and Joseph Banks, 1954

SEPTEMBER 17

On 17 September 1954, Mrs Camille Banks, a wealthy middle-aged divorcée, was found dead in her home at

Stinson Beach, California, in the company of her former husband; they had both been murdered. Mrs. Banks was in her bedroom, and had been battered over the head; her ex-husband, an alcoholic, lay on the settee in the living-room, surrounded by empty bottles.

Joseph Banks had been stabbed with a fourteen-inch kitchen knife. A suicide note left beside his body was found to be a forgery, and its wording indicated that it had been written by Mrs. Banks' Filipino houseboy, Bart Caritativo. Banks, in any case, was found to have been far too drunk to stab himself.

A typewritten will was also found. This had ostensibly been written by Mrs. Banks, and said that her entire estate was to go to Caritativo. However, it was written in broken English and contained misspellings of simple words. A letter which accompanied it had been written in the same fashion.

Bart Caritativo, aged forty-eight, had arrived in America in 1926. Mrs. Banks had been kindly disposed towards him, having found that, irrespective of his broken English and misspellings, he had literary aspirations; she had had similar aspirations herself. But following her divorce in 1954, she decided to sell her home and live abroad. The murders were discovered when a real estate agent arrived at her home to discuss the sale of the property.

Caritativo expressed shock at the murders and surprise at his apparent bequest. But handwriting experts were certain that he had forged the documents, and he was arrested for the murders. He was brought to trial in January 1955, convicted and sentenced to death. His execution took place in the gas chamber at San Quentin on 24 October 1958.

The prison psychiatrist later revealed that Caritativo, while under sentence of death, had confessed to the crimes.

Body found in Crypt, 1953

On the morning of 21 September 1953, a party of police officers and firemen equipped with arc-lights, picks and shovels began digging in the crypt of a Congregational Church in Halifax, Yorkshire. The crypt was huge, with extensive tunnels, but the work was confined to one particular corner. Before long the body of a little girl was discovered, and the men had to stop digging to await the arrival of a pathologist.

The body was that of Mary Hackett, aged six, who had been reported missing from her home in Lister Lane on 12 August after being allowed out to play in some nearby sand. She had died from head injuries caused either by blows with a blunt instrument, or through being repeatedly dashed against a wall or floor. As her face was unrecognizable, her parents had to identify her from her clothes.

The church was just across the road from Mary's home, and the crypt had been searched several times before without any trace of the missing girl being found. But the caretaker, a white-haired man named George Albert Hall, had aroused suspicion, and that corner, in which chairs and pews had been stacked and two tins of paint left open, had also been regarded with interest. To the police officers concerned, it seemed possible that the tins had been left open deliberately, so that the paint fumes would hide the smell of decomposing flesh.

Hall, who claimed to have heard 'whisperings' from the crypt on the day of Mary's disappearance, was already under constant surveillance. Now, in the light of this discovery, he was asked whether he knew anything which would assist the police in their investigation, and said that he did not.

253

But the following day he was followed to a mental hospital where he had once been a patient. There, it was afterwards learnt, he spoke to the resident medical superintendent for over an hour, during the course of which he said he had had nothing to do with Mary Hackett's death and that he had been told by a police officer, shortly after the body was found, that the little girl had died from injuries to the back of her head. This was clearly a lie, as the police officer — whom he named — had not known the cause of death at that time.

During subsequent interviews the caretaker made voluntary statements to the police which reinforced the belief that he was the murderer. He said, for example, that on the day Mary disappeared he had heard a child screaming, and that he had seen a strange man in the church grounds. He had mentioned this strange man before and even given a description of him, but had said nothing about the screaming. Eventually he was charged with the crime, and brought to trial at the Leeds Assizes.

Mary Hackett had not been sexually assaulted, and no motive could be found for her murder. The accused, however, was shown to be 'a glib liar' who had known the cause of her death before it was made public, and the jury found him guilty. He was hanged, at the age of forty-eight, at Leeds Prison in April 1954.

Body of Mary Jane Bennett discovered, 1900

SEPTEMBER 23

On the morning of 23 September 1900, a young woman's body was found on the beach at Yarmouth. She had been strangled with a bootlace during the course of the previous night, the disarrangement of her clothes indicating that she had also been the victim of a sexual assault. A local landlady recognized the body as that of a Mrs. Hood, who had been spending a holiday in Yarmouth since 15 September. But laundry marks on the victim's clothes led to her being identified as Mary Jane Bennett, the wife of Herbert John Bennett, who was later found in Woolwich.

Bennett and his wife, though separated for some time, had been seen together in the town on the night of the murder, and a booking-clerk at Yarmouth Station claimed that Bennett had travelled back to London on the 7.20 train the following morning. A gold chain which, according to her landlady, Mrs. Bennett had been wearing on the evening of 22 September, was found in her husband's lodgings. It was also discovered that Bennett, who had been unfaithful to his wife many times, had entered into a liaison with a parlourmaid named Alice Meadows whom he intended to marry.

Bennett had met his wife in Northfleet, Kent, some years earlier; he was a grocer's assistant at the time and she became his music teacher. Following their marriage in 1897, they bought old violins cheaply for Mrs. Bennett to hawk from door to door, pleading near-starvation. The £400 which they made in one year by this means enabled them to set up a grocery business — the premises conveniently catching fire after being insured. Bennett later went to South Africa, from where he was soon deported on suspicion of being a spy for the Boers.

At the time of his arrest, he was working at Woolwich Arsenal, but had far more money in his possession than could have been obtained from this employment; he refused to say where it had come from and the police were unable to discover the source of it themselves. As Mrs. Bennett had given a false name and other false information to her landlady in Yarmouth, it is possible that she and her husband, despite their separation, were engaged in a further joint venture just before her death.

Brought to trial for murder at the Old Bailey, Bennett

pleaded not guilty, but the evidence against him was overwhelming. In view of his character and apparent inability to tell the truth about anything, his barrister did not dare to call him as a witness in his own defence, for fear of making the prosecution's case even stronger.

Bennett, aged twenty-two, was hanged at Norwich Prison on 21 March 1901. When the black flag was raised to show that the execution had been carried out, the flagstaff snapped. Some took this to be a sign that a miscarriage of justice had just taken place.

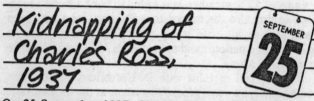

Kidnapping of Charles Ross, 1937

SEPTEMBER 25

On 25 September 1937, Charles Ross, a wealthy Chicago businessman aged seventy-two, was kidnapped at gunpoint by two men while driving with his secretary in Franklin Park, Illinois. The kidnappers forced his limousine to a halt by swerving in front of it, then ordered Ross to get into their own car. His secretary, who was left behind, reported what had happened.

Ross was taken to Wisconsin and made to write to a friend, asking him to raise a ransom of $50,000. After a second note had been received the money was delivered, Mrs. Ross inserting an advertisement in a Chicago newspaper as instructed by the kidnappers. A third note then stated that Ross would be released when the money had been spent. But he was never seen alive again.

The FBI carried out a full-scale search, with J. Edgar Hoover personally in charge of it. The ransom notes were found to have been written on a new typewriter, and inquiries were made about recent sales in Chicago. The purchaser of one model was traced to a rooming-house, and fingerprints which were discovered there matched others found on the notes.

By this time marked bills in which the ransom had been paid had started turning up at racetracks, their disposal following a definite pattern. It was this pattern which resulted in the arrest of John Henry Seadlund at a track in Los Angeles on 14 January 1938.

Seadlund, an occasional labourer with a record of petty crime, admitted his part in the kidnapping and said that he had murdered his accomplice, James Atwood Gray, as well as Charles Ross. He led the FBI to a pit in Spooner, Wisconsin, where the bodies of both men had been buried. 'Will I be hanged or fried?' he asked indifferently.

He was executed in the electric chair later the same year, at the age of twenty-eight.

Murder of a Shepherd's wife 1947

SEPTEMBER 26

On 26 September 1947, Catherine McIntyre, forty-seven-year-old wife of a head shepherd, was found murdered at her home in Kenmore, near the small Perthshire town of Aberfeldy. She had been bound, gagged and battered over the head, and her murderer had escaped with £90 in cash — the wages of the shepherds in her husband's charge — as well as Mrs. McIntyre's wedding ring.

Though no fingerprints had been left at the scene, the police found various items in a nearby area of bracken, which had evidently been used as a hideout. These included a sawn-off shotgun, a bloodstained handkerchief, a used razor blade and the return half of a railway ticket of a special type issued to members of the Armed Forces.

Following appeals to the public for information, the gun was recognized by a farmer in Old Meldrum, Aberdeenshire, who said that he had borrowed it from a neighbour but afterwards found it to be missing from his farm. A Polish soldier named Stanislaw Myszka had been casually employed there at the time and was suspected of having stolen it, the farmer added.

A taxi-driver then revealed that he had driven a man of Myszka's description from Aberfeldy to Perth on the afternoon of 26 September and the police announced that they wished to interview this man in connection with the crime.

Myszka, a twenty-three-year-old deserter from the Polish Army in Exile, was arrested at an old RAF camp near Peterhead on 2 October, and a wedding ring similar to Mrs. McIntyre's was found hidden in one of his shoes. He had been staying with a Polish couple at Ardallie, in the same county, but fled after hearing that the police wanted to question him.

He denied having committed the crime, but hairs taken from a razor with which he had been shaved in prison appeared to be identical in structure to others found on the discarded razor blade near the scene. This, together with other incriminating pieces of evidence, led the jury at his trial to find him guilty, and he was hanged in Perth on 6 February 1948.

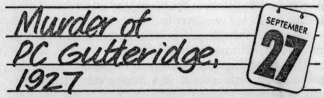

Murder of PC Gutteridge, 1927

SEPTEMBER 27

On the morning of 27 September 1927, the body of PC George Gutteridge was found in a country lane between

Romford and Ongar in Essex. He had been shot four times — twice through the left cheek and once in each eye. His pencil was clutched in his hand and his pocket-book was found nearby. It was assumed from this that he had been taken by surprise as he was about to write something in the pocket-book. His death was estimated to have occurred between 4 and 5 a.m.

About 2.30 the same morning a car belonging to Dr. Edward Lovell had been stolen from a garage at the owner's house in London Road, Billericay — about ten miles away. When this was later found abandoned in Brixton, south London, there were bloodstains on the runningboard by the driver's door; there was also an empty cartridge case under one of the seats. Following these discoveries, the police began to keep known car thieves under surveillance.

One of these thieves was Frederick Guy Browne, a forty-six-year-old mechanic who had a garage near Clapham Junction. Browne, a married man with one daughter, had served several prison sentences and was known to be violent. In January 1928 he was arrested in connection with the theft of a Vauxhall two months earlier. Police searches then led to the discovery of two loaded Webley revolvers in his garage and two other guns, also loaded, in his rooms off Lavender Hill.

The police at first said nothing to him about the murder, but on finding these weapons they strongly suspected that he had been involved in it. A few days later his former accomplice, William Henry Kennedy, who was believed to have taken part in the same theft, was arrested in Liverpool.

Kennedy, a thirty-six-year-old drunkard, also had a criminal record, his offences including burglary, housebreaking, theft and indecent exposure. He had a pistol in his possession and tried to shoot the police officer who confronted him, but the safety catch was in position and the gun merely clicked. He was quickly overpowered.

Taken to New Scotland Yard, Kennedy was asked if he

259

had any information to give about the murder of PC Gutteridge. He asked to be allowed to think for a few minutes before answering, and then to see his wife. When Mrs. Kennedy, whom he had only married a few days previously, told him to tell the truth about what had happened, he made a long statement, admitting that he had been present at the crime but blaming Browne for it.

He and Browne, he said, had stolen Dr. Lovell's car and were driving it back to London by a route which avoided main roads when PC Gutteridge saw them and signalled to them to stop. They drove on, but stopped when they heard a police whistle and waited until he came over to speak to them.

Not satisfied with the answers to his questions, Gutteridge took out his pocket-book and was about to begin writing in it when Browne, who had been driving, fired two shots at him at close range. The two thieves then got out of the car and Browne, with Kennedy trying to restrain him, fired two more shots as his victim lay groaning on the ground.

Browne and Kennedy were both charged with murder and brought to trial at the Old Bailey on 23 April. Ballistics evidence was given with great effect, the Crown's expert, Robert Churchill, demonstrating that the cartridge case found in the stolen car had markings which matched others produced by test shots fired from one of Browne's revolvers. Powder discoloration on the victim's skin had been found to match the powder used in one of two obsolete types of ammunition found in the same gun.

Browne said that Kennedy's statement was a 'pack of wilful or imaginative lies', claiming that he had been at home in bed at the time of the murder. Kennedy stuck to his story that Browne alone was responsible for the murder, concluding, 'I can only now express my deep regret to Mrs. Gutteridge that I should have been in the car on the night of the crime.' Both men were found guilty and sentenced to death. They were hanged on 31 May 1928 — Browne at Pentonville Prison and Kennedy at Wandsworth.

Kennedy, the night before the executions, had written to his wife, urging her to join him in heaven.

Kidnapping of Bobby Greenlease, 1953

On 28 September 1953, Bobby Greenlease, the six-year-old son of a millionaire car-dealer, was taken from his convent school in Kansas City, Missouri, by a woman pretending to be his aunt. The boy's mother had suffered a heart attack and wanted to see him at once, according to the woman in question. But later, when the acting Sister Superior called Bobby's home to inquire about his mother's condition, Mrs. Greenlease answered the telephone herself. It was then realized that the boy had been abducted.

Shortly afterwards a ransom note was received, demanding $600,000 in $10 and $20 bills from each of the twelve federal reserve districts. Robert C. Greenlease Sr, the boy's father, immediately made arrangements to comply with this instruction, and during the next few days received a number of telephone calls from a man calling himself 'M', who promised that he would get Bobby back when the ransom had been paid.

Eventually the money, crammed into an army duffel bag, was thrown into a culvert outside Kansas City, and Mr. and Mrs. Greenlease waited anxiously for news that their son had been released. But they waited in vain, for Bobby was already dead.

On 6 October, two days after delivery of the ransom, police in St Louis, in the same state, learnt that a man had been parting with large sums of money in a casual manner

Carl Austin Hall, a convict on parole, was promptly arrested in a hotel suite, and found to have nearly $300,000 in cash in two suitcases. He admitted that he was one of the kidnappers, and led police to his mistress, Mrs. Bonnie Brown Heady, a forty-one-year-old alcoholic. It was Mrs. Heady who had taken Bobby from school and, though Hall said that she hadn't known the boy was being kidnapped, her fingerprints were found to match those on the ransom note.

It later emerged that Bobby had been shot and his body buried in quicklime in the backyard of Mrs. Heady's house in St. Joseph, Missouri — in a grave which had been dug beforehand. Hall had originally intended to strangle him, but the piece of rope which he had brought along for this purpose had proved to be too short, and his little victim had put up a fierce resistance. He had been dead at the time the ransom was demanded.

Hall and Mrs. Heady were quickly brought to trial and sentenced to death. They made no appeal, but likewise showed little remorse until the day of their execution drew near. They then wrote letters to Robert Greenlease Sr, begging his forgiveness for the suffering which they had caused. They were jointly executed in the gas chamber at the Missouri State Penitentiary on the night of 17 December 1953.

The rest of the ransom money was never recovered.

Human remains found near Moffat, 1935

SEPTEMBER 29

On 29 September 1935, a woman standing on a bridge near Moffat, on the Carlisle to Edinburgh road, saw a human arm lying on the bank of the stream below. When this was reported to the police a search of the area began and further human remains, including two heads and a trunk, were discovered.

Though these had been mutilated in order to hinder identification, some of them had been wrapped in a special edition of the *Sunday Graphic*, which had been distributed in Morecambe and Lancaster on 15 September.

This led police officers to suspect that the remains were those of the common-law wife of Dr. Buck Ruxton, a general practitioner in Lancaster, and their children's nursemaid, Mary Rogerson, neither of whom had been seen since 14 September.

Ruxton, aged thirty-six, was a Parsee who had qualified at the Universities of Bombay and London; his name had originally been Bukhtyar Hakim. He had acquired his practice in 1930, by which time Isabella Ruxton, then aged twenty-nine, had been living with him for two years. By 1935 they had three children.

It was known to the police that the couple often quarrelled and that Ruxton, who suspected his wife of infidelity, had several times used violence and threatened to kill her.

Prior to the discovery of the remains he had given various explanations for the absence of the two women, finally claiming that they had gone to Edinburgh together. Then, when the remains were found, he denied that they were the bodies of his wife and Mary Rogerson, and asked the police if a statement could be issued to that effect. 'All this damned nonsense is ruining my practice!' he complained.

But one of his female patients, who had been asked to scrub his staircase on 15 September, showed a police officer some carpets, felt stair-pads and a suit of clothes — all bloodstained — which Ruxton had given to her.

More bloodstained carpets were found in the possession of his charwoman, Mrs. Oxley, and a georgette blouse in which some of the remains had been wrapped was identified as having belonged to Mary Rogerson.

263

Following Ruxton's arrest on 13 October, fingerprints and palmprints found in his house proved to be identical to those taken from the left hand of one of the murder victims; bloodstains were found on the bathroom floor and in other parts of the house, and blood and human debris were found in his drains.

Ruxton was brought to trial at the Manchester Assizes the following March, the prosecution contending that he had strangled his wife in a fit of rage and then killed Mary Rogerson because she had witnessed or discovered the crime. Though Ruxton denied this, he was convicted and sentenced to death. His execution took place at Strangeways Prison on 12 May 1936, his confession being published the following Sunday.

Execution of Patrick Higgins, 1913

OCTOBER 1

On 1 October 1913, Patrick Higgins, a widower, was hanged in Edinburgh for the murder of his two small sons. The crime had taken place nearly two years earlier, but had not been discovered until June 1913, when the two bodies, tied together with sash-cord, were found in a water-filled quarry near Winchburgh, in West Lothian. Higgins, a former soldier who had served in India, admitted the justice of his sentence and awaited execution with little concern. He blamed his heavy drinking for his downfall.

Some years earlier, following his discharge from the army, he had returned to Winchburgh and married a local girl; their first son, William, was born in December 1904, their second, John, in August 1907. But, though employed at the Winchburgh Brickworks, where he earned 24s

(£1.20) a week, Higgins neglected his family — and later, after his wife's death in 1910, began to get into trouble with the law for failing to maintain the children.

On one occasion, in 1911, he was jailed for two months; then, when he boarded them with a widow in nearby Broxburn but failed to pay for their keep, he was warned that he would be prosecuted again. He therefore took the boys away from the widow, but was unwilling to pay for their keep elsewhere. It was then, in November 1911, that he murdered them, the children having evidently walked out to the secluded quarry with him, without any inkling of his intention.

Higgins, by this time, was spending most of his money on drink. He stayed at a lodging-house when he could afford it, but often had to sleep at the brickworks, making soup in his pail and using his spade as a frying-pan. He explained the disappearance of his sons in various ways, generally by saying that he had given them away to two women he had met on a train. He was arrested within a few days of the discovery of the bodies, the stamp of a poor-house on one of the boy's shirts having helped the police to identify them.

Besides being a heavy drinker, Higgins had a history of epilepsy: it was for this reason that he had been discharged from the army, and several witnesses at his trial stated that they had seen him having fits. The defence counsel argued that because of this illness he had been of unsound mind at the time of the crime, but the jury found him to be sane and their recommendation of mercy proved unavailing.

Higgins's execution was carried out on a scaffold which had been erected in the well of a staircase next to the condemned cell. It was Edinburgh's first execution for many years, and caused much excitement among the inhabitants. However, the crowds outside the prison dispersed without incident as soon as the black flag appeared, many of them to go to the Musselburg Races. The prison governor later published a letter from Higgins, thanking him for the kindness which he had received during his incarceration.

On 7 October 1942, troops exercising on Hankley Common, near Godalming in Surrey, found the decomposed body of a young woman lying under a mound of earth at the top of a hill. The back of her head had been smashed in with a heavy, blunt instrument and there were also stab wounds in her head and forearm. It was quickly established that the murder had taken place some weeks earlier and that the body had been dragged to the place where it was buried.

The body proved to be that of nineteen-year-old Joan Wolfe who, having run away from home several months before, had been living in a little hut made of branches, twigs and leaves in nearby woods. A search of the area resulted in the discovery of a letter which she had written to a French-Canadian soldier named August Sangret, stationed about two miles away at Witley Camp, telling him that she was pregnant and making it clear that she expected him to marry her.

The blunt instrument, a heavy stake of birch wood, was also found; it had hairs attached to its thicker end which matched those of the victim, but its surface was too rough to provide any fingerprints. The knife which had been used, which was known to have a distinctive hooked point, did not come to light until some weeks later.

August Sangret, an illiterate man with Red Indian ancestors, admitted having been intimate with Joan Wolfe and identified her clothes and belongings. He said that he had not seen her for weeks and did not know what had become of her. Finally, after making a statement running to 17,000 words — it had taken him five days, during the course of which he had not been told that she was dead —

he remarked, 'I guess you found her. I guess I shall get the blame.'

Even so, there was not enough evidence to justify a charge against him. No knife had been found among his possessions; stains found on one of his blankets and also on his battledress trousers could not be positively shown to be blood. Though strongly suspecting him of the crime, the police had no choice but to let him go free while they continued to search for the knife.

Then, on 26 November, a black, bone-handled clasp-knife with a hooked blade was found blocking a drain of the washhouse attached to the guardroom at Witley Camp. Sangret, on being questioned about it, was tricked into making statements which incriminated him. The fact that he had hidden the knife, which he said had belonged to Joan Wolfe, was regarded as evidence of his guilt because he would not have known of the victim's stabbing injuries at the time unless he had inflicted them himself.

Sangret was arrested and brought to trial for the 'Wigwam Murder' at the Kingston Assizes the following February. It was alleged by the prosecution that he had killed Joan Wolfe because she was pregnant, and had then — in keeping with a Red Indian tradition — dragged her body 400 yards in order to bury her on high ground. The jury found him guilty and, in spite of a recommendation of mercy, he was hanged at Wandsworth Prison in April 1943. He was thirty years old.

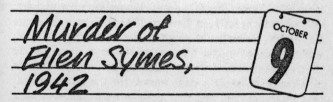

Murder of Ellen Symes, 1942

Taking her four-year-old son home on the night of 9 October 1942, Mrs. Ellen Symes, of Strood, Kent, was attacked and stabbed in the neck by a soldier in uniform. The crime took place close to her home in Brompton Farm Road, the owner of a nearby house going out to investigate after hearing screams. Mrs. Symes, who had collapsed in the road, died shortly afterwards, but her little boy was unharmed. The attacker fled from the scene.

The following morning a soldier in the Gravesend Road was seen acting suspiciously and taken to Rochester police station. He was Gunner Reginald Buckfield, a married man with three children whose constant smiling and good nature had earned him the nickname of 'Smiler'. Having deserted from an anti-aircraft unit at Gravesend, he had been working as a casual labourer on farms, his most recent job having been at Hoo, three miles from Strood, just before the murder.

Buckfield was held in custody by the police prior to being handed over to the military authorities. He spent his time writing a crime story, called *The Mystery of the Brompton Road Murders*, with a character named 'Smiler' who was presented in flattering terms. On leaving police custody under military escort, he handed the unfinished story to a detective, assuring him that he would find it very interesting.

Though he claimed that the story was fictitious, Buckfield had written into it details of the murder of Ellen Symes which only the murderer himself could have known, he was therefore regarded as a suspect. Later he was found to be the owner of a table-knife which had been discovered in a garden near the scene of the crime. So, four weeks after Ellen Symes' death, he was charged with her murder.

Two months later, in January 1943, he was tried at the Old Bailey. He smiled throughout the proceedings, though witnesses called to give him an alibi failed to do so and he contradicted his own statements. Despite the failure of the prosecution to show a clear motive for the attack, Buckfield was convicted and sentenced to death. He was later judged to be insane and committed to Broadmoor.

Murder of Mr and Mrs Goodman 1949

At ten o'clock on the night of 10 October 1949, Leopold Goodman, a wealthy forty-nine-year-old Russian Jew, and his wife Esther, aged forty-seven were found murdered in the dining-room of their home in Ashcombe Gardens, Edgware, Middlesex. They had both been battered over the head, the same weapon — the base of a television aerial — being used in each case. There were no signs of robbery; in fact, large sums of money had been left untouched in different parts of the house. The murder weapon was found in the scullery.

Earlier that evening Mr. and Mrs. Goodman had visited their daughter and her four-day-old son at a maternity home in Muswell Hill, leaving the building about 9 p.m. Their son-in-law Daniel Raven, a twenty-three-year-old advertising agent, had been there too, and had left shortly after them. Raven lived with his wife in nearby Edgwarebury Lane, their house having been bought for them by his father-in-law. On being asked by telephone to come to the Goodmans' house straight away, he arrived immaculately dressed in a light grey suit.

'Why did they tell me to go?' he asked, as he sat crying on the stairs. 'Why didn't they let me stop?'

He said that he had driven his wife's parents back from the maternity home and had wanted to stay with them as they had recently had a burglary and were worried about the possibility of another; he had only returned to his own home at their insistence, he continued. However, the police officer in charge of the case was suspicious of Daniel Raven's account, and on learning from another source that the young man had been wearing a different suit earlier, he took him to Edgware police station for further questioning.

Raven, on being asked for the keys of his house, handed them over, telling Detective Inspector J. Diller that he would find nothing there. 'I only had a bath,' he said. But on entering the house at 11.45 p.m., Diller noticed a smell of burning coming from the kitchen and managed to retrieve part of a dark blue suit from the blazing boiler. This was later found to be bloodstained, the blood being of the same rare group as the Goodmans'. In the bathroom there was no evidence of anyone having recently had a bath.

A search of the premises resulted in the discovery of a pair of shoes which had been washed and hidden in the garage; it was also found that the driver's seat of Raven's car had been scrubbed. Bloodstains of the same type were discovered on both articles.

When Daniel Raven was asked to explain the suit he admitted that it was his own, but said that he did not know how the blood had got on to it. He had left it in the bathroom, he said. On being charged with his father-in-law's murder, he protested his innocence, claiming that Leopold Goodman had made enemies by engaging in crooked business practices.

Raven was brought to trial at the Old Bailey on 22 November 1949. Despite the failure of the prosecution to show that he had a motive for the crime, he was found guilty two days later. It was afterwards contended, in support of an appeal, that he was insane, medical evidence being produced to show that he had a history of 'blackouts and brainstorms'. He was, however, hanged, the execution taking place at Pentonville Prison on 6 January 1950.

Execution of Linwood Briley, 1984

OCTOBER 13

On 13 October 1984, Linwood Earl Briley, aged thirty, was executed in the electric chair at the state penitentiary in Richmond, Virginia, for the murder of a disc jockey five years earlier. It was not his only crime, for he had also received seven life sentences for eleven other murders and robberies. Moreover, he had led the biggest escape from Death Row in the United States' history only five months before his death.

The escape had taken place at the Mecklenberg Correctional Centre in Boydton, in the same state, on 31 May, when Briley, his brother James and four other convicted murderers had overpowered six guards, stolen their uniforms and driven out of the institution in an official van, pretending that they were removing a bomb.

Though the other four were all back in custody within eight days, the two brothers remained at large until 19 June, when they surrendered to FBI agents after being discovered in a garage owned by a relative in Philadelphia.

Linwood Briley behaved calmly at his execution, maintaining that he was innocent of the crime for which he had been condemned. His brother James, who had murdered a pregnant woman and her five-year-old son during the course of a robbery, followed him to the electric chair six months later.

A third brother, Anthony, had also been convicted of murder and was serving a life sentence.

Murder of Mrs Greenhill, 1941

OCTOBER
14

On 14 October 1941, Mrs. Theodora Greenhill, sixty-five-year-old widow of an army officer, was found murdered in the drawing-room of her self-contained flat in Elsham Road, West Kensington. She had been struck on the head with a beer bottle as she sat at her writing bureau, then strangled with a ligature as she lay unconscious on the floor. On the bureau, which had been ransacked, lay a sheet of paper bearing the words: 'Received from Dr. H.D. Trevor the s . . .' The writing ended abruptly with a jagged line.

Mrs. Greenhill had been trying to let the flat so that she could move out of London, and it appeared that her murderer had pretended to be a prospective tenant. After killing the old lady he had covered her face with a handkerchief; he had also gathered up some of the broken glass and put it into a waste-paper basket. The contents of a cash-box had been stolen from the victim's bedroom.

Detective Chief Superintendent Fred Cherrill, Scotland Yard's fingerprint expert, thought that the name Trevor seemed familiar, and asked the Criminal Record Office to send all files bearing it to the scene of the crime.

By the time they arrived Cherrill had found fingerprints on some of the pieces of glass, on a table near the body and on the cash-box. After spending a few minutes comparing these with the prints in the CRO files, he was able to say to the officer in charge of the investigation, 'The man we want is Harold Dorian Trevor.'

Trevor, aged sixty-two, was well known to the police. A tall, slim man with grey hair and a monocle, he had a long record of fraud and theft and had been free for a total of only forty-eight weeks during the previous forty-two years.

He was arrested as he left a telephone kiosk in Rhyl four days later.

'It wasn't murder,' he said after being cautioned. 'There was never any intent to murder. I have never used violence to anyone in my life before. What came over me I do not know. After I hit her my mind went completely blank and is still like that now. Something seemed to crack in my head.'

He was brought to trial at the Old Bailey the following January, a plea of insanity being made on his behalf. On being found guilty, he made a long, impassioned speech which the spectators found very moving.

'If I am called upon to take my stand in the cold, grey dawn of the early morning, I pray that God in His mercy will gently turn my mother's face away as I pass into the shadows,' he said. 'No fear touches my heart. My heart is dead. It died when my mother left me.'

It was to be the last of many courtroom speeches made by Harold Trevor, and could make no difference to the sentence that was passed on him. He was hanged at Wandsworth Prison on 11 March 1942.

Disappearance of John and Phoebe Harries, 1953

OCTOBER 16

On 16 October 1953, John Harries, aged sixty-three, and his fifty-four-year-old wife Phoebe disappeared from their farm at Llanginning, near St Clears in Carmarthenshire, shortly after attending a local harvest thanksgiving service. Ronald Harries, their twenty-four-year-old adopted nephew, claimed that they had gone to London for a holiday, leaving him to look after the place. But they were never seen alive again, and three weeks after their disappearance the Carmarthenshire police asked Scotland Yard to help in the search for them.

Ronald Harries, who claimed to have driven the missing couple to Carmarthen railway station on the morning of 17 October, was regarded with suspicion. The discovery that Phoebe Harries had left an uncooked joint of meat in her oven suggested that she had not left the farm intentionally. Then a cheque written by John Harries was found to be fraudulent when presented for payment by his nephew: it had originally been made out for £9, but this sum had afterwards been changed to £909.

The police suspected that John and Phoebe Harries had been murdered and their bodies buried near Cadno Farm, where Ronald Harries lived. In the hope that Ronald would lead them to the bodies, they tied cotton threads across every exit, then made a lot of noise in the vicinity of the farmhouse, causing him to fear that the bodies had already been discovered.

The next morning, at dawn, they found that one of the threads had been broken. The bodies of the missing couple were then found buried in the adjoining field; they had both been battered to death. Ronald Harries was charged with their murders.

Four days after his arrest the murder weapon — a hammer which he had borrowed from a Mr. Lewis on the night of 16 October — was found buried in the undergrowth around the farm.

Ronald Harries was brought to trial at the Carmarthen Assizes in March 1954. It was clear from the evidence that he had killed his uncle and aunt for the sake of their money and property at a time when he was in financial difficulties, and that he had taken over their farm immediately afterwards. He was convicted and sentenced to death, his execution being carried out at Swansea Prison.

On 18 October 1982, Arnfinn Nesset, a forty-six-year-old former nursing-home manager, was brought to trial in Trondheim, accused of twenty-five murders and a number of other offences. It was alleged that between 1977 and November 1980, he had murdered fourteen women and eleven men, all of whom were patients at the Orkdal nursing home for the elderly, by injecting poison into their veins.

The trial lasted nearly five months, becoming the longest criminal trial in Norwegian history, with over 150 witnesses. The accused, a thin, bespectacled man, pleaded not guilty to all charges. Finally, in March 1983, the jury found him guilty of the murder of twelve women and ten men and the attempted murder of one woman.

Nesset's victims, aged between sixty-seven and ninety-four, had been killed with curacit. The court was told that after his arrest on 9 March 1981, the prisoner had admitted not only the twenty-five murders with which he was charged, but also five others. The jury of six women and four men found that in addition to the crimes of murder and attempted murder, he was guilty of forgery and embezzlement of about 13,000 kroner (£1200) from patients.

Though declared sane by medical experts, Nesset appeared to have had no real motive for the murders. Following his conviction, arguments were entered on whether they had been mercy killings, but the court found that they had not been. It was then accepted that he was suffering from permanently impaired mental faculties. The maximum sentence of twenty-one years' imprisonment and up to ten years' preventive detention was nonetheless passed on him.

275

It was the worst case of mass murder in any of the Nordic countries in modern times.

Death of Matilda Clover, 1891

On 20 October 1891, Matilda Clover, a twenty-six-year-old prostitute, was found writhing in agony in a brothel in Lambeth Road, south-east London. She managed to say that a man named Fred had given her some white pills, but little attention was paid to this at the time, and when she died shortly afterwards, her death was put down to alcohol poisoning. She was buried in a pauper's grave at Tooting.

The previous week, on the evening of 13 October, another prostitute, nineteen-year-old Ellen Donworth, had died on the way to hospital after collapsing on a pavement near her lodgings in Duke Street, off Westminster Bridge Road. Before her death she was able to say that a tall, cross-eyed gentleman with a silk hat had given her some 'white stuff' to drink from a bottle earlier the same evening. In this case, a post-mortem revealed that the girl had died from poisoning with strychnine.

Nobody seems to have suspected that 'Fred' and this cross-eyed gentleman were the same person until the following April, when two other young prostitutes died, also from strychnine poisoning. Emma Shrivell, aged eighteen, and Alice Marsh, twenty, both lived at a brothel in Stamford Street and claimed to have been visited by a doctor named Fred, who had given them some pills. It was after these deaths that Matilda Clover's body was exhumed and she, too, was found to have been poisoned with strychnine.

While the newspapers speculated wildly about the murderer's identity, Dr. Thomas Neill Cream, who since 9 April had been living in lodgings at 103, Lambeth Palace Road, began accusing a fellow lodger — a medical student named Walter Harper — of being responsible for the deaths.

Cream, who at this time was known as Thomas Neill, wrote to Harper's father, a doctor in Barnstaple, saying that he had evidence of his son's guilt. He offered to sell this evidence to him for £1500, but said that he would otherwise give it to the coroner concerned. The letter led to Cream's arrest on a charge of attempted extortion on 3 June.

But by this time Cream was suspected of the murders himself, and had been under police surveillance following inquiries into the rumours which he had spread in his own neighbourhood. He was later charged with the murder of Matilda Clover, and brought to trial at the Old Bailey on 17 October the same year.

The evidence against him was overwhelming, and included the testimony of Louise Harvey, a prostitute, who told the court that one evening in October 1891 the prisoner, who had spent the previous night with her, had given her some pills which she pretended to swallow but actually threw away. Other evidence was given of the doctor buying *nux vomica* — containing strychnine — and gelatine capsules from a chemist, and the finding of seven bottles of strychnine at his lodgings.

The jury was left in no doubt that the accused had murdered not only Matilda Clover, but the other three prostitutes as well, and on being found guilty he was sentenced to death.

Cream, a Scotsman who had graduated in Canada, had been in trouble before. While practising as a doctor in Chicago in 1881 he had poisoned a patient named Daniel Stott, with whose wife he had been having an affair. His other known crimes included arson, abortion, blackmail, fraud and theft.

Having received a life sentence for Stott's murder, he had been released from Joliet Prison, Illinois, in July 1891, shortly after inheriting $116,000 from his father. The murder of Ellen Donworth had taken place less than two weeks after his arrival in England.

On 15 November 1892, Neill Cream, aged forty-two, was hanged at Newgate Prison. Just before the trap opened he started to say that he was 'Jack the Ripper', but in view of his life sentence in America the claim is not generally taken seriously.

After his death his clothes and belongings were sold to Madame Tussaud's for £200.

Torso found in Essex Marsh, 1949

OCTOBER 21

On 21 October 1949, a farm labourer hunting wildfowl on the Essex marshes near Tillingham found a human torso wrapped in felt floating on the water. Horrified though he must have been by the discovery, Mr. Sidney Tiffin had the presence of mind to secure the bundle to a stake driven into the mud, before going off to inform the police. The following morning, when the tides permitted, the bundle was taken away in a boat and examined at a mortuary in Chelmsford. The post-mortem was later carried out at the London Hospital Medical School.

A bloodstained silk shirt and the remains of a pair of blue trousers clung to the torso; the head and legs were missing. There were five stab wounds in the chest, and a large number of bones had been broken after death. Fingerprints obtained by spraying glycerine under the skin enabled Scotland Yard to identify the dead man as Stanley

Setty, a second-hand car dealer of Lancaster Gate, London, who had been missing from his home since 4 October. The pathologist Francis Camps found that the broken bones were crash injuries, and suggested that the torso had been thrown out of an aeroplane into water.

Stanley Setty was a forty-six-year-old man of Turkish birth; his name had originally been Sulman Seti. He had a criminal record for fraudulent bankruptcy, and had been suspected of using his business as a cover for a variety of criminal activities. It was known that on the day of his disappearance he had sold a car and cashed a cheque at the Yorkshire Penny Bank, receiving £1000 in £5 notes.

The suggestion that his torso had been thrown from an aeroplane led to inquiries being made at airports in the east of England, and before long it was discovered that on the day following his disappearance, a former RAF pilot named Brian Donald Hume had hired a sports plane for a flight from Elstree — a private airport in Hertfordshire — to Southend, carrying two parcels.

Having said that he would return the plane before dark, Hume had left it overnight at Southend where, the following afternoon, he lifted a third bundle into it before taking off again, apparently with the intention of flying back to Elstree. This time, after three hours, he landed at Gravesend airport, claiming that he had lost his way. He finally asked officials at Elstree to send somebody to collect the plane.

Hume, aged thirty, lived with his wife and baby daughter in a maisonette in Finchley Road, Golders Green. He had a record of petty crime and was suspected of having taken part in large-scale robberies. An examination of the plane which he had hired led to the discovery of bloodstains on the floor behind the co-pilot's seat. Moreover, a £5 note which he had used to pay a taxi fare was found to have been part of the money received by Setty at the Yorkshire Penny Bank.

On being questioned by the police, Hume admitted that he had known Setty and said that he had been bribed into disposing of the bundles by three strangers, who gave him £50 in £5 notes. He had thrown them out of the plane while flying over the Channel, he explained. He was held in custody while a search was made for the three men he had described, but it soon became clear that no such men existed. It was also discovered that a large quantity of blood had been spilt on his dining-room floor.

In January 1950 Hume was brought to trial at the Old Bailey, charged with murder. The prosecution, in seeking to prove that Setty had been killed and dismembered in the prisoner's maisonette, relied on Hume being unable to account for all the blood in any other way. But Hume *did* manage to account for it; he said that he had dropped the bundle containing the torso and that the blood had escaped from it when one end fell open. He was acquitted of murder, but sent to prison for twelve years for being an accessory to the crime.

Shortly after his release in 1958 Hume published a newspaper confession, stating that he *had* committed the murder. Setty, he said, had been employing him to steal cars and fly arms illegally, but often insulted him. On 4 October 1949, Setty, according to this new account, visited the maisonette to give him a new assignment, but Hume, enraged by his remarks, attacked him with a dagger and killed him. Having done so, he drove the dead man's car back to his garage, then dismembered the body with a saw and a kitchen knife.

The confession, published in the *Sunday Pictorial*, made Hume £2000, enabling him to live extravagantly in Zürich for a while. But on 30 January 1959, he shot and killed a taxi-driver there, while escaping from a bank which he had robbed. For this he was sentenced to life imprisonment.

He remained in jail in Switzerland until August 1976, when he was found to be insane. He was then returned to Britain and committed to Broadmoor.

On the night of 23 October 1929, Mrs. Rosaline Fox, aged sixty-three, died at the Hotel Metropole in Margate following a fire in her bedroom. The fire alarm had been raised by her thirty-year-old son Sidney, who was staying at the hotel with her, and Mrs. Fox was still alive when she was dragged from the smoke-filled room by another guest. But she died almost immediately afterwards, her death being put down to shock and suffocation, and was buried in her native village of Great Fransham in Norfolk a few days later. There were, however, grounds for suspecting that her death had not been the result of an accident.

Mrs. Fox and her son had arrived at the hotel almost penniless and without luggage earlier the same month. Two accident policies on the dead woman's life, their value totalling £3000, had been due to expire on 22 October when Sidney Fox had extended them for the surprisingly short period of thirty-six hours — until midnight on the 23rd. Moreover, an investigation by the insurance company led to the discovery that the blaze had not originated in the gas fire, as had been supposed, but had almost certainly been started deliberately with the use of petrol.

A police investigation followed. The body of Mrs. Fox was exhumed eleven days after her funeral and a post-mortem was carried out by Sir Bernard Spilsbury, who gave the cause of death as manual strangulation. Sidney Fox, a homosexual with a record of petty crime, was then arrested and charged with murder. He was brought to trial at the Lewes Assizes on 12 March 1930.

During the course of the trial a serious disagreement between Spilsbury and two of his colleagues emerged; Spilsbury claimed to have found a bruise 'about the size of half a crown' at the back of the dead woman's larynx, but Professor Sydney Smith and Dr. Robert Brontë both said that no such bruise existed. However, the prisoner gave a poor impression of himself, telling the court that after finding his mother's room on fire he had gone out and closed the door so that 'the smoke should not spread into the hotel'.

Though the judge's summing-up was largely in the prisoner's favour as far as the forensic evidence was concerned, the circumstantial evidence against him was very strong and the jury found him guilty. He was hanged at Maidstone Prison on 8 April 1930.

Mrs Phoebe Hogg murdered, 1890

OCTOBER 24

On 24 October 1890, Mrs. Phoebe Hogg, thirty-one-year-old wife of a furniture remover living in Prince of Wales Road, Kentish Town, received a note inviting her to visit Mrs. Mary Eleanor Pearcey, a twenty-four-year-old friend of the family, in her rooms in Priory Street in the same district of London.

She went to the house, taking her eighteen-month-old daughter — also named Phoebe — whose pram she left in the hall. But not long after her arrival she was savagely murdered, her skull being fractured with a poker and her throat cut so deeply that her head was almost severed from her body.

Her child was also killed — by suffocation — though it is not known at what stage this happened, or whether it was done deliberately or by accident.

At any rate, Mrs. Pearcey, having done her best to

remove bloodstains from her top-skirt, an apron, her kitchen curtains and a rug, took the two bodies from the house in the little girl's pram and wheeled them through the streets covered with an antimacassar. It was dark by this time, and she was able to push the pram for some miles without anyone stopping or reporting her.

She finally left Mrs. Hogg's body at a building site in Crossfield Road, near Swiss Cottage, where it was found by a police constable later that night. The child's body was placed on waste ground in Finchley Road, where it was not discovered until the morning of 26 October. The pram was abandoned in Hamilton Terrace, between Maida Vale and St John's Wood.

Mrs. Pearcey, whose real name was Mary Eleanor Wheeler — she had assumed that name while living with a man named Pearcey who had since left her — had committed the murder, or murders, out of jealousy. Phoebe Hogg's husband Frank had been her lover since before his marriage, and had only married Phoebe because she was pregnant.

Eleanor Pearcey, though she had another lover — a man who paid for her rooms in Priory Street — had continued to entertain Hogg in secret whenever the opportunity arose. She hoped that with Phoebe out of the way she would have him entirely to herself.

The following morning, on hearing that an unknown woman had been murdered, Frank Hogg's sister Clara, who also lived in the house in Prince of Wales Road, called on Eleanor Pearcey to ask if she knew Phoebe's whereabouts. Mrs. Pearcey said that she did not, but agreed to go with Clara to the Hampstead police, to ask to see the murdered woman's body. But when they were taken to the mortuary she became hysterical, trying to drag the sister-in-law away from the corpse.

Clara identified the dead woman and, on being shown the pram which had been found in Hamilton Terrace, said that it had belonged to Phoebe. She and Eleanor Pearcey were then taken to the house in Prince of Wales Road, where Frank Hogg and his landlady were questioned about the murder.

When Hogg was searched a key to the house in Priory Street was found in his possession.

That afternoon, while her rooms were being inspected, Eleanor Pearcey played the piano, sang and talked about her 'poor dear dead Phoebe'. The police found broken windows and blood on the walls and ceiling of the kitchen; two carving-knives were bloodstained; the poker had blood and matted hair on it; a bloodstained tablecloth was found in an outhouse, and the stained rug smelt of paraffin, with which an attempt had been made to clean it.

Mrs. Pearcey's neighbours informed them that they had heard 'banging and hammering' about 4 p.m. the previous day, but had not realized where the noise was coming from.

Mrs. Pearcey was taken to Kentish Town police station, where she was charged with murder. When she was searched it was found that her hands had cuts on them and her underclothes were heavily bloodstained; a wedding ring on one of her fingers was identified as having belonged to Phoebe. Eleanor Pearcey was brought to trial at the Old Bailey on 1 December, her trial lasting four days. She was convicted and sentenced to death.

While she waited for the date of her execution to arrive, permission was obtained for Frank Hogg to visit her but he failed to do so.

Maintaining her innocence to the end, Eleanor Pearcey was hanged at Newgate Prison on 23 December 1890, the crowd outside cheering as the black flag appeared.

On 26 October 1921, Oswald Martin, a thirty-two-year-old solicitor of Hay-on-Wye in Brecknockshire, called at the home of Major Herbert Rowse Armstrong, an older member of the same profession, at his home in the nearby village of Cusop. The two men were involved in a professional dispute over the uncompleted sale of an estate at the time, and it seemed that Armstrong, a widower of fifty-two with three children, had invited his young rival to tea in an attempt at conciliation.

However, they found that they had little to say to each other and neither of them raised the subject of the dispute. Later, after returning to his own home, Oswald Martin began to feel ill. He retched and vomited throughout the night, his illness continuing for some days afterwards.

His family doctor, Dr. Tom Hincks, was uneasy about his patient's symptoms, and became even more so after learning from Martin's father-in-law, a local chemist, that Major Armstrong regularly bought large quantities of arsenic from his shop. It was then remembered that a month earlier Martin had received a box of chocolates through the post, apparently from an anonymous well-wisher.

These chocolates had been placed on the table at a dinner-party at Martin's home on 8 October, but were eaten only by one of his sisters-in-law, who afterwards became ill.

In view of the suspicions which had suddenly been aroused, it was thought advisable to have the remaining chocolates, as well as a sample of Martin's urine, sent to the Clinical Research Association in London to be analysed. When both were found to contain arsenic, a secret police investigation began, Major Armstrong being finally arrested in his office on 31 December and charged with attempted murder.

But by this time Armstrong was also suspected of having poisoned his wife, whose death on 22 February previously had been put down to heart disease. On 2 January 1922, Mrs. Armstrong's body was exhumed and a post-mortem carried out by Dr. Bernard Spilsbury revealed arsenic in her remains. Armstrong was subsequently charged with her murder.

He was brought to trial at the Hereford Assizes on 3 April, the case lasting ten days. The prisoner, a neat little man weighing only about seven stone, was confident that he would be acquitted, but could give no satisfactory explanation for having a packet of arsenic in one of his pockets, and a further two ounces of it in his desk at the time of his arrest. He was therefore found guilty.

His execution took place at Gloucester Prison on 31 May 1922.

Last crime of an Axe-man, 1919

OCTOBER
27

On 27 October 1919, Mike Pepitone, a New Orleans grocer, was brutally murdered in his own home by an unknown intruder. The crime was discovered by his wife, who rushed into the room in time to see the murderer escaping. The man had gained entry to the couple's home by chiselling out a door panel.

It was to prove to be the last of a series of violent crimes which had begun eight years earlier, the person responsible being known as the 'Axe-man of New Orleans'. A year later the victim's widow shot and killed a man named Joseph Mumfre in a Los Angeles street, declaring that *he* was the Axe-man.

The police found that Mumfre had a criminal record, and that all of the Axe-man's crimes had been committed during his brief periods of freedom following prison sentences. But no real evidence connected him with the crimes, and the identity of the culprit remains unknown.

The first four deaths attributed to the Axe-man had occurred in 1911; the victims were an Italian grocer named Tony Schiambras, his wife and two other grocers whose names were Cruti and Rosetti. These crimes were followed by a lull lasting until 23 May 1918, when somebody murdered another couple running a grocery store. Joseph Maggio and his wife were both struck with an axe as they slept, their assailant afterwards cutting their throats with a razor. In this case, the brothers of the dead man were accused but afterwards released.

Then, in the early hours of 28 June, Louis Besumer, another grocer, and his common-law wife were both attacked with a hatchet. Mrs. Besumer died of her injuries a few days later, and on 5 August her husband who had survived the attack, was arrested for her murder. But the same night, the Axe-man attacked a pregnant woman, Mrs. Scheider, whose husband found her unconscious when he returned home from work.

Mrs. Scheider recovered from the attack and gave birth to her child a week later. By this time the Axe-man had committed a further murder — that of Joseph Romano, a barber, who died of head wounds inflicted at his home on 10 August.

Louis Besumer, on being tried for his wife's murder, was acquitted.

On 10 March 1919, the Axe-man broke into the home of a family named Cortimiglia, injuring the husband and wife and killing their baby. Rosie Cortimiglia accused two members of an Italian family, Iorlando Jordano and his son Frank — who lived opposite them and, in fact, had found them after the attack — of killing her child, but Charles Cortimiglia was equally insistent that neither of the Jordanos was responsible.

They were, however, brought to trial on 21 May 1919 and convicted, Frank being sentenced to death and his father to life imprisonment. But a few days after the shooting of Joseph Mumfre, Rosie Cortimiglia, whose husband had since left her, confessed that the Jordanos had *not* committed the crime and that she had accused them falsely out of malice. The two men were then set free.

In the meantime the Axe-man had attacked and injured a man named Steve Boca on 10 August 1919, had been disturbed in the act of trying to break into the home of a chemist on 2 September, and had attacked a nineteen-year-old girl in her bed on 3 September.

The Axe-man, having entered a building by chiselling out one of the door-panels, generally attacked his victims with an axe found on the premises, and invariably left the weapon at the scene of the crime. The motive for the attacks was never discovered, and the reason for their sudden cessation is also unknown.

Mrs. Pepitone was sentenced to ten years' imprisonment for shooting Mumfre, but served only three years before being released.

Wrotham Hill murder, 1946

OCTOBER 31

During the early morning of 31 October 1946, Dagmar Peters, a poor spinster aged forty-seven, left her home — a small bungalow which was really just a hut — at Kingsdown in Kent, to visit her sister-in-law in London. She did this every week, hitching lifts on lorries, but this time did not complete the journey. Later the same day her body was found in a shrubbery on Wrotham Hill on the A20. She had been strangled.

The murder had been committed while Miss Peters was sitting upright, and scratches on her legs, sustained after death, indicated that her body had been dragged or carried to the place where it was found. There was no apparent reason for the crime, for she had not been sexually assaulted and had been too poor to rob.

However, certain items known to have been in her possession — an attaché case, a purse, a key and a yellow string handbag — were missing, and the police appealed to the public in their attempts to trace them. At the same time inquiries were made about lorry-drivers known to have driven along that stretch of road between 5 a.m. and 8 a.m. on the day of the murder.

It was soon learnt that the yellow handbag had been found in a lake some distance from the road by a fifteen-year-old boy who had given it to a neighbour. She (the neighbour) had given it to another woman who, in turn, had given it to a third. The bag had thus changed hands three times within forty-eight hours, each of the three women scrubbing it as it came into her possession. Shortly after this discovery parts of the dead woman's attaché case were found further along the A20.

From subsequent inquiries it seemed that the yellow handbag had been carried downstream from the village of East Malling, where an old mill had been turned into a cider works. While discussing this possibility with his assistant, Detective Chief Inspector Robert Fabian noticed a pile of bricks standing at the factory gates. These were found to have been delivered on 31 October by a firm of haulage contractors in Cambridge which had so far been overlooked in connection with the investigation.

The driver who had delivered them, a man calling himself Sydney Sinclair, was interviewed at Cambridge Police Station. He was a tough-looking character and

Fabian, sensing that he was an old lag, soon got him to admit that his real name was Harold Hagger. He had sixteen convictions, including one for an assault on a woman.

Hagger admitted having handled the attaché case, saying that he had found it and then thrown it away. On being driven along the route, he pointed out the place where he had thrown it and then, surprisingly, showed Fabian where he had thrown a man's woollen vest which had also been owned by the victim. Miss Peters had bought it in Maidstone two days before her death and had been using it as a scarf when she set out to visit her sister-in-law. It proved to be the murder weapon.

On being questioned further, Hagger agreed that he had given the dead woman a lift in his lorry and said that he had 'got mad at her' and killed her by accident when she tried to steal his wallet from his jacket pocket. The jacket, according to him, had been hanging on a peg in the cab of the lorry at the time, but this was not believed, as on the morning in question it had been bitterly cold.

Harold Hagger was brought to trial for murder and, in spite of his apparent lack of motive, convicted and sentenced to death. He was hanged at Wandsworth Prison on 18 March 1947.

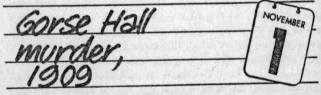

Gorse Hall murder, 1909

NOVEMBER 1

The unsolved murder of George Harry Storrs, a wealthy mill-owner and building contractor, took place at the victim's home, Gorse Hall, near Stalybridge in Cheshire, on the evening of 1 November 1909. Storrs, a generous and kindly man of forty-nine, had many friends and was liked by his employees; his coachman was so grieved by his death that he committed suicide a few days later. However, there is reason to believe that Storrs knew that he was in danger and it is generally assumed that he knew the identity of his murderer. If so, he died without revealing it.

A few weeks earlier, on 10 September, a man had broken into the grounds of Gorse Hall and fired a shot through one of the dining-room windows while the mill-owner, his wife and his wife's niece, Marion Lindley, were having dinner. Storrs, being healthy and vigorous, had gone after the intruder himself but been unable to prevent him escaping; he said afterwards — none too convincingly — that he did not know the culprit.

The incident led to the installation of an alarm bell which could be heard in Stalybridge on the roof of the hall. This was heard ringing two days before the murder, but when police arrived in response to it Storrs apologized, saying that he had rung it himself as a test. Clearly, he was apprehensive of the intruder returning.

When this happened on 1 November, the man got inside the house, armed with a revolver. Storrs once again tried to tackle him and Mrs. Storrs, managing to snatch the gun from his hand, ran upstairs to sound the alarm. But the intruder attacked the mill-owner with a knife, stabbing him repeatedly. By the time help arrived, Storrs lay dying and the man had fled.

The killer had been seen not only by Mrs. Storrs but also by Miss Lindley, the cook and the maid, and two weeks later, following their descriptions, the police arrested a young man named Cornelius Howard, living in Huddersfield, who turned out to be a cousin of the deceased.

Howard, a butcher with a record for burglary, was picked out at an identity parade and charged with the crime. But if he was guilty of it, his motive was unknown, for Mrs. Storrs and Miss Lindley both said that they had never seen him before the night of the murder and the deceased was not known to have had any contact with him.

On being brought to trial, Howard was acquitted.

Some months later a local man, Mark Wilde, was arrested after attacking another man with a knife similar to that with which Storrs had been murdered. Though Wilde was alleged to have owned the gun which had been taken from the killer's hand, and he, too, was identified by witnesses, he appeared to have had no connection at all with the inhabitants of Gorse Hall and was also acquitted.

No further arrests were ever made in connection with this baffling case, which is the subject of *The Stabbing of George Harry Storrs* by Jonathan Goodman.

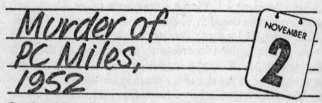

Murder of PC Miles, 1952

On the night of 2 November 1952, two youths from south London, Christopher Craig, aged sixteen, and Derek Bentley, nineteen, attempted to break into a confectioner's warehouse in Croydon, Surrey, intent on burglary. Craig, whose older brother Niven was serving a long prison sentence for armed robbery, was carrying a revolver and a sheath knife; Bentley, who was illiterate and had a criminal record for shop-breaking, was armed with a knife and a knuckle-duster. The warehouse was in Tamworth Road.

They did not get into the premises unobserved, and ten minutes later a police van arrived at the scene, closely followed by a police car. Detective Constable Frederick Fairfax climbed on to the flat roof, twenty-five feet above the ground, where the two youths were hiding behind a lift-house. He called on them to give themselves up and, when they refused, rushed towards the lift-house and dragged Bentley out into the open.

Bentley, breaking free, shouted, 'Let him have it, Chris!' Craig then fired his gun, grazing the police officer's shoulder from a distance of six feet.

Fairfax, having fallen, got up and chased after Bentley, knocking him down with his fist. He took possession of his knife and knuckle-duster and held on to him firmly, calling out to Craig to drop his gun. 'Come and get it!' Craig called back to him from the other end of the roof.

Further shots were fired as other policemen closed in on him, and PC Sidney Miles, who had obtained the warehouse keys from the confectioner's manager, was killed as he stepped on to the roof from an interior staircase.

'Come on, you brave coppers!' shouted Craig. 'Think of your wives!' A moment later, after a truncheon, a milk-bottle and a piece of wood had been thrown at him, he continued: 'I'm Craig! You've just given my brother twelve years! Come on, you coppers! I'm only sixteen!'

By this time police reinforcements had arrived, some of the newcomers being armed. Bentley was taken from the roof, Fairfax returning with a gun. Shots were exchanged as he moved closer to Craig, taking cover behind roof-lights. Suddenly Craig found that his gun was empty. Rather than wait to be overpowered, he swung himself over the railings at the edge of the roof and jumped to the ground, fracturing his spine, breastbone and forearm. He and Fairfax spent the night in adjacent cubicles at the Croydon General Hospital.

On 9 December Bentley and Craig — the latter still using crutches — were brought to trial at the Old Bailey, charged with the murder of PC Miles. Both pleaded not guilty, Bentley on the grounds that he was under arrest at the time of the fatal shooting and had not known beforehand that his accomplice was armed, Craig on the grounds that he had not intended to kill Miles, or any of the other policemen, and had only fired shots in order to frighten them off.

After considering the cases for seventy-five minutes the jury found both prisoners guilty. Bentley was thereupon sentenced to death, while Craig, as he was under eighteen years of age, was to be detained 'at Her Majesty's pleasure'. Though many pleas were made for Bentley's life to be spared, he was hanged at Wandsworth Prison on 28 January 1953.

Christopher Craig was released on licence in May 1963 and settled in Buckinghamshire. He married in 1965, at the age of twenty-eight.

Death of Alice Thomas, 1930

NOVEMBER 4

During the early hours of 4 November 1930, Mrs. Alice Thomas, of Trenhorne Farm, Lewannick, in Cornwall, died at the Plymouth City Hospital shortly after being admitted. Her death gave rise to rumours, and when a post-mortem revealed the presence of arsenic in the body Mrs. Annie Hearn, a widow residing at Trenhorne House, 200 yards from the farm, was suspected of having poisoned her.

Mrs. Hearn, who was from the Midlands, had lived alone since the death of her sister, Lydia Everard, known as 'Minnie', on 21 July previously. Before that she and her sister had lived together at Trenhorne House, and both had been on good terms with Alice Thomas and her husband William.

On 18 October the couple had taken Mrs. Hearn for a drive to Bude, and during the course of that outing Mrs. Thomas had been ill after eating tinned-salmon sandwiches which Mrs. Hearn had prepared. Mrs. Hearn had afterwards stayed at the farm to look after her and had remained there to run the house when Mrs. Thomas'

294

mother arrived to take over the nursing on 29 October.

However, it was said locally that Annie Hearn had been 'too friendly' with William Thomas, and this, together with the story of the salmon sandwiches, caused pointed remarks to be made by relatives attending the funeral on 8 November.

Two days later, Mrs. Hearn disappeared after writing a letter to the dead woman's husband, declaring her innocence. Her coat was found on the cliffs at Looe, on the Cornish coast, where it had apparently been left in order to give the impression that she had committed suicide.

The inquest on Alice Thomas was held on 24 November, the jury deciding on a verdict of murder by some person or persons unknown. This was followed on 9 December by the exhumation of Lydia Everard's body, in which arsenic was also found. Some weeks later Annie Hearn was discovered in Torquay, Devonshire, where she had been working as a housekeeper under a different name. She was arrested and charged with two murders.

At her trial at the Bodmin Assizes in June 1931, she faced only the charge of murdering Alice Thomas, though evidence concerning the death of her sister was introduced. But Crown witnesses had to agree that Lydia Everard's symptoms were consistent with chronic gastric catarrh, from which she had suffered for many years and which the doctor attending her had certified as the cause of her death.

It was also admitted that the organs taken for analysis had been left uncovered in the churchyard, thus exposing them to contamination by dust in an area in which the arsenic-level of the soil was exceptionally high due to the presence of tin.

The prosecution fared no better with its evidence concerning the death of Alice Thomas, for it was pointed out that, had the salmon sandwiches been poisoned with weed-killer, as alleged, they would have turned blue within a short time and nobody would have eaten them. A second dose of arsenic, from which Alice Thomas had finally died, might not have been administered during the period in which the accused was nursing her.

Annie Hearn told the court that she had not murdered anyone and denied the suggestion that she had hoped to marry William Thomas. She made a good impression, answering questions clearly and without faltering. After retiring for less than an hour the jury returned a verdict of not guilty and the prisoner was released.

The pathologist Sir Sydney Smith, who attended the trial as an adviser to Norman Birkett, the defence counsel, later described Annie Hearn as 'a foolish woman but not a murderess'. His comments on the case, in *Mostly Murder*, seem to imply that he suspected William Thomas of being the real culprit.

Body in blazing car, 1930

NOVEMBER 6

During the early hours of 6 November 1930, two young men walking towards the village of Hardingstone in Northamptonshire after attending a Guy Fawkes' Night dance, saw a fire a short distance ahead of them. As they approached it, a respectably-dressed man climbed out of a nearby ditch and hurried past them on the opposite side of the lane, remarking, 'It looks as if someone has had a bonfire!' But the young men found that it was a car which was burning, with flames leaping to a height of fifteen feet, and ran to the village to report the matter. Later, when the flames had been extinguished, a charred corpse was found lying across the two front seats.

Though the body was unrecognizable, the ownership of the car was traced to Alfred Arthur Rouse, a thirty-six-year-old commercial traveller of Buxted Road, Finchley in north London. When the police contacted Mrs. Rouse, she said that her husband had left home on business the previous night, and also that she believed she recognized pieces of clothing retrieved from the wreckage as belonging to him. However, the police were suspicious and, following extensive publicity of the case, soon learnt that Rouse was still alive. He was apprehended at Hammersmith Bus Terminus on the night of 7 November and taken to the nearest police station for questioning.

Rouse claimed that on the night of 5 November he had given a lift to a stranger who wanted to go to Leicester. He had stopped the car in the lane near Hardingstone and asked his passenger to refill the petrol tank while he himself went into a nearby field to relieve his bowels. Shortly afterwards, he said, he had realized that the car was on fire with the man still inside it. Unable to open the door, he had then panicked and run away.

Sir Bernard Spilsbury's examination of the body had revealed that the man was still alive when the fire started. But a scrap of cloth found in the car smelled of petrol, and an expert fire-assessor found that the carburettor had been tampered with and a trail of petrol on the roadside ignited. The two young men from the village identified Rouse as the man who had climbed out of the ditch at the time of the fire.

It was discovered that Rouse had been wounded in the head with shrapnel during the First World War, and had been a compulsive womanizer ever since. He had mistresses in many towns, and his life had become increasingly complicated by maintenance orders and promises of marriage which he could not keep, though on one occasion he had committed bigamy. It seemed that he had suddenly decided to fake his own death and assume a new identity.

Charged with the murder of an unknown man, Rouse appeared for trial at the Northampton Assizes on 26 January 1931. The case lasted six days, the accused

297

showing himself to be callous and boastful; the jury was left in no doubt that he was guilty. He was hanged at Bedford, at the age of thirty-seven, on 10 March the same year and his confession, in which he claimed to have strangled his victim after getting him drunk, was later published in the *Daily Sketch*.

The identity of his victim was never discovered.

Double murder in Cornwall, 1952

On 7 November 1952, Miles Giffard, a twenty-six-year-old unemployed man of Porthpean in Cornwall, murdered both of his parents. The crime was evidently premeditated, but so clumsily committed that it is hard to believe that he expected to get away with it. Indeed, his conduct afterwards was so careless that his arrest was inevitable, and when it happened he immediately confessed. The crime may therefore be said to have been characteristic of Giffard, for had he not been a failure in other respects it would not have taken place.

The Giffards lived in a large house on the cliffs overlooking Carlyon Bay, two miles from St. Austell, where Charles Henry Giffard was Clerk to the Magistrates. Miles Giffard had been sent to Rugby, but was afterwards removed, suffering from mental deterioration; his illness was diagnosed as a form of schizophrenia, but he was never treated for it. Later he studied law for a while, then gave it up in favour of a course in estate management; but at twenty-five, on inheriting £750, he gave that up as well, and made no further attempt to study anything.

He spent the next four months squandering his inheritance in Bournemouth, worked for a few weeks selling ice-cream, then in June 1952 returned to Porthpean to live off his parents. By now he was a constant disappointment to his father, if he had not been before, and there were some differences between them. In an attempt to assert his independence, Miles Giffard moved to London in the middle of August and rented a furnished room. But he failed in this as well, and after being reduced to living from hand to mouth, he decided to return home once again and ask his father for help.

While in London, however, he had become attached to nineteen-year-old Gabrielle Vallance, who lived in Tite Street, Chelsea; it was his desire to go on seeing her after his return to Porthpean which led to the final conflict between his father and himself. For Charles Giffard, though he gave his son the use of his car, forbade him to make trips to London. And Miles, at the age of twenty-six, was so dependent on his father that he did not dare to disobey him.

'I am dreadfully fed up as I was looking forward to seeing you,' he wrote to Gabrielle on 3 November. 'Short of doing him in, I see no future in the world at all.'

Four days later, however, he telephoned her at 5.30 p.m., saying that he would probably be travelling to London within a few hours on his father's behalf, and that he would call her again at 8.30 p.m. to confirm this. At 7.30 he found his father in the garage, working on Mrs. Giffard's car, and knocked him unconscious with an iron pipe. He then went into the kitchen and, approaching his mother from behind, struck her down with the same weapon.

At this point he telephoned Gabrielle again and said that he would be driving to London in his father's Triumph; he asked if he could have a wash and shave at her house on arrival. After the phone call, he struck both parents several more times, killing his father but not his mother. He pushed his mother to the edge of the cliff in a wheelbarrow and tipped her over, then disposed of his father's body in the same way, pushing the wheelbarrow over after him.

Before leaving Porthpean Giffard tried to clear up all the blood from the kitchen and garage; he also took pieces of jewellery from his mother's room and money from his father's coat pocket. He disposed of the murder weapon and some bloodstained articles of clothing on the way to London, and later stopped to give a lift to a couple of hitch-hikers. He rang Gabrielle's door bell at 8 a.m. on 8 November after resting for three hours in the car. He sold his mother's jewellery for £50 shortly afterwards.

On the evening of the 8th Giffard took Gabrielle to a pub and suddenly, under the influence of drink, told her that he had killed his parents. He said afterwards that 'it upset her, and we just moved on to further public houses, drinking'. The bodies, in the meantime, had been discovered; so, too, had the Triumph which had been left in Tite Street. So when Giffard took Gabrielle back to her home after closing time, he found the police waiting for him.

'I can only say that I have had a brainstorm,' he said in his statement. 'I cannot account for my actions. I had drunk about half a bottle of whisky on the Friday afternoon — before all this happened. It just seemed to me that nothing mattered as long as I got back to London.'

Miles Giffard was brought to trial at the Bodmin Assizes, a plea of insanity being made on his behalf. However, the jury deliberated for only a short while before returning a verdict of guilty. A panel of psychiatrists appointed by the Home Secretary afterwards declared him to be sane. He was therefore hanged at Bristol on 24 February 1953.

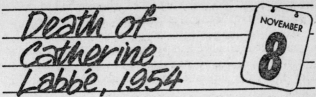

On the afternoon of 8 November 1954, Catherine Labbé, an illegitimate child aged two and a half, was drowned in a stone washing-basin in the courtyard of her grandmother's house at Vendôme, near Blois, in France. Denise Labbé, the child's mother, was in charge of her at the time and claimed that the drowning had been an accident. But suspicions were aroused and an examining magistrate was appointed to conduct an inquiry into the circumstances of it.

Denise Labbé, a twenty-eight-year-old secretary who worked in Paris, was arrested soon afterwards, and in January 1955 was charged with having attempted to murder her daughter on three earlier occasions. She then made a statement to the examining magistrate, admitting that she had killed her daughter and claiming that it had been a 'ritual murder'.

'I am the mistress of Jacques Algarron, Second Lieutenant in the School of Artillery at Châlons-sur-Marne,' she said. 'It was he who asked me to kill my child in order to prove my love for him ...' She went on to explain that Algarron, whom she had first met on 1 May the previous year, had cast a spell over her, saying, 'The price of our love must be the death of your daughter. Kill for me. An innocent victim must be sacrificed.' The attempts on Catherine's life had all been made since then and against Denise's own will.

Algarron, who was four years younger than Denise Labbé, denied having been in any way involved in the child's death, but was arrested and held in custody. A week later he was confronted with his accuser in the examining magistrate's chambers. He listened calmly as she repeated her allegations and, on being asked what he had to say in reply, answered, 'The girl is completely out of her head.'

The examining magistrate, however, continued his inquiry, Denise Labbé and Jacques Algarron remaining in prison in Blois. They were eventually brought to trial on 30 May 1955, the accusations and denials being repeated in court.

'He wanted our union to go from suffering to suffering until we became the ideal couple,' said Denise. 'One day, in a Paris restaurant, he asked me whether I would kill my child for him. I replied, "Yes."'

She went on to tell the court that he had told her to take sick leave from her job and throw Catherine into the river at Rennes. 'It was terrible for me because I wanted to keep my child,' she said, sobbing uncontrollably.

Algarron dismissed the whole idea as incredible. 'Doubtlessly I was at fault for not having realized what she really was — a girl without culture or finesse,' he said coldly. 'But my fault went no further than that. I would never have wanted the death of Catherine.' He described the murder as 'the most monstrous act that anyone could have committed', and said that he found it impossible to explain to himself how she could have done such a thing. Later a number of his former mistresses, of whom there were many, were called to testify that he had been a normal lover and had made no extraordinary demands on them.

But Madame Laurent, a professional foster-mother who had looked after Catherine at Agly, near Paris, told the court that Denise had been a devoted mother, and concluded her testimony by screaming at Algarron, 'Beast! Beast! Beast!' She was followed to the witness stand by Madame Thébault, who had been Denise's best friend. This witness told the court how Denise had returned to Algarron after one of the unsuccessful attempts on her daughter's life.

'She and Algarron looked at each other without saying a word when she arrived. Then she broke down in tears, throwing herself into her lover's arms. But she had exactly the attitude of a woman who was imploring her lover's pardon.'

The Advocate General described the crime as being exceptional not only for its horror but also for the absence of any easily-discernible motive. He said that Algarron, having realized Denise Labbé's 'exceptional sensuality', had inspired the crime out of a perverse desire to experiment with her and convince himself that she was in his power.

The jury deliberated for nearly three hours before returning to give their verdict. Denise Labbé, who was found guilty of murder with extenuating circumstances, was sentenced to penal servitude for life. Jacques Algarron, who was found guilty of having provoked the crime, was given twenty years' hard labour.

Denise Labbé's use of the phrase 'ritual murder' in connection with the affair was never explained.

WAAF found murdered 1944

NOVEMBER 9

During the early morning of 9 November 1944, the body of WAAF Winifred Evans, a twenty-seven-year-old wireless operator, was found in a ditch by the roadside at an aerodrome near Beccles in Suffolk. She had been suffocated, the person responsible having held her face down in the mud during the course of a brutal sexual attack. The case was investigated by Scotland Yard.

It was learnt that the previous evening Winifred Evans had been to a dance at a nearby American camp with Corporal Margaret Johns, a friend in the same unit as herself; they had returned to their station about midnight.

Winifred Evans had then visited the WAAF quarters before going off in the direction of the aerodrome where she was due to relieve another operator.

A moment or two afterwards Margaret Johns had found a man in an RAF uniform lurking in an ablution hut at the WAAF quarters; he was drunk and claimed to have lost his way back to his own camp, less than a mile away. She had given him directions and he had set off along the same road as Winifred Evans, and only a short distance behind her. It was on this road that the crime had taken place.

The police soon discovered that the airman in question was LAC Arthur Heys, a married man aged thirty-seven with a young family. He had been seen returning to his quarters after 1 a.m. on the night of the murder, and had spent a lot of time cleaning his clothes the following morning. Without Heys' knowledge, the police used his next pay parade for the purpose of identification, and Corporal Johns picked him out without difficulty.

Heys' clothing was examined by a pathologist, who found bloodstains on his tunic, rabbit hairs on his trousers — as on the clothes of the dead girl — and brickdust from the ditch on his shoes. Though Dr. Keith Simpson warned that the scientific evidence was far from conclusive, Heys was arrested and charged with the crime.

Before he was brought to trial his commanding officer received an anonymous letter, written in block letters with a blue pencil. It was a confession to the murder, stating that Heys had been wrongly accused and containing details which only the murderer could have known.

On comparing this with samples of Heys' own lettering, Superintendent Fred Cherrill, the fingerprint expert, found proof that the prisoner had written it himself. It had been written in Norwich Prison and smuggled out.

Heys was brought to trial in Bury St Edmunds in January 1945, the anonymous letter proving to be the most damning piece of evidence against him. The jury took forty minutes to find him guilty and he was afterwards hanged.

Murder of Angela Woolliscroft, 1976

On 10 November 1976, a man wearing sunglasses and armed with a sawn-off shotgun entered the branch of Barclays Bank in Upper Ham Road, Richmond, Surrey, and demanded money. After being given £2500 in notes by one of the cashiers he fired the gun at her, shattering the glass partition and wounding her in the chest and hand. He then turned and fled, dropping a woman's yellow raincoat and an empty plastic fertilizer bag in his haste to get away. The wounded cashier, Angela Woolliscroft, aged twenty, died on the way to hospital.

The owner of the raincoat, a Miss Marshall, was traced from two pieces of paper which had been left screwed up in the pocket. She told police that she had taken her sister-in-law shopping on the morning of the murder, leaving her faded maroon A40 car in a store car park in Kingston with the passenger door unlocked. On returning to it soon after 2 p.m. she had found the car in a different position with her raincoat and a pair of sunglasses missing, she explained. She had also found a lot of mud on the back of the car, some of it sticking to the number plate.

Further inquiries revealed that the car had been seen near the bank and that the driver had narrowly avoided a collision with another car immediately after the crime. It was learnt, too, that on returning the car to the car park, he had drawn attention to himself in his attempts to make other drivers give way to him. The fertilizer bag was found to have been taken from a small green opposite the bank, where it had been left by a part-time gardener who had been clearing leaves.

The police received many pieces of information from people hoping to claim a large reward offered by Barclays, one informant stating that he had seen a man named Michael George Hart taking a shotgun from one car to another in Basingstoke, Hampshire, twenty-five miles from the bank. The man in question was interviewed and his house was searched, but no evidence was found connecting him with the murder. He was, however, a known criminal, so arrangements were made for him to be kept under observation by the local police.

On 22 November the same man was recognized as the driver of a car which had just been involved in an accident. He had left the scene and, on being pursued, managed to get away. But the car was afterwards found abandoned, with an automatic pistol and seventy-two rounds of ammunition in the boot. The gun had been stolen, together with a double-barrelled shotgun and another pistol, during a burglary at a gun-shop in Reading, Berkshire, on 4 November.

Hart avoided arrest until 20 January 1977, when he tried to collect money owed to him for some work which he had carried out as a self-employed builder several months previously. He was then taken into custody and, following an unsuccessful suicide attempt, made a confession. He had driven to the car park in Kingston in a borrowed car and chosen Miss Marshall's A40 for the robbery because he had an ignition key which fitted it, he said. He had taken the yellow raincoat to hide the shotgun, and had intended to put the money into the fertilizer bag. He had afterwards covered the rear number plate of the car with mud to hinder identification.

Hart also revealed that he had blackened his face with boot polish and worn a wig as well as Miss Marshall's sunglasses. He maintained that he had shot Angela Woolliscroft by accident, though forensic evidence proved otherwise. The shotgun was later recovered from the Thames at Hampton Court.

At the time of the murder Hart was already awaiting trial on burglary charges in Basingstoke, and was wanted for attempted murder in France. He had been refused bail four times but granted it on his fifth application, on condition that he reported to the Basingstoke police twice a day. He had committed a further thirty-nine offences since the murder, including burglary, fraud, theft and receiving stolen property, some of them in association with a young woman.

On 3 November 1977, Hart, aged thirty, was convicted of murder at the Old Bailey. He was sent to prison for life, with a recommendation that he should serve at least twenty-five years. His female accomplice was sent to prison for three years for issuing worthless cheques.

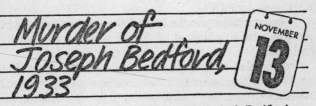

Murder of Joseph Bedford, 1933

NOVEMBER 13

On the evening of 13 November 1933, Joseph Bedford, an eighty-year-old bachelor, was attacked and robbed in his dingy general store in Portslade, Sussex, receiving head injuries from which he died in hospital the following morning. The crime was committed about 8 p.m., as the old man was about to close the shop, but was not discovered until two hours later. About 9.50 a neighbour reported that the light in the shop was still on and that some of Mr. Bedford's stock was still out on the pavement. A police constable arrived to investigate the matter.

He found the door locked, but heard sounds from the dimly-lit interior — 'as if someone were stumbling against something'. Flashing his torch through the glass, he saw the shopkeeper inside with his face covered with blood. At that moment the old man staggered and fell against a showcase, and by the time the door had been forced open he was lying on the floor. His assailants had got away with about £6.

Two young men, both of them strangers to the neighbourhood, had been seen hanging about outside the shop just before the attack. They were later found to be in police custody in Worthing, where they had been arrested on a charge of loitering with intent to commit a felony.

When interviewed about the attack on Mr. Bedford, Frederick William Parker, a twenty-one-year-old labourer, admitted that he and his accomplice, Albert Probert, a fitter aged twenty-six, were the men concerned. He and Probert, he said, had held up the old man with an unloaded gun after locking the shop door, and had stolen the money from two chocolate boxes which he used as a till.

'I wish it had been a bigger job,' he said. 'It was not worth doing for £6.'

It was not until after he had admitted being involved in the crime that he learned of the old man's death, but he had blamed Probert for the violence from the outset.

Probert denied having had anything to do with it. But on 23 November, after they had each been given a nominal sentence of one day's imprisonment for the offence for which they had been arrested, the two men were jointly charged with murder.

They appeared for trial at the Sussex Assizes in Lewes on 14 March the following year. Both pleaded not guilty, a suggestion being made on their behalf that Mr. Bedford may have died of misadventure, having fallen and fractured his skull as a result of being frightened by the police constable's torch. But they were convicted of murder, the jury having retired for thirty-five minutes.

They were hanged at Wandsworth Prison on 4 May 1934.

Murder in Agra, 1912

On the night of 17 November 1912, four thugs entered the home of Henry Clark, a doctor in the Indian Subordinate Medical Service in Agra, and killed his wife with a sword. Clark was not there at the time and later told police that he had been seeing Mrs. Augusta Fullam, the widow of a military accounts examiner who had died the previous year. The police questioned Mrs. Fullam as a matter of course, and then decided to search her bungalow.

Finding a metal box which Clark had left in her care, they insisted upon having it opened. They thus discovered about 400 love letters, suggesting not only that Clark and Mrs. Fullam had been having an affair, but also that they had poisoned Mrs. Fullam's husband. Subsequent inquiries revealed that the four thugs who murdered Mrs. Clark had been hired to do so by Clark himself.

The affair had started during the summer of 1909 when Henry Clark, aged forty two, and Augusta Fullam, thirty-five, met at a ball in Meerut where they were both then living. They quickly fell in love and remained so after Clark had been posted to Agra about a year later. Following a brief reunion in April 1911, Clark began sending Mrs. Fullam supplies of arsenic — referred to as 'tonic powders' in their letters — for the purpose of disposing of her husband.

Edward Fullam, whose doctor was worried by his symptoms, was sent to the Agra Station Hospital on 8 October the same year. There, on 10 October, he died, having been given an injection of the same poison by Henry Clark, who also signed the death certificate. The true cause of Fullam's death was not discovered until nearly fourteen months later when a court order was obtained for the body to be exhumed

309

Henry Clark and Augusta Fullam were brought to trial in two separate cases before the Allahabad High Court, the second case being against the four thugs as well as themselves. The letters found in Clark's metal box provided the prosecution with a good deal of evidence, and Mrs. Fullam sought to save herself by accusing her lover of the crime. But both were convicted, and Clark was hanged on 26 March 1913.

Mrs. Fullam, who was pregnant at the time of the trial, was sentenced to life imprisonment. She served only fifteen months before dying of heat-stroke on 29 May the following year.

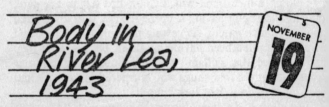

Body in River Lea, 1943

NOVEMBER 19

On the afternoon of 19 November 1943, corporation sewer men working in Luton, Bedfordshire, noticed a roughly-tied bundle wrapped in sacks in a few inches of water near the edge of the river Lea. Discovering that it contained a corpse, they informed the police; it was then found to be the body of a woman who had been dead for between twelve and twenty-four hours. She had been beaten to death with a blunt instrument, following an unsuccessful attempt to strangle her.

The woman's face had been badly battered and had to be treated in order to restore the features to their original appearance. There were no items of clothing or jewellery to help the police identify her; even her false teeth were missing. Moreover, a check on her fingerprints revealed that she had no criminal record. The police had therefore to resort to public appeals and exhaustive routine inquiries in the hope of identifying her. For three months, during the course of which they took thousands of statements, these proved unavailing.

Then, in February 1944, a large assortment of rags and pieces of clothing, collected from dustbins and rubbish dumps, was re-examined in the hope that some clue, previously overlooked, would come to light. Part of a black coat with a dyer's tag attached to it was then investigated further and found to have belonged to a Rene Manton, of Regent Street, Luton.

Detective Chief Inspector Chapman of Scotland Yard, acting upon instinct, went to Rene Manton's address personally and the door was opened to him by a little girl of eight who appeared to him to bear a strong resemblance to the dead woman. Learning from her that her mother had 'gone away', he interviewed her father, Horace William Manton — known as 'Bertie' — a lorry-driver employed by the National Fire Service.

In answer to a question regarding the whereabouts of his wife, Manton replied, 'Oh, she left me some time ago, and is working somewhere in London.' He produced a number of letters which she had apparently sent him from Hampstead during the previous three months. But Chapman did not regard these as proof that Mrs. Manton was still alive, and arranged for Superintendent Fred Cherrill to search the house for fingerprints.

Cherrill examined every object and every surface in the whole house without finding a single one of Mrs. Manton's fingerprints until he came to the very last object of all — a pickle bottle in the cellar, covered with dust. On this he found a thumbprint which corresponded with one of the dead woman's.

Bertie Manton was arrested and charged with his wife's murder. He then made a confession.

'I killed her,' he said. 'But it was only because I lost my temper. I didn't intend to. She left me about last Christmas twelvemonths, and was away for five months ... I persuaded her to mend her ways and come back to me for the children's sake. She was very grumpy and quarrelsome because she thought she was going to have a baby.'

On the day of her death, he said, they had been sitting together by the fireside when a quarrel started and his wife suddenly threw a cup of hot tea in his face, saying that she hoped it would blind him.

'I lost my temper, picked up a very heavy wooden stool, and hit her about the head and face several times,' he continued. 'When I came to and got my senses again I saw what I'd done. I saw she was dead and decided I had to do something to keep her away from the children. I undressed her and got four sacks from the cellar, cut them open, and tied her up in them. I carried her down to the cellar and left her there.'

He went on to state that he had washed up all the blood and hidden the bloodstained clothing before the four children came home, and then, when they had all gone out again, wheeled his wife's body to the river on his bicycle. The next day he burnt the bloodstained clothing, together with his wife's false teeth, in the copper.

Since then he had managed to keep up the pretence that she was still alive by writing letters, ostensibly from her, and making trips to London to post them.

Bertie Manton was brought to trial at the Bedford Assizes. He pleaded not guilty to the charge of murder, claiming that he was guilty only of manslaughter, as he had had no intention of killing his wife and had been provoked into attacking her. However, the marks on her neck, which indicated that he had tried to strangle her, caused the jury to believe otherwise and he left the court under sentence of death.

His sentence was afterwards commuted to life imprisonment, but he died three years later, in November 1947, at Parkhurst Prison.

About three o'clock in the morning on 21 November 1931, Peter Queen, the son of a bookmaker, rushed into a Glasgow police station and reported that the woman he called his wife was dead. The police went to his home and found the body of Chrissie Gall with whom he had been living for almost a year: she had been strangled with a piece of clothes-line. There were no signs of a struggle. Chrissie Gall was lying in bed with the bedclothes pulled up over her chest; her false teeth were in place in her mouth. But at 5.30 that morning Peter Queen was charged with her murder.

Queen, a clerk in his father's office, had married at eighteen, but he and his wife — an alcoholic — had only lived together for two years. Chrissie Gall, who had once been employed by his father as a nursemaid, began living with Queen in December 1930, when he was thirty years old and she was twenty-seven. Chrissie, however, was tormented by the fear that others would find out about this. Drinking heavily, she began to suffer from depression, several times attempting suicide. But the two pathologists who carried out a post-mortem both said that she had been murdered.

The trial of Peter Queen began in Glasgow on 5 January 1932. It was stated by police witnesses that, on going to report Chrissie Gall's death, the accused had said, 'Go to 539, Dumbarton Road. I think you will find my wife dead. I think I have killed her.' Queen disputed this, telling the court that what he had actually said was, '*Don't* think I have killed her.' It was reluctantly admitted by the police that the statement had not been put into writing.

The medical evidence given for the prosecution was

challenged by Sir Bernard Spilsbury and Sir Sydney Smith, who both appeared as defence witnesses. Spilsbury declared that Chrissie Gall had committed suicide; Smith was inclined to the same view, though with less certainty. Other witnesses told the court of the prisoner's love and kindness towards her, and also of Chrissie's suicidal tendencies.

In spite of all this, the jury found the accused guilty of murder, but added a recommendation of mercy. Peter Queen was sentenced to death, the sentence afterwards being commuted to life imprisonment. He died in 1958.

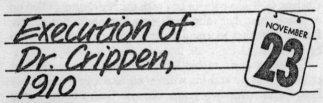

Execution of Dr. Crippen, 1910

NOVEMBER 23

Dr. Hawley Harvey Crippen, who was hanged on 23 November 1910, was an American doctor who had settled in London ten years earlier, making his living from the sale of patent medicines. He was a little man with a sandy moustache and gold-rimmed glasses, polite and considerate but very discontented. His first wife had died about 1890, and his second marriage, to the ill-fated Cora Turner, had taken place two or three years later. This was the main cause of his dissatisfaction.

Cora was the daughter of a Russian Pole; her real name, prior to her marriage, had been Kunigunde Mackamotzki. She was stout and flamboyant, and sang in music halls, calling herself Belle Elmore; she had many friends and admirers in the theatrical world. But to Crippen, who was obliged to do most of the housework, she was domineering and bad-tempered. He often quarrelled with her.

For three years he found consolation in the company of

his typist, Ethel le Neve, a younger woman who had become his mistress. But then he lost his job and his wife threatened to go and live with another man, taking their joint savings. Crippen was thus faced with serious financial difficulties and suddenly decided upon a desperate course.

On 19 January 1910, he obtained five grains of hyoscine, a poison, from a chemist's in New Oxford Street. Less than a fortnight later his wife disappeared, and Crippen began telling friends that she had returned to America because one of her relatives was ill. But he also pawned some of her jewellery and, within a few weeks, moved Ethel le Neve into their home in Hilldrop Crescent, Holloway. Finally, towards the end of March, he announced that Mrs. Crippen had died in America.

It was not until another three months had elapsed that Scotland Yard was asked to investigate the matter, and even then a search of the house by Detective Chief Inspector Walter Dew revealed no incriminating evidence. However, the visit alarmed Crippen and his mistress, and they immediately fled the country. During a more thorough search of the premises, the police then found human remains under the floor of the cellar.

The remains, from which the head, limbs and skeleton had been removed, were those of Cora Crippen: they were identified from a piece of scar tissue, the result of abdominal surgery. The presence of hyoscine in her organs proved that she had been poisoned, and a warrant was issued for the arrest of her husband and Ethel le Neve for 'murder and mutilation'.

A few days later the captain of the SS *Montrose*, sailing from Antwerp to Quebec, recognized two of his passengers as the fugitives. Crippen had shaved off his moustache and Ethel was dressed as a boy: they were travelling as Mr. John Robinson and his sixteen-year-old son. The captain sent a wireless message to the ship's owners in Liverpool, informing them of this, and Scotland Yard was notified. Chief Inspector Dew then boarded a faster ship, the SS

Laurentic, and arrested the couple in Canadian waters on 31 July.

It was, as most accounts point out, the first time that wireless had been used during the course of a murder hunt, and it was also the first major case in which the renowned pathologist Dr. Bernard Spilsbury, was involved.

Crippen, aged forty-eight, was tried at the Old Bailey in October 1910. Shortly before he was hanged at Pentonville Prison he made a public statement, declaring his love for Ethel le Neve and maintaining that she was entirely innocent. She, in the meantime, had been tried on the charge of being an accessory after the fact, and acquitted. It is not known for certain what became of her afterwards.

John Barleycorn murder, 1943

NOVEMBER
29

On the morning of 29 November 1943, Mrs. Rose Ada Robinson, a sixty-three-year-old widow who managed the John Barleycorn public house in Portsmouth, was found strangled in her bedroom. The room had been ransacked and two large handbags in which she kept money from the till were empty. The crime had been committed in the early hours, the murderer having entered the premises by forcing open a window at the back. No fingerprints had been left at the scene and the only possible clue to his identity was a small black button which had been pulled from his coat as he climbed through the window. It was later ascertained that the sum of money stolen was about £450.

The police checked on all known criminals who lived locally, but made no progress on the case until three weeks later, when Harold Loughans, a man with a long record of crime, was arrested trying to sell a stolen pair of shoes in Waterloo Road, London. Loughans, apparently suffering from remorse, told the arresting officers, 'I'm wanted for things far more serious than this. The Yard wants me. It's the trap-door for me now.' He went on to confess that it was he who had killed Mrs. Robinson, after being discovered in the act of burgling the pub.

'I had to stop her screaming, but I didn't mean to kill the old girl,' he said. 'But you know what it is when a woman screams.' He went on to declare that he had since committed a dozen other burglaries — 'to get it off my mind'.

There were no buttons on his coat to match the one found on Mrs. Robinson's window-sill — he had pulled the others off and replaced them — but various fibres found on his clothes were identified as having come from the scene of the crime. Loughans, in the meantime, had dictated and signed a confession. He was therefore charged with the murder.

Brought to trial in Winchester in March 1944, he pleaded not guilty, claiming that the confession had been fabricated by the police and producing witnesses to swear that he had spent the night of the murder at a London Underground station, which was then being used as an air-raid shelter. The jury failed to agree on a verdict, so a retrial was ordered.

This took place at the Old Bailey a fortnight later, the judge refusing to allow new evidence collected by the police to rebut Loughans' alibi on the grounds that it should have been presented at the first trial. However, Sir Bernard Spilsbury, who had not given evidence in the previous trial, was allowed to appear as a defence witness and stated his belief that the accused, who had a mutilated right hand — the four fingers were merely stumps, although the thumb was intact — could not have committed the murder. This time Loughans was acquitted.

As he left the court a free man, he was immediately

arrested again, this time for another of the crimes to which he had confessed: a burglary in St. Albans, during the course of which he had almost killed a second woman by tying her up with wire. For this he was sent to prison, having been convicted of attempted murder. He later fell foul of the law again and was given fifteen years' preventive detention.

He was still in prison in December 1960 when the *People* newspaper published extracts from the autobiography of J.D. Casswell, who had appeared for the prosecution in both trials arising out of the John Barleycorn case. These, according to Loughans, suggested that he was guilty of the murder and said clearly that he had been lucky to be acquitted. He accordingly started libel proceedings, and the case was heard in 1963.

Loughans was now sixty-seven years old and suffering from cancer of the stomach; his appearance was that of a weak and tired man. But the jury, after hearing much of the evidence which had been given in the two John Barleycorn trials, *and also evidence of Loughans' crime at St. Albans a fortnight after Mrs. Robinson's murder*, found for the defendants — saying, in effect, that the plaintiff was guilty of the crime of which he had been acquitted.

Even this was not the end of the matter, for a few months later Loughans approached the *People* and offered that newspaper an article admitting that he *had* murdered Mrs. Robinson. The *People* published his story together with a photograph of him writing it.

Harold Loughans died at the age of sixty-nine in 1965.

On 30 November 1946, the body of John McMain Mudie, a thirty-five-year-old hotel barman, was found lying in a trench in a chalkpit near Woldingham in Surrey. He had died of asphyxia, caused by hanging, about forty-eight hours earlier, and an unsuccessful attempt had been made to cover his body with soil. There were no signs of anyone having been hanged from a tree in the vicinity, and there were several minor bruises and abrasions on the body which had not been caused by the hanging itself. A straight line round Mudie's neck, visible only in photographs, showed that the noose had been tightened before he was suspended.

Mudie had worked at the Reigate Hill Hotel, about twelve miles from the chalkpit, for the previous few months, before that he had lived in Wimbledon. He was said to have been quiet and inoffensive, and there appeared to have been no reason for his murder. However, when the police appealed to the public for information, two gardeners came forward, saying that they had seen a man behaving suspiciously at the chalkpit on 27 November — the day before Mudie's death.

He had been standing on a hill overlooking the pit until he saw them, they said, and had then run down the side of it at great speed, jumped into a parked car and driven out hastily in reverse. The car, according to these witnesses, had been a small dark saloon with the figures 101 in its registration number.

On 14 December, following further publicity, an ex-boxer named John William Buckingham went to Scotland Yard and confessed that he and another man, Lawrence Smith, had abducted Mudie, having been hired to do so by

Thomas Ley, the sixty-six-year-old chairman of a property company.

'Ley told me Mudie was blackmailing a young woman and her mother who lived in Wimbledon, and that he wanted to make Mudie sign a confession and leave the country,' said Buckingham.

He went on to explain that on the day of his disappearance, Mudie had been decoyed to Ley's house in Beaufort Gardens, Kensington, by means of a bogus invitation to a cocktail party, and on arrival had been pushed into the front room and held against his will. Ley had then paid Buckingham £200 for his part in the affair and Buckingham had left the house.

When Lawrence Smith, a foreman joiner, was confronted with Buckingham's statement, he agreed that the abduction had taken place, but said that Buckingham's part in it had been greater than the statement suggested. He said that when Mudie arrived at the house he and Buckingham had thrown a rug over his head and tied him up with a clothes line. They had afterwards left him bound and gagged in Ley's presence, Smith leaving the house — also with £200 — shortly after Buckingham.

Thomas Ley, an extremely fat man, was a qualified solicitor who had once been Minister of Justice in New South Wales. Mrs. Maggie Brook, one of the directors of the property company, was his former housekeeper and mistress, and was known to have stayed for a short while in the same lodging-house as Mudie in Wimbledon. It was also known that Ley, an intensely jealous man, had accused her of having sexual intercourse with Mudie, who was over thirty years her junior, and two other young men in the same house as well.

On being informed of the allegations which had been made against him, Ley denied that there was any truth in them. The police did not believe that he was a fit enough man to have moved Mudie's body on his own, and hesitated to make an arrest until more evidence came to light. Finally, they discovered that a few days before the murder, Lawrence Smith had hired a dark Ford car with the registration number FGP 101. He was afterwards identified by one of the gardeners — though not the other — as the man who had been seen at the chalkpit.

Ley and Smith were brought to trial at the Old Bailey on 19 March 1947, charged with murder. Buckingham, who had also been accused, was allowed to turn King's Evidence, as it was feared that all three would otherwise be acquitted. Both prisoners, on being found guilty, were sentenced to death, but Ley was then found to be insane and committed to Broadmoor, where he died of a stroke on 24 July the same year. Smith's sentence was commuted to life imprisonment.

Body of Sergeant Watters found, 1953

DECEMBER 1

During the early hours of 1 December 1953, Reginald Watters, a sergeant serving with the British Occupation Forces in Germany, was found dead in his barracks in Duisburg, having apparently hanged himself. It was rumoured at the time that his German-born wife Mia was having an affair with his Irish fellow sergeant, Frederick Emmett-Dunne, and the verdict of suicide recorded at the inquest did not satisfy everyone in the unit. A few months later, when Mia and Emmett-Dunne — now stationed in England — were married, Watters' body was exhumed and a second post-mortem carried out.

This time it was found that his death had been caused not by hanging but by a blow to his throat — the sort of blow delivered with the edge of the hand in unarmed combat. The body had been hanged afterwards in order to conceal the true cause of death.

Emmett-Dunne, who had been in a commando unit during the Second World War, denied knowing anything about Watters' death, but an investigation of his movements on the evening of 30 November led to his arrest for murder. When committal proceedings started at Bow Street he pleaded that as a citizen of Eire he could not be tried before an English court for a crime which had taken place abroad. This was accepted, and he was returned to Germany, where he stood trial before a military court in Düsseldorf, at the age of thirty-three, in June 1955.

It was revealed that Emmett-Dunne had left his camp for a short time on the evening in question, and that following his return he had been seen cleaning his car outside one of the barrack blocks while a bundle large enough to contain Watters' body lay just inside the block entrance. Later he had asked his half-brother, Private Ronald Emmett — also stationed in Duisberg — for help, saying that he had killed Watters by accident and wanted to make it look as if he had committed suicide.

Emmett, reluctant to become involved in the matter, had agreed only to fetch a bucket which was to be left on its side below the corpse. He had then watched as Emmett-Dunne hung the body from a bannister with a piece of rope.

The guardroom time-sheet was found to have been altered in order to give the impression that Emmett-Dunne had been away from the camp for longer than he actually had been.

Emmett-Dunne's counsel tried to show that his client had struck Sergeant Watters in self-defence after being threatened with a revolver, but this was not believed and the prisoner was found guilty of murder. As there was no death penalty in West Germany, he was given a sentence of life imprisonment, to be served in England.

Frederick Emmett-Dunne remained in prison until July 1966, and afterwards went to work at a garage in Fulham

Road, Chelsea. In October 1969 he pleaded guilty to a charge of obtaining goods by deception having, by his own account, been blackmailed by two other ex-convicts; he asked for two similar offences to be taken into consideration. He was fined a total of £75, and advised to go to the police if anyone tried to blackmail him in future.

Haarmann and Grans brought to trial, 1924

DECEMBER
4

On 4 December 1924, two depraved and predatory men were brought to trial in Hanover, charged with the murder of twenty-seven teenage boys. The trial lasted sixteen days, with nearly 200 witnesses being called, and the revelations which were made were shocking to the point of incredibility. Fritz Haarmann, aged forty-five, and his accomplice, twenty-five-year-old Hans Grans, were shown not only to have murdered a large number of refugees from other parts of Germany, but also to have cut up and sold their bodies as meat. It was one of Europe's most astonishing series of crimes for centuries.

Haarmann, a homosexual, had been a criminal since his youth. He had served prison sentences for various types of theft and fraud, and also for sex offences involving children. Following the completion of a five-year sentence in 1918, he had started to trade in smuggled meat, operating as a police spy at the same time in order to avoid prosecution for his own activities. He also started selling second-hand clothes.

The murders, for which Haarmann, at first was solely responsible, began soon afterwards. Haarmann befriended refugees arriving at Hanover's central railway station and selected individuals to take back to his lodgings at 27, Cellarstrasse. There they were killed in a frightful manner, Haarmann biting through their throats, sometimes after sexually assaulting them. Their flesh was then cut up for sale, their skulls and bones being thrown into the river Leine.

Haarmann met Grans, who was also a homosexual and a thief, in September 1919, and they took rooms together in Neuestrasse, later moving to an alley called Rothe Reihe. Grans, the son of a librarian, was emotionless and cynical; he regarded Haarmann as his inferior and often taunted him. Haarmann was to say that Grans had instigated and taken part in many of his subsequent crimes, sometimes choosing a particular victim because he wanted his clothes.

The meat-trader had some narrow escapes. In September 1918 police officers went to his rooms in Cellarstrasse at the insistence of a missing youth's parents who claimed to have seen their son in Haarmann's company, but they made such a cursory search that nothing was found to incriminate him. Haarmann, at his trial, revealed that at the time of this visit he had had the youth's head wrapped in newspaper behind his oven.

On another occasion a customer took a piece of meat which had been purchased from Haarmann to a police analyst, suspecting that it was human flesh, only to be assured that it was pork!

In spite of these and other such incidents, Haarmann and Grans became increasingly incautious: it was estimated by a police officer that during their last sixteen months of freedom they were committing two murders every week — and sometimes they sold the clothes of the victim within a day or two of acquiring them.

Many reports were made of young people disappearing on arrival in Hanover, one newspaper claiming that there had been as many as 600 such disappearances in one year. Reports were also received from suspicious acquaintances of Haarmann and Grans, stating that while many youths

nd boys had been seen entering their lodgings, none had
ver been seen leaving. But Hanover's chief of police,
nowing that Haarmann had friends in positions of author-
y, was reluctant to take action against him.

Then, on 17 May 1924, the first of many human skulls
as found by the river. This was followed by a second skull
n 29 May, and two more on 13 June. Finally, the police
hief decided that something had to be done, and arranged
or Haarmann to be kept under surveillance by two detec-
ves from Berlin.

On 22 June Haarmann approached a boy named
romm, but a quarrel started between them and then they
egan to fight. They were promptly arrested by the two
etectives and Haarmann was held in custody, charged
ith indecent behaviour. The arrest was followed by a
earch of his rooms and the discovery of many items of
othing and personal possessions. The landlady's son was
und to be wearing a coat which belonged to a boy who
ad been reported missing. Haarmann, on being
uestioned, confessed to several murders, implicating
rans, who was then arrested too.

Further human remains were discovered by boys play-
g in a meadow on 24 July, and later, when the river-bed
as dredged, an assortment of 500 bones was recovered.

At the trial there were many scenes which were painful
watch, with grief-stricken parents identifying items
hich had belonged to the victims. Haarmann was allowed
interrupt the proceedings almost as he pleased, and did
frequently — sometimes jocularly, sometimes with
dignation. At one point he was even allowed to smoke a
gar. As for Grans, he denied everything, though with
tle chance of being believed.

Fritz Haarmann, fearing that he might be sent to an
ylum, insisted that he was sane and demanded to be
ecuted. Having heard the evidence of two psychiatrists,
th of whom declared that he was sane, the court decided
at death was the appropriate punishment in his case. But
ans Grans was dealt with more leniently, being given a

325

sentence of life imprisonment, which was later reduced to twelve years.

Haarmann's execution, by beheading, was carried out without delay, perhaps because it was feared that an attempt might otherwise be made to lynch him.

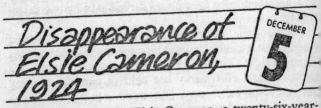

Disappearance of Elsie Cameron, 1924

DECEMBER 5

On 5 December 1924, Elsie Cameron, a twenty-six-year-old unemployed typist, left her parents' home in Kensal Rise, north London, to go and stay with her fiancé, Norman Thorne, on his chicken farm near the village of Crowborough in Sussex. The couple had been engaged for almost two years, and although Thorne had since fallen in love with a local girl, Elsie was determined to become his wife. However, her parents received no news from her during the next few days, and her father, on sending Thorne a telegram, received a reply saying that she had not arrived at the farm. The police were then informed that Elsie had disappeared.

Thorne, who was two years younger than Elsie, was a mechanic by trade, but had set himself up as a chicken farmer after being forced to go on the dole in the summer of 1921. His home was hardly an ideal one; he lived in squalor in one of the huts on the farm. Nor were his prospects good, for the business was not doing well and he was in financial difficulty. But Elsie, a plain and nervous woman, had been willing to tolerate this, and had even tried to convince him that she was pregnant — which she was not — in order to hurry him into marrying her. She did not realize that Thorne was equally determined to avoid

326

loing so.

On being questioned about Elsie's disappearance,
Thorne repeated his claim that she had not been to the
arm that day and that he did not know her whereabouts —
nd he persisted in this story in spite of being told that two
lower-growers had seen her in the vicinity on the day in
uestion. But a few weeks later, when it was discovered
hat a neighbour had actually seen Elsie entering the farm
n 5 December, he was arrested on suspicion and a search
f the premises was started.

The police found Elsie's wrist-watch, which had been
amaged, and some of her jewellery in a tool-shed, and the
ollowing morning unearthed an attaché case which she
ad been carrying when she left her parents' house for the
st time. Norman Thorne then made a statement, admit-
ng that she was dead but denying that he had killed her.
lsie's remains were afterwards discovered in the ground
nder a chicken-run. Her body had been dismembered
ith a hack-saw.

According to Thorne's statement, Elsie had arrived at
e farm unexpectedly and a quarrel had taken place
etween them over his association with the local girl. Later
e had left her alone in the hut for nearly two hours, and
uring that time she had hanged herself from a beam with
piece of cord. 'I was about to go to Doctor Turle and
nock up someone to go for the police and I realized the
osition I was in,' the statement continued. He had then
t up her body and buried it.

John Norman Holmes Thorne was brought to trial at
e Lewes Assizes on 4 March 1925. Sir Bernard Spils-
ury, appearing as a prosecution witness, said that he had
und evidence of several injuries on Elsie's head and body,
d that a 'crushing blow' on her forehead could have been
used by an Indian club found outside the hut. He also
id that he had found no evidence of hanging. This
idence was challenged by medical experts for the
fence, but Thorne was found guilty and sentenced to death.

He was hanged at Wandsworth Prison on 22 April 1925.

Execution of Martha Marek, 1938

Martha Marek, an Austrian murderess executed on 6 December 1938, was a woman of great beauty and few scruples. Born to unknown parents about 1904, she was adopted by a poor couple named Löwenstein in Vienna and later became the ward of Moritz Fritsch, a wealthy store-owner who found her working in a dress shop in 1919. She was then sent to finishing schools in England and France and, when Fritsch died, inherited a substantial sum of money. However, she was extravagant, and soon after her marriage in 1924 to Emil Marek, an engineering student, she had nothing left.

To remedy this, she and Marek made an incredible attempt at fraud — an attempt which required a sacrifice on her husband's part and became known as the 'Case of the Chopped-off Leg'. Marek, having been insured against accident for £10,000, allowed Martha to hack one of his legs with an axe, so that he could claim to have injured himself while cutting down a tree. The wound thus inflicted was serious, and the leg had to be amputated below the knee. But the surgeon performing the operation found that it had been caused by three separate cuts, and that the angle of these was inconsistent with Marek's story.

The police investigated the matter, and the couple were charged with attempted fraud. Though they were both acquitted when the case came to court, the insurance company forced them to accept a settlement of only £3000. At the same time, they were both given short prison sentences for bribing a hospital orderly into accusing the surgeon of misconduct.

Emil and Martha Marek later went to Algiers, where they became destitute after the failure of a business venture. They returned to Vienna, where Martha, who now had two children, was reduced to selling vegetables from a street barrow. In July 1932 Marek died in a charity ward, his death being put down to tuberculosis. The following month Martha's baby daughter Ingebrog also died. But these deaths aroused no suspicion, and Martha became the companion of an elderly relative, Susanne Löwenstein.

Frau Löwenstein died after making a will in Martha Marek's favour, but again Martha spent most of her money within a short time. She began letting rooms in her house, taking in a Frau Kittenberger, who died after Martha had insured her life for £300. This time, however, poisoning was suspected, and Frau Kittenberger's son demanded an investigation. His mother's body was exhumed and found to contain thallium.

This discovery led to the bodies of Emil Marek, Ingeborg Marek and Frau Löwenstein all being exhumed, and each was found to have died of the same poison. Moreover, the police found that Martha's son Peter, who had been boarded out, was also suffering from thallium poisoning. A chemist stated that Martha had bought the poison from him. She was beheaded, her execution being carried out with an axe.

The death penalty, previously abolished in Austria, had been restored by Hitler.

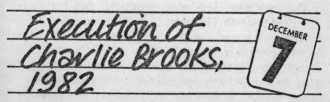

Execution of Charlie Brooks, 1982

DECEMBER
7

On 7 December 1982, Charlie Brooks, a forty-year-old black convicted of the murder of a second-hand car salesman six years earlier, was executed by lethal injection at

329

Huntsville Prison, Texas. As he was the first prisoner to die by this method in the United States, the execution naturally aroused much public interest and curiosity.

It was carried out in that part of the prison which had formerly been the gas chamber, the apparatus of death comprising a medical trolley, to which the prisoner was strapped, an intravenous needle inserted into his right arm and a rubber tube leading across the floor of the execution chamber to an adjacent room, where the executioner — a medical technician — was hidden.

The executioner opened a valve at his end of the rubber tube and administered a dose of sodium pentathol, causing the condemned man to lose consciousness; this was followed by quantities of pavulon and potassium chloride. Within minutes Charlie Brooks was pronounced dead, the execution having apparently been carried out efficiently and painlessly.

The crime for which Charlie Brooks was executed had taken place shortly before Christmas 1976. Brooks and another man, Woody Lourdres, had set out in the company of a prostitute with the intention of shoplifting. When their car broke down they tried to steal another from a garage by taking it for a trial run and not returning it, but the garage insisted that one of its employees should go with them. Brooks and Lourdres then took the salesman to a motel, bound him hand and foot and shot him through the head. It was never discovered which of the two actually fired the shot.

The two men were tried separately, and both were sentenced to death. However, Lourdres managed to obtain a retrial and agreed to a plea-bargain, as a result of which he was given a sentence of forty years' imprisonment. Brooks appealed repeatedly against his death sentence, the news that his last attempt had failed being received while he was strapped to the trolley in the execution chamber.

Brooks' execution was attended by a twenty-seven-year-old nurse with whom he was in love: they had both committed themselves to each other 'for the next life', and the prisoner had asked that she be allowed to be present as a witness. Having become a Muslim during the time he had spent on Death Row, he was also attended by two Islamic priests with whom he went through a brief ritual. He remained calm throughout his final ordeal.

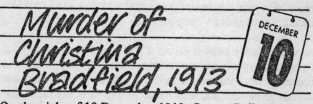

Murder of Christina Bradfield, 1913

DECEMBER 10

On the night of 10 December 1913, George Ball, a twenty-two-year-old tarpaulin packer also known as George Sumner, battered his forty-year-old employer, Christina Bradfield, to death in her shop in Old Hall Street, Liverpool. With the assistance of the shop's other employee, Samuel Angeles Elltoft, aged eighteen, he then sewed her body into a sack in readiness to dispose of it in the Leeds and Liverpool Canal. But before it could be taken from the premises a shutter from the shop window blew down, falling on to a man who was standing in the street.

The man, a ship's steward named Walter Eaves, was waiting to meet a girl and, fortunately, was wearing a bowler hat. This took the force of the blow, but was damaged by it, and when Samuel Elltoft came out to replace the shutter, Eaves told him what had happened. Elltoft told Ball, who came out to apologize and paid Eaves 2s (10p) compensation. However, when Ball and Elltoft left the shop a few minutes later, pushing a handcart covered with tarpaulin, the unlucky ship's steward was still waiting in the street and could hardly fail to notice what they were doing.

Though the sack had been weighted with pieces of iron, it was found obstructing one of the gates of a lock the following day and pulled ashore; the body was then identified without difficulty from a medallion round its neck. Elltoft was arrested at his home, but Ball, realizing that he had little chance of avoiding a murder charge, had absconded.

During the course of the ten-day search which followed Ball's photograph was shown on cinema screens all over Liverpool, and it was as a result of this that he was recognized. On being arrested, he was found to have Christina Bradfield's watch in his possession and bloodstains on his clothes.

In February 1914 Ball and Elltoft were brought to trial at the Liverpool Assizes, charged with murder. Ball was found guilty and sentenced to death; Elltoft, though acquitted of murder, was found guilty of being an accessory after the fact and sentenced to four years' imprisonment.

George Ball, having finally confessed to the murder, was hanged at Walton Prison on 26 February.

Brenda Nash found murdered, 1960

DECEMBER
11

On 11 December 1960, Brenda Nash, an eleven-year-old Girl Guide, was found dead in a ditch on Yately Common, in Hampshire, about twenty-five miles from her home in Heston, Middlesex. She had been reported missing after failing to return home on the night of 28 October previously, and it was estimated that she had been dead for about six weeks. She had been strangled during the course of a struggle, evidently while trying to resist a sexual assault.

Three months earlier, on 9 September, a Girl Guide

living in Twickenham — about three miles from Heston — had been abducted and raped by a man driving a black Vauxhall car, and police suspected that the same man was responsible for the disappearance of Brenda Nash. So far, in spite of interviewing about 5000 owners of black Vauxhalls registered in Middlesex and Surrey, they had been unable to discover his identity. They therefore began a re-examination of all the statements that had been taken.

However, the news that the body had been discovered prompted a young woman hairdresser in London's West End to tell them that a fellow employee had been asked by her uncle, who fitted the wanted man's description, to provide him with an alibi for the day of the girl's disappearance. This piece of information led to the arrest of Arthur Albert Jones, aged forty-four, a married man with a sixteen-year-old son.

Jones, who lived in Hounslow, a mile from Brenda Nash's home, was identified by the girl who had been raped in September. He was formally charged with that crime and remanded in custody.

Arthur Jones had been among the 5000 car-owners interviewed by police before the discovery of Brenda's body. On that earlier occasion he had claimed that he and his wife had been to visit his sister-in-law in Beckenham, Kent, on 28 October. But his sister-in-law, having confirmed this, now confessed to having given him a false alibi.

There was evidence to connect him directly with the murder, for green fibres found on the victim's clothes were similar to those of a rug in Jones' car, and a piece of chain found under her head matched other pieces from his house. But the police hesitated to charge him with murder in the hope of further information coming to light.

In March 1961 Jones was tried at the Old Bailey for rape, convicted, and sentenced to fourteen years' imprisonment. The publication of his photograph in the newspapers the following day led to a number of witnesses coming forward to say that they had seen him in Heston on the evening of Brenda Nash's disappearance. Then a fellow prisoner named Roberts reported that Jones had confessed the murder to him.

Jones was charged with the murder on 10 May after two witnesses had picked him out at an identity parade, and brought to trial on this charge on 17 June. The jury, after retiring for only seven minutes, returned a verdict of guilty, and he was sentenced to life imprisonment.

Beginning of the Boyle murder case, 1935

DECEMBER 13

On 13 December 1935, police in Boyle, Co. Roscommon, received a report that Patrick Henry, a sixty-seven-year-old local man, had not been seen for three months. Henry, known as 'Old Pat', was the tenant of a two-roomed cottage on the outskirts of the town — a hovel without electricity, sanitation or even running water. His landlady, who lived in another part of Boyle, had been there several times since his disappearance and found it locked on each occasion. Having received no rent from him since the end of August, she now wanted to be free to let the place to somebody else.

Two policemen accompanied the landlady to the cottage, forced the padlock by which the door was secured, and found the old man's decomposed body inside. Patrick Henry had been brutally beaten with a blunt instrument; his skull had been fractured and his jaw and other facial bones also broken. His body had been burnt in several places, some of the burns having been sustained while he was still alive. The pathologist who examined the body expressed the opinion that his death had occurred two or three months previously.

Despite the squalid conditions in which Henry had lived, the motive for his murder had clearly been robbery, for his gold watch had been stolen and the linings of his jacket and waistcoat cut open — undoubtedly in the hope that they would be found to contain money. A fifty-six-year-old man named Thomas Kelly, who had lodged with the victim for some months, had left about the time that Henry was last seen alive, and the police were certain that he was the person responsible. But they had no idea where he had gone, and it was several months before they succeeded in tracing him.

Kelly was finally apprehended in Coatbridge, near Glasgow, in June 1936, after it had been learnt that he was expected to visit a bank there. On being taken to a nearby police station, he suddenly produced a cut-throat razor, slashed the side of his neck and then put up a fierce struggle before being overpowered. He was kept under guard in a Glasgow hospital until he was well enough to be taken back to Ireland to stand trial for murder.

The trial began on 10 November, the prosecution contending that the murder had been committed on 11 September the previous year, and producing evidence that Kelly and Henry had not been on good terms. A woman living in the adjoining cottage said that she had seen Henry for the last time on 10 September, and also that she had seen Kelly the following afternoon. The manager of the local labour exchange stated that neither of the men had collected their unemployment benefit on 11 September though both had signed on the day before. But after hearing further evidence to the effect that Kelly had talked about leaving Boyle on 9 or 10 September, the prosecution obtained permission to change the date on which the murder had allegedly taken place to 10 September.

Thomas Kelly denied the offence, saying that he had left Boyle on 11 September, and that Henry had still been alive at the time of his departure. He was unable to explain satisfactorily why he had left Boyle without luggage, why he had failed to collect his dole, or why he had been using a false name and wearing spectacles which he did not need at the time of his arrest. On being found guilty, he was sentenced to death.

But later, when seven new witnesses came forward, claiming to have seen Patrick Henry alive two days after the date specified in the charge, i.e. on 12 September 1935, the Court of Criminal Appeal set aside the conviction and ordered a fresh trial. This was held in April 1937, when the defence also produced medical evidence that Henry had not been dead for as long as three months at the time the body was discovered. On this occasion the jury was unable to agree on a verdict.

On 15 November 1937, Thomas Kelly was brought to trial yet again, and this time the court heard *eleven* witnesses state that they had seen Henry alive on 12 September 1935 — but, astonishingly, the prisoner was found guilty and once more sentenced to death. It was perhaps in keeping with the character of this confusing case that the judge omitted to put on the black cap before sentence was pronounced.

Thomas Kelly was afterwards reprieved, his sentence being commuted to life imprisonment. He remained in prison for the next ten years, and was released on 17 December 1947.

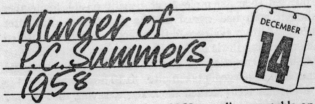

Murder of
P.C. Summers,
1958

DECEMBER
14

On the night of 14 December 1958, a police constable on patrol duty in Holloway, north London, found two rival gangs of youths engaged in an affray outside a dance-hall in Seven Sisters Road. It was a frightful battle, with about twenty people, some armed with choppers, hammers or bottles, screaming and striking out at each other. PC Raymond Summers, aged twenty-three, immediately dashed in among them, ordering them to desist.

Many of them did so and took to their heels, but one man drew a ten-inch knife and thrust it into the policeman's back. Then he, too, ran off and PC Summers, tended by two teenage girls, lay dying on the pavement.

A hunt began for those who had taken part in the fighting, and before long a large number of young people were being questioned at Caledonian Road police station. Among them was Ronald Henry Marwood, a twenty-five-year-old scaffolder with cuts on his left hand, who claimed to have been involved in a fight elsewhere. Though allowed to go home after making a statement, Marwood was later found to have lied about his movements, and when police went to see him again they found him to be missing from his home.

On 20 December Scotland Yard announced that they wished to interview him in connection with the murder, but it was not until 27 January 1959 that he was seen again. He then gave himself up and made a second statement, admitting that he had struck the blow which killed PC Summers but denying that he had done so intentionally.

His story was that he and some friends had gone to the dance-hall and found a scuffle taking place outside on the pavement. Someone had aimed a blow at him with a chopper and his hand had been cut when he shielded his head with it. Afterwards, while he had his hands in his pockets, PC Summers had punched him, he said. His statement then continued:

'I must have had my hand on the knife in my right-hand pocket. I struck out, with the intention of pushing him away from me. I remember striking him with the knife and the policeman fell ... I ran away and kept on running.'

At his trial, which began at the Old Bailey on 12 March, Marwood pleaded not guilty and retracted his second state-

337

ment, saying that the police had fabricated parts of it. He had had nothing in his hand when he hit PC Summers, he said; he had merely punched him and run off. He told the court that he had drunk about ten pints of brown ale beforehand. The jury nonetheless found him guilty of murder and he was sentenced to death.

Marwood was not a habitual criminal and was not even connected with either of the gangs involved in the fighting. There was therefore widespread sympathy for him when his appeal was dismissed, and many protests were made. On the morning of his execution, 8 May 1959, hostile crowds gathered outside Pentonville Prison, and mounted police had to be called to keep order.

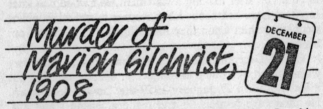

Murder of Marion Gilchrist, 1908
DECEMBER 21

On the evening of 21 December 1908, Helen Lambie, twenty-one-year-old servant to an elderly spinster living in Queen's Terrace, West Prince's Street, Glasgow, went out as usual to buy a newspaper. When she returned about ten minutes later, she found a neighbour, Arthur Adams, standing outside the flat; he told her that he had heard noises from inside. Helen, apparently unconcerned, unlocked the door and entered, leaving Adams standing at the threshold.

At that moment another man appeared from the spare bedroom, walked towards the door and left hurriedly, without speaking to either of them. It was only after he had made good his escape that Helen found her employer lying in front of the dining-room fireplace with a rug over her head.

Miss Marion Gilchrist, aged eighty-two, had been savagely battered, sustaining injuries from which she died shortly afterwards. A diamond crescent brooch had been stolen and a wooden box containing private papers wrenched open, but other valuables had been left untouched on Miss Gilchrist's dressing-table. In his haste to get away from the scene of the crime, the murderer had almost run into Mary Barrowman, a fourteen-year-old messenger girl walking along the street. However, the description which this third witness gave of him was markedly different from that provided by the other two.

Appealing for information, the police learnt that Oscar Slater, a German Jew in his thirties, had been offering to sell a pawn-ticket for a diamond brooch. They went to his flat in St. George's Road, a few minutes' walk from the home of the victim, but found that he had left in the company of his mistress. When further inquiries revealed that he had boarded a ship bound for the United States on 26 December, extradition proceedings were started and the three witnesses travelled to New York to give evidence against him.

Oscar Slater, whose real name was Leschziner, denied the offence. The brooch which he had pawned had *not* been Miss Gilchrist's at all and had, in fact, been in his possession some weeks before the murder took place. But, for reasons of their own, the Glasgow police were determined that he should be convicted, and Slater suddenly gave up contesting the extradition and declared himself willing to return to Scotland to face trial. He arrived back in Glasgow in the custody of a police officer on 21 February 1909, and his trial took place in Edinburgh early in May.

Various witnesses were produced by the prosecution to identify the prisoner as a man they had seen lurking near Miss Gilchrist's flat during the weeks preceding the crime. Helen Lambie and Mary Barrowman both identified him as the man they had seen on the evening of the murder, the servant more positively than she had done so in New

York and the messenger admitting that she had been shown photographs of him before making her identification. Arthur Adams could only say that Slater bore a resemblance to the man in question.

As for the medical evidence, there was disagreement among the witnesses over whether a light hammer found in the prisoner's luggage could have been the murder weapon, and none could state with certainty that clothes which he had allegedly worn at the time of the murder were blood-stained, even though the victim had been struck over fifty times.

The most important pieces of evidence produced by the prosecution were therefore far from satisfactory, and, to weaken the case still further, Slater's mistress and *their* servant both claimed that he had been at home when the murder took place. But, unfortunately for him, the prisoner was also shown to be an unsavoury character, who had lived partly by gambling and partly on immoral earnings, and the jury found him guilty by a majority verdict. He was sentenced to death.

Two days before he was due to be hanged, Slater's sentence was commuted to life imprisonment. But many believed him to be innocent and some, including Sir Arthur Conan Doyle, campaigned tirelessly for an inquiry into the case. Even so, he served over eighteen years in prison before being finally vindicated on appeal and awarded £6000 compensation.

He died twenty years later, in 1948, at the age of seventy-four.

Murder of Stephanie Baird, 1959

On the evening of 23 December 1959, police went to a YWCA hostel in Birmingham to investigate a report that a young woman had been attacked by an intruder. The attack had taken place in the ground-floor laundry room, where the victim, twenty-one-year-old Margaret Brown, had been working. The intruder had entered the room, switching off the light, and struck at her in the darkness. But he had not managed to hurt her, and had run off when she screamed.

However, during a search of the premises, the police found one of the rooms locked and, forcing open the door, discovered that the occupant, twenty-nine-year-old Stephanie Baird, had been murdered in a revolting manner. Her head, which had been severed from her body, was lying on the bed. Her body, which was naked and hideously mutilated, was on the floor. And beside these gruesome remains lay a note scribbled on an envelope. It read: 'This was the thing I thought would never come.'

Stephanie Baird was found to have been strangled before her body was mutilated, but it was clear from the nature of the mutilations that her murder had been the work of a sadist. But apart from the note which had been left, there were no clues to his identity, and the police had to make extensive house-to-house inquiries in the hope of obtaining further evidence. It was after 20,000 other men had been interviewed that Patrick Byrne, a twenty-eight-year-old Irish labourer, was seen.

Byrne, who was staying with his mother in Warrington, had worked in Birmingham and lodged near the YWCA hostel at the time of the murder: it was his landlady there who had given police the address at which he could be found. But the police had no reason to suspect that he was the culprit until they asked as a matter of course, if they could take his fingerprints. He then became agitated and, following further questions, admitted that he was the person who had killed Stephanie Baird.

His handwriting was found to match that of the note left in the victim's room, and he also gave details of the crime which had not been revealed to the press. He was charged with murder.

In his confession, Byrne admitted to being a fantasist preoccupied with sadistic ideas, and also to feeling compelled to terrify women 'to get my own back on them for causing my nervous tension through sex'. On the evening in question, he said, he had peered through one of the windows of the hostel hoping to see one of the occupants undressing, and had seen Stephanie Baird, wearing an underskirt and pullover, packing a suitcase. He had then broken into the building and stood on a chair in order to watch her through the fanlight, but she had heard a noise and opened the door.

He tried to kiss her and when she resisted, pushed her back into the room and strangled her. He then took off her clothes and raped her before finding a tableknife in a drawer and mutilating her body. Having cut off her head, he held it up by the hair, watching himself in a mirror. Afterwards the sight of Margaret Brown in the laundry room excited him afresh and he tried to hit her with a stone wrapped in a brassiere from a clothes line outside.

Brought to trial at the Birmingham Assizes in March 1960, Patrick Byrne was found guilty of murder, the jury having evidently been impressed by evidence that he was sexually abnormal but not insane. This verdict was changed on appeal to one of manslaughter, but Byrne's sentence of life imprisonment was not reduced.

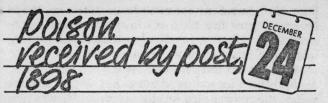

On 24 December 1898, Harry Cornish, sports director of New York's exclusive Knickerbocker Athletic Club, received a silver toothpick holder and a bottle of what appeared to be bromo-seltzer through the post. The package had been sent anonymously and was thought to have been a joke on the part of one of his acquaintances. A couple of days later Cornish took both articles home and gave them to his cousin who, like her mother, lived with him in his apartment on West 84th Street. The following morning his aunt, Mrs Katherine J. Adams, collapsed and died after drinking some of the 'bromo-seltzer' in a glass of water. An autopsy revealed that she had died from cyanide poisoning.

Two months earlier Henry C. Barnett, another member of the Knickerbocker Club, had received a box of Kutnow's powder — 'pleasant-tasting effervescent salts' — also sent anonymously through the post; this was analysed after he became ill and found to contain cyanide of mercury. Although Barnett had died in November, it appeared that his death had not been caused by poisoning but by diphtheria. Even so, an attempt at poisoning *had* been made, and it was remembered now that only eleven days after his death, Blanche Chesebrough, whom Barnett had been courting, had married his rival, Roland B. Molineux, the manager of a factory in Newark, New Jersey.

Molineux, a third member of the Knickerbocker Club, was the son of General Edward Leslie Molineux, a hero of the Civil War and a prominent figure in New York. He had enough knowledge of chemistry to have prepared the fatal substance; it was also known that he disliked Cornish intensely and had tried unsuccessfully to get him removed from his position as sports director. Moreover, seven experts declared that his handwriting had characteristics identical to that of the package sent to Cornish which, fortunately, had not been thrown away.

When this was revealed at the inquest into Mrs. Adams' death, the jury found that Molineux had, in fact, sent the poison; the coroner then ordered his arrest. He was later alleged to have murdered Barnett as well, but the charge on which he was eventually brought to trial concerned the murder of Mrs. Adams only.

The trial took place in New York City's Central Criminal Court and lasted from 14 November 1899, to 11 February 1900. Molineux, aged thirty-two, was alleged to have murdered Mrs. Adams by mistake, having intended the poison for her nephew. The handwriting evidence proved to the most important part of the prosecution's case, and during the course of an eight-hour retirement the jury asked to be supplied with a set of the exhibits. Finally, Molineux was found guilty of murder in the first degree and sentenced to death.

In October 1901 the verdict was set aside on appeal and a fresh trial ordered. This took place in 1902, with Molineux producing an alibi for the time that the package was posted, and further handwriting experts appearing to challenge the evidence of those called by the prosecution. Another new witness claimed to have seen the package being posted and said she was 'pretty sure' that *Cornish* was the man who had posted it. This time the verdict was one of not guilty and Molineux was released.

While under sentence of death Molineux had written a book, *The Room with the Little Door*, recording his impressions of prison life. When this was published, it became quite popular, and he afterwards wrote romantic fiction for Sunday newspaper supplements. However, he was hardly romantic in real life, for he contracted syphilis and became insane, his wife having obtained a divorce in the meantime. He died in a lunatic asylum on 2 November 1917.

Murder of Harry Michaelson, 1948

DECEMBER 26

During the early hours of 26 December 1948, Harry Michaelson, a lightning cartoonist known as 'One Minute Michaelson', was found fatally injured at the entrance door of his basement flat in the Paddington district of London. He had been attacked by an intruder in his bedroom but had managed to stagger outside in search of help. He was bleeding from a deep wound on his forehead and was later found to have fractured ribs as well as a fractured skull. He died in hospital without being able to give any information about the attack.

It was learnt from the porter of the block that Mr. Michaelson had been staying in his flat alone, as his wife was out of London. He had evidently been awakened by the noise of the intruder, who had entered by an open window, and had switched on the light and challenged him. His jacket and trousers were found lying on the floor, and there was no money in any of the pockets. The murder weapon, a tubular steel chair, was taken away for examination and a single fingerprint was found on it.

Though fingerprint experts tried to identify the culprit from this, they got no immediate results due to the difficulty of checking individual prints. But just over three weeks later a young man was seen acting suspiciously in the St John's Wood area and taken into custody. When his fingerprints were sent to Scotland Yard one of them was found to match the one on the steel chair. The man was found to be Harry Lewis, a twenty-one-year-old Welshman and a known thief. He had no fixed address.

On being questioned about the murder, Lewis made a full confession. He said that on the night in question he had been wandering the streets penniless when he saw the open window and decided to break into the flat. He managed to get into the victim's bedroom and had taken some money from one of the trouser pockets when Michaelson woke up and began to remonstrate with him. Lewis then panicked and began to hit him with the chair — the first object that came to hand. He afterwards left the flat by the same window as he had used before.

Harry Lewis, who had gained £5 8s 9d (£5.44) by the crime, was brought to trial at the Old Bailey on 7 March 1949. He pleaded not guilty to the murder charge, his counsel contending that Michaelson had died as a result of his hospital treatment rather than the blows struck by the prisoner. But a pathologist appearing for the prosecution said that he would have died irrespective of his operation, and Lewis was found guilty. Despite a recommendation of mercy from the jury, he was hanged at Pentonville Prison on 21 April.

Detective Chief Superintendent Peter Beveridge, who investigated the crime, later remarked that the victim had been a kindly man, and that if Lewis had asked him for money — especially at Christmas — he would almost certainly have been given some.

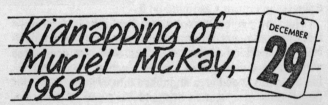

Kidnapping of Muriel McKay, 1969

DECEMBER 29

On the evening of 29 December 1969, Alick McKay, deputy chairman of the *News of the World* newspaper, found his fifty-five-year-old wife Muriel missing from their home in Arthur Road, Wimbledon. No note had been left for him, the telephone in the hall had been disconnected and the contents of his wife's handbag lay scattered on the stairs. Mr. McKay informed the police who, though far from convinced that it wasn't a publicity stunt, treated the disappearance as a case of possible kidnapping. Some hours later, after his telephone had been reconnected, Mr. McKay received the first of many calls from a coloured man claiming to speak for a group called 'Mafia M3'.

The man said that Mrs. McKay was in the hands of his group and would be killed unless a million pounds was paid for her return. When Mr. McKay said that he could not raise so much money the man insisted that that was the sum the group wanted, and that it should be ready in two days. He added that they had intended to kidnap the wife of Rupert Murdoch, the newspaper's millionaire chairman, but being unable to do this, had decided on Mrs. McKay instead. The call was made from a public call-box in Epping.

Two days later, following a second call, Mr. McKay received a letter from his wife which had been posted in north London. It read: 'Please do something to get me home. I am blindfolded and cold. Only blankets. Please co-operate for I cannot keep going ... I think of you constantly ... What have I done to deserve this treatment?' In further telephone calls, the kidnappers continued to insist that Mr. McKay should pay a ransom of £1 million, but it was some time before they gave instructions for its delivery.

The case was highly publicized from the start, with the result that the culprits knew the police were involved and Mr. McKay's telephone was frequently occupied with nuisance calls from other people. At one stage even the kidnappers complained, in a letter to the editor of the *News of the World*, that they had tried to contact Mr. McKay several times but found his number engaged on each occasion.

On 22 January two further letters from Mrs. McKay were received, together with a ransom note from the kidnappers giving detailed instructions about what should be done with the money. In one of the letters Mrs. McKay said that she was 'deteriorating in health and spirit', and pleaded with her husband to keep the police out of the affair.

The ransom note said that half the money should be handed over to the kidnappers on 1 February. But in the meantime, following three more telephone calls, Mr. McKay received another note from them, together with two more letters from his wife which had been written in a state of despair.

On the night of 1 February a suitcase containing £500,000 — most of it in forged notes — was taken to a telephone box in Edmonton, on the A10, by a police officer pretending to be Alick McKay's son, Ian. There he received a call directing him to another call-box along the same road, where he found further instructions written in a cigarette packet. In accordance with these, the suitcase was left on a bank at High Cross. However, the kidnappers failed to collect it, and two days later Ian McKay received a telephone call in which he was accused of setting a trap for them. Police cars had been seen near the place where the money had been left, the caller said angrily.

Ian McKay denied that there had been a trap, and on 5 February fresh instructions were received for the money to be paid the following day. This time police officers impersonating Alick McKay and his married daughter Diane went to one of the A10 call-boxes and were then directed to another box in London's East End. There they received instructions to go on the Underground to Epping, where they would receive a further call. They were then told to go to Bishop's Stortford, where they were to leave the money — this time in two suitcases — beside a mini-van parked in a garage forecourt.

They arrived at the garage in a mini-cab. But before the money was left the mini-cab stopped on the other side of the road and a third police officer, who had been hiding on the floor, crawled out and disappeared behind a hedge. Other policemen later took up positions close by.

Once again the kidnappers did not collect the money,

this time because the suitcases were taken off to the local police station after being reported by a couple who thought that somebody must have lost them. But in the meantime a dark blue Volvo had been seen passing the garage several times, the driver apparently taking an interest in them. This car was afterwards found to belong to Arthur Hosein, a thirty-four-year-old Muslim from Trinidad, who lived with his family and his twenty-two-year-old brother, Nizamodeen, on a farm near Stocking Pelham in Hertfordshire.

Arthur Hosein's fingerprints were found to match those of the ransom notes, the envelopes and the cigarette packet from the call-box on the A10, and various items found in the seventeenth-century farmhouse connected the two brothers with Mrs. McKay's disappearance. But Mrs. McKay was not there and, despite a search of the farm and its surroundings lasting several weeks, no trace of her body was found.

The two brothers were brought to trial at the Old Bailey in September 1970, and found guilty of murder, kidnapping and blackmail, the jury recommending leniency in the case of Nizamodeen Hosein, as he had been dominated by Arthur. Both were given life sentences for Mrs. McKay's murder, Arthur Hosein receiving a further twenty-five years and his brother a further fifteen years on the other charges.

Though there is no certainty of what became of Mrs. McKay's body, it is generally believed that it was cut up and fed to Arthur Hosein's pigs.

On the afternoon of 30 December 1950, Carl and Thelma Mosser, driving along Highway 66 between Tulsa and Oklahoma City, stopped to give a lift to a young man who was hitch-hiking. The family came from Atwood, Illinois, where Carl was a farmer, and were on their way to visit relatives in Albuquerque, New Mexico. However, the hitch-hiker pulled out a gun and, getting into the car, forced them to drive according to his instructions.

The gunman had nowhere in particular in mind, and during the next three days made the frightened Mossers drive from town to town in Oklahoma, New Mexico, Texas and Arkansas, until finally he shot all five members of the family and threw their bodies into a disused mineshaft near Joplin, Missouri. He then drove the car back to Tulsa himself, abandoned it and went back to hitch-hiking on the morning of 2 January.

The car was found in a ditch on 3 January by a deputy sheriff of Osage County, who afterwards examined it and found bloodstains, bullet holes and used bullets on the inside. When this became known to the inhabitants of the county, witnesses reported having seen the hitch-hiker near the car the previous morning, and roadblocks were set up in the hope that he was still in the area.

Information was received from a man running a combined filling station and grocery store in Wichita Falls, Texas, of a struggle which had taken place there on the evening of 30 December when Mosser tried to overpower the hitch-hiker after they had stopped to fill the tank.

Another man revealed that earlier the same day he had given the gunman a lift from Lubbock, Texas, to the outskirts of Oklahoma City. Then, he said, he had been

350

forced into the trunk at gunpoint, but had later managed to escape. A receipt from a pawnshop in El Paso, made out to W.E. Cook, had been discovered in the car when it was found abandoned on Highway 66.

As a result of this last piece of information, the hitch-hiker was quickly identified as William E. Cook, a twenty-three-year-old Joplin man with a criminal record who had been released from the Missouri penitentiary in June 1950. A complaint was accordingly filed, charging Cook with the kidnapping of the motorist who had escaped.

Cook, who was of medium height and build and had a drooping eyelid, was known to have been staying at a motel in Blythe, a small town in east California, less than a fortnight earlier, and on 4 January a deputy sheriff who knew him called there to see if he had returned. To his surprise, Cook came to the door with a gun in his hand and ordered him to get back into his car. The two men then drove out into the desert, where Cook left the deputy tied up on the roadside before driving off on his own. Eleven days later he was arrested in Mexico; the bodies of the five members of the Mosser family were discovered shortly afterwards.

While in custody in San Diego William Cook confessed not only to those five murders but also to the killing of another man, whose body had been found thirty-five miles south of Mexicali, in southern California. Robert H. Dewey, aged thirty-two, of Seattle, Washington, had also been abducted and forced to drive according to Cook's instructions; he had been shot dead during the course of a struggle. It was for this murder that Cook was brought to trial and sentenced to death.

He was executed in San Quentin's gas chamber on 12 December 1951.

☐	True Crime Diary Vol 2	James Bland	-	£4.99
☐	Crime Strange But True	James Bland		£4.99
☐	The Book of Executions	James Bland		£4.99
☐	Fatal Passions	Adrian Vincent		£4.99

Warner now offers an exciting range of quality titles by both established and new authors. All of the books in this series are available from:

Little, Brown and Company (UK) Limited,
P.O. Box 11,
Falmouth,
Cornwall TR10 9EN.

Alternatively you may fax your order to the above address. Fax No. 0326 376423.

Payments can be made as follows: cheque, postal order (payable to Little, Brown and Company) or by credit cards, Visa/Access. Do not send cash or currency. UK customers and B.F.P.O. please allow £1.00 for postage and packing for the first book, plus 50p for the second book, plus 30p for each additional book up to a maximum charge of £3.00 (7 books plus).

Overseas customers including Ireland, please allow £2.00 for the first book plus £1.00 for the second book, plus 50p for each additional book.

NAME (Block Letters) ....

....

ADDRESS ....

....

....

☐ I enclose my remittance for _____

☐ I wish to pay by Access/Visa Card

Number ☐☐☐☐☐☐☐☐☐☐☐☐☐☐☐☐

Card Expiry Date ☐☐☐☐